INTELLECTUAL PROPERTY LAW IN THE SPORTS AND ENTERTAINMENT INDUSTRIES

INTELLECTUAL PROPERTY LAW IN THE SPORTS AND ENTERTAINMENT INDUSTRIES

WALTER T. CHAMPION, KIRK D. WILLIS, AND PATRICK K. THORNTON

 PRAEGER

AN IMPRINT OF ABC-CLIO, LLC
Santa Barbara, California • Denver, Colorado • Oxford, England

4/4/16
ww
$60.00

Library of Congress Cataloging-in-Publication Data

Champion, Walter T., Jr., 1950-, author.
  Intellectual property law in the sports and entertainment industries / Walter T. Champion, Kirk D. Willis, and Patrick K. Thornton.
     pages cm
  ISBN 978-0-313-39163-7 (hardback) — ISBN 978-0-313-39164-4 (ebook)
1. Intellectual property—United States. 2. Sports—Law and legislation—United States. 3. Performing arts—Law and legislation—United States. I. Willis, Kirk D., author. II. Thornton, Patrick K., author. III. Title.
  KF2979.C43 2014
  346.7304'8—dc23   2013042814

ISBN: 978-0-313-39163-7
EISBN: 978-0-313-39164-4

18 17 16 15 14   1 2 3 4 5

This book is also available on the World Wide Web as an e-book.
Visit www.abc-clio.com for details.

Praeger
An Imprint of ABC-CLIO, LLC

ABC-CLIO, LLC
130 Cremona Drive, P.O. Box 1911
Santa Barbara, California 93116-1911

This book is printed on acid-free paper ∞

Manufactured in the United States of America

To Charles, Samuel, and George—three fine young sons

and to

My late, great friend, Patrick Thornton

Contents

CHAPTER 1

Introduction

Intellectual property is the glue that ties capitalism together. Without the protection of intellectual property, corporations are less willing to develop their products so that they are readily identifiable. It's Pavlovian: as soon as we see the Golden Arches, we salivate. Is there really a difference between brand name milk and a generic product? Yes: the former is more expensive, but the product comes from the same tanker.

Intellectual property rights of athletes and entertainers are essential to their careers; their publicized ephemeral "image" is, after all, the only thing they're selling. And don't get me started with so-called reality stars. They neither reap nor sow. The shelf lives of athletes and entertainers can be very brief. In the blink of an eye, a tailback can blow out his knee. Longevity is the exception; brevity is the norm. The rule is to make hay while the sun shines, and that's where intellectual property enters.

In sports and entertainment, especially the former, it's the logo that drives the market. One thinks of the Yankees' emblem, or the Nike Swoosh, or the MGM Lion, when one chooses a particular product for purchase. It may be subliminal, but it's as effective as a lure that secures corporate growth. They say that the only two words that are universally understood throughout the world are "okay" and "Coca-Cola®."

In the U.S. Supreme Court case of *American Needle, Inc. v. National Football League*, 130 S.Ct. 2201 (2010), the Court decided that for purposes of trademark identification, each team logo is not interchangeable. The Court held that the licensing activities of a separate corporation that licenses the NFL intellectual property is a separate "concerted action" and violates the Sherman Antitrust Act.

The Dallas Cowboys won a trademark infringement case to protect their phrase, "America's Team," even though the other side registered first; the Cowboys proved "trademark priority by using the phrase previously in a 1979 season highlight film" (*Dallas Cowboys Football Club v. America's Team Properties,* 616 F. Supp. 2d 627 [N.D. Tex. 2009]).

In a gross overview, copyright is key to entertainment, and trademark is vital to sports. "Intellectual property" is a catchall phrase that includes ideas and subjects such as patents, trademarks, copyright, trade secrets, and trade dress. It also encompasses other subjects, such as publicity rights, misappropriation, false advertising, and unfair competition. Intellectual property attempts to protect the creation of ideas. In sports, the marketing of both athlete and team is formed and controlled by the laws of intellectual property. Sports marketing is a huge industry. The Super Bowl and marketing of the Super Bowl are American phenomena, the essence of sports marketing, with corporate sponsors lining up for the right to advertise their products to the game's millions of spectators. Patents are governed by the Federal Patent Act. Copyrights are protected by the Copyright Act, which protects original works of authorship embodied in a tangible medium of expression. Trademarks are a type of symbol used to identify a particular set of goods and to distinguish them from another's goods. Trade dress protection is available for nonfunctional features if they distinguish the good's origin. Broadcasting and licensing rights are controlled by the various intellectual property protections and are integral to sports dissemination.[1]

Davy Jones is dead. He was a member of the Monkees, "a band that became a cross-generational piñata for musical commerce over musical artistry—absorbing whacks and spilling forth sugary pop . . . ," according to Andrew Dansby of the *Houston Chronicle.*[2] "Yet the band never shook its prefab origins as four people assembled for a pop-music TV show designed to cash in on the success of the Beatles." To the Monkees, TV was a promotional medium, a first for a "rock" band. The show spawned copyrighted music, movies, and books and registered trademarks for lunch pails, trading cards, and Halloween costumes.

From sports, remember James Earl Jones's soliloquy in the mystical baseball movie, *Field of Dreams*: "The one constant through all the years, Ray, has been baseball. America has rolled by like an army of steamrollers; it's been erased like a blackboard, rebuilt and erased again. But baseball has marked the time. This field, this game, is a part of our past, Ray. It reminds us of all that once was good and could be again."[3]

The logos, marks, and copyrights in sports and entertainment are shorthand for our cumulative culture. According to a recent *Science* article, a study with children and chimpanzees suggests that cultural leaps occur in humans because we work together and use shared experiences and memories as a social exercise by giving verbal (and visual) instructions to one another. Intellectual property protects products, words, and logos—leitmotifs for communication—and when communication helps solve puzzles, the children share the rewards. "Humans . . . have ratcheted up their culture by teaching one another, imitating the successful behavior of others."[4]

Unlike other "law," like a penal statute, intellectual property must be shaped by advocacy. The Yankees must punish rip-offs of their trademarked logo. Bette Midler must sue to protect her commercial image. From the moment a patent is approved, a mark is registered, or a song is copyrighted, the battle begins to protect and advocate the importance and/or uniqueness of the intellectual property. The trial begins at the moment of conception! Intellectual property in sports and entertainment must be acted on, in some way, to be valuable. It is not a passive process. Litigation strategy should be considered at the moment of creation or at least when the intellectual property is legally memorialized. So when Jeremy Lin registers Linsanity®, he should conceptualize advocacy, litigation, and trial strategy, not only to maximize rewards but also to lessen theft that besmirches glory (and profits).

Why Is Intellectual Property Essential to the Sports and Entertainment Industries?

In our capitalistic rat race, nothing is done without the hope of economic gain. We write books to make money. Teams design logos to establish a brand to make money. Intellectual property secures potential monetary remuneration, which is the impetus for creativity.

The question has been effectively posed by Paul Goldstein thusly: "The term itself [intellectual property] suggests the nature of the challenge."[5] "How can a product of the mind—an invention, a song, a brand, a business secret—become the subject of precise, bounded property rights?" Nothing is new; not the Bible, not Shakespeare. Directors, writers, teams, leagues, athletes, musicians, and producers look to themes, incidents, remembered phrases, and other elements from earlier works, etc. Again, Goldstein asks, "Which of these elements is in the public domain, free for the taking, and which are not?" The Nike "Swoosh," Adidas's three stripes, and the names Nike, Adidas, and MGM are all little more than common words, descriptions, or amalgamations—nothing fancy, nothing worthy of the title "Genius of Invention." So why does Nike get the exclusive use of "the Swoosh?" Or when an employee leaves a sport shoe manufacturer with knowledge of air-filled cushioned soles (or some such nonsense), which he then uses to start a boutique company in Taiwan, what part of that information rightfully belongs to the shoe giant and what knowledge is a product of his own savvy and invention? Trade secrets are usually filtered through contracts such as non-compete agreements and negative covenants. "Marking off the boundaries of intellectual assets," Goldstein has noted, "is like drawing lines in water." In sports and entertainment, the delineation of assets is even more difficult, given the nature of the beast. Why is Lady Gaga popular? Why was Davy Jones a "teen idol" for many years? Why is A-Rod worth $32.5 million a year? Careers in sports are very short—injury, age, drugs, indifference, whatever. Eighty percent of all athletes are broke in six years. Allen Iverson did it in less than that. Careers are short, and tastes change. What is the flavor of the day? Think of Adam "Pacman" Jones or Mark "the Bird" Fidrytch. The NCAA paid $40 million for the phrase "March Madness." Enough said. Mel Gibson pocketed close to $6 billion for *Passion of Christ* and could afford a $400 million divorce.

Sports in America has been compared to a religious experience. As the eminent French philosopher/historian Jacques Barzun said, "Whoever wants to know the hearts and minds of America had better learn baseball." In *The Meaning of Sports,* Michael Mandelbaum concurs with the almost mythical view of sports in America as seen in *Field of Dreams* or *The Natural.* We live vicariously through our sports heroes (and teams).

Could you live without football on Saturday and Sunday? Is college about sports or education? Can you imagine homecoming based on cross country? One co-author of this book, Walter Champion, has taught Sports Law more than fifty times and begins each course with questions such as these. The tale of Barry Bonds can be educational: an IRS agent who worked out at his health club (also the club of Barry's trainer) thought Barry looked "too strong." An investigation was begun by the Attorney General's officer, costing upwards of $100 million and, on the way, mocking the federal rules of evidence by forcing Barry's mistress to testify about the relative size of certain physical attributes. In a court of law! Our theory is that baseball recovered from the 1994 strike (which eliminated the World Series) by actively ignoring steroid abuse, which produced the Sosa–McGwire home run derby and lifted the sport from the doldrums. In his 2004 State of the Union address, George W. Bush (former co-owner of the Texas Rangers in 1994) stated that steroid use in professional sports was America's worst problem. International terrorism, the search for Bin Laden, nuclear proliferation, etc., were all relegated to lesser importance than sports.

Some cynics and conspiracy theory advocates believe that this struggle against steroids in sports was an attempt to push the wars off the front page (which it did) and hide the fact that Iraq's alleged weapons of mass destruction (WMD) were nonexistent. Only sports could make this happen!

Babe Ruth was the first sports marketing superstar. He was paid vast sums of money to endorse an array of consumer products, from pajamas to automobiles—not to mention the fact that he was associated with a very tasty candy. When asked in 1930 if it was proper that he was paid more than the President of the United States, he said, "I had a better year than he did." The story might be apocryphal, but his popularity, even in his own lifetime, was legendary, and his persona entered popular culture by defining any prodigious feat as "Ruthian."[6]

Michael Mandelbaum discusses the significance of logos and branding by commenting that Dallas's mascot, the cowboy, emphasizes rugged individualism and suggests sufficient virtues to earn the nom de guerre of "America's team." The Cowboys were the first team to wear white while playing in their opponent's stadium, thereby creating a lasting association with the color of purity. Their logo was a lone star, the type a sheriff might have worn in the Old West. In contrast, the Oakland Raiders wore black with a pirate wearing an eye patch with crossed swords behind him. The Raiders' symbol developed a near-cult following, which typified the style of play of the team and the behavior of its fans.[7]

Don Garber, Commissioner of Major League Soccer, looked at the relationship between teams and branding this way:

Sports leagues and their teams, like most businesses, deliver a product to a consumer and strive to be profitable for an owner or group of investors. To be successful, sports organizations require strong branding and effective marketing. With these strategies in place, fans will hear and read about their teams every day and will care deeply about the players and the team.

While many American consumers are very connected with countless household brands (Coke, Tide, M&M's, McDonald's, etc.), sports leagues, teams, and players have a different and a more complicated relationship with their consumers or "fans." It's a relationship that can last for many years, through wins or losses, player trades, name changes, and other forms of new branding.

Once the bond between a team and fan is forged, it can last for many years and is often passed from one generation to the next. It thrives with victory and survives defeat. It's a relationship built on loyalty and trust, fueled by hope and excitement . . .

Sports teams and leagues succeed or fail by their relationships with the average fan. Rarely is there a consumer product that is as important as it is to children; that spans widely diverse ethnic groups and is as important to the CEO in the corner office as it is to the employee on the factory floor.

Team branding, player personnel decisions, marketing strategies, pricing policies, in-stadium operations, and day-of-game practice logistics and entertainment must take into account their impact on every segment of the fan base.[8]

There is a unique relationship among fans and their local teams, such that, to the fans, the teams exist in the public domain, with the associated branding also belonging to (and representing) the fans.

Something a Little Different: Copyright in Sports

Copyright in sports is a step-child to copyrights in entertainment or trademarks in sports. Copyright in sports is interesting because there any many types of intellectual property that are also included in a declaratory or infringement lawsuit. Copyrights are usually associated with screenplays or books that are the basis for films, music, compositions, and music in recordings. However, there are books about sports too that also need copyright protection. This is often the nexus between sports and entertainment. For example, a book on sports like *Ball Four* was made into a movie. Not to mention John Feinstein's *The Punch: One Night, Two Lives, and the Fight That Changed Basketball Forever* (Boston: Little, Brown & Co., 2002), which was an account of the punch thrown by Kermit Washington that shattered Rudy Tomjanovich's face. (Note: Rudy Tomjanovich's successful trial lawyer, Nick C. Nichols, a friend of the co-authors, successfully argued the novel theory that the Los Angeles Lakers branded Kermit Washington as an enforcer as seen through the cover photo [of Kermit and other NBA "enforcers" photographed in suitably menacing poses] of *Sports Illustrated* and corresponding lead story. The case was eventually settled for $2 million.)

In *Open Source Yoga Unity v. Choudhury,* the question was whether the defendant had valid copyright or trademark rights in a series of yoga exercises that he compiled under the name "Bikram yoga." This type of yoga consists of a sequence of 26 yoga positions ("asanas") and two breathing exercises performed at a room temperature of 105 degrees Fahrenheit.

The asanas themselves are in the public domain, but Choudhury was the first to select and arrange this particular sequence of asanas in this particular way.

This is a very unusual case; yoga is an ancient physical practice, and the individual asanas of the Bikram yoga sequence have been in the public domain for centuries. On first impression, it thus seems inappropriate that a sequence of yoga positions could belong to one person's intellectual property.

Copyright does not protect factual or functional information or information in the public domain; however, copyright does extend to an arrangement of information in the public domain assembled in a sufficiently creative fashion. Choudhury successfully argued that his arrangement aesthetically creates a dispute of fact on the issue of whether sufficient creativity exists in the Bikram yoga routine so that copyright protection attaches.[9]

In *Reed v. Peterson*, 2005 WL 1522187 (N.D. Cal.), the plaintiff is "Football Clock Management," which instructs players and coaches on various offensive and defensive strategies for time management. Defendants subsequently authored *The Football Coach's Guide to Clock Management*. Plaintiff Reed claims copyright infringement and unfair competition and seeks injunctive relief, damages, and attorney's fees. Plaintiff's claim for copyright infringement fails on the basis of a lack of substantial similarity.[10]

A classic "sports book" is *Green Bay Love Stories and Other Affairs*, which describes plaintiffs'/groupies' personal experiences with certain members of the Green Bay Packers. Plaintiff's distribution agreement gave defendants the exclusive right to publish, distribute, and sell the book. Although the parties terminated the agreement, the defendants continued to sell copies. Plaintiff sues on copyright infringement, alleging that defendant distributed copies of her book without authorization, and thus infringes on her copyright.[11]

Another form of potential copyright infringement involves the surrealistic world of fantasy sports, which began with "Rotisserie Baseball." In these games, each participant receives a budget to draft 23 players from either league, filling roster spots by position. The commercial use of statistics generated by the athletes could constitute a violation of federal copyright law. Sports leagues also claim that the use of the names of professional athletes, along with performance statistics, size, and uniform identification, violate the athletes' publicity rights.[12]

Playbooks in sports are also protected by intellectual property. A scripted play is a creative idea not unlike a theatrical play or a musical song. The coach is the author, who directs and demonstrates to the team how to carry out the play. Football, of course, has a great variety of offensive and defensive plays, formations and strategies. The question is whether copyright protects the use of the play script. Also, it appears that individual sport moves and routines are afforded copyright protection. The argument is that football possesses sufficient innovation to be comparable to the artistic nature inherent in choreography; for example, the "Icky Shuffle" or Usain Bolt's "Lightning Bolt" posture.[13] Do these sports moves contain sufficient educational and aesthetic value to merit intellectual property protection? What about Michael Jordan's tongue gesture when he dunks? Copyright protection also includes substantial non-literal copying. For example, Michael Buffer's copyright of "Let's Get Ready to Rumble" in his unmistakable "Bolero"-type vocal phrasing would also protect "Let's Get Ready to . . . Dance," or whatever. Back to "Celebration moves," the Copyright Act specifically protects choreography's ballet dance movements. "Sports moves" are dance-like since they consent to multi-layered moves and maneuvers. But the Copyright Act excludes those moves that are purely functional and utilitarian. Another question is whether a particular athlete's "signature" moves constitute a privacy right violation. Trademark protection encompasses Pat Riley's "THREE PEAT." There also is the possibility of patenting sports moves, for example, a "patented vault."[14]

Sports logos and symbols fuel the passion and create the gut-level response that triggers fan loyalty and their accompanying emotions. The National Football League announced that the Cleveland Browns were moving to Baltimore. The team, of course, would need a new name and logo. Bouchat, a Baltimore security guard and amateur artist, began drawing logo designs based on the various names that the team was considering, including the name "Ravens." Eventually, he created a drawing of a winged shield as a "Ravens" logo.

The Baltimore team adopted the name "Ravens." Bouchat sent the shield drawing via fax to the Maryland Stadium Authority. The question is whether his shield drawing was mistakenly used by National Football Properties, Inc., in the production of the Ravens' logo, the "Flying B." The Court held that the use of the logo was determined to be fair use within the meaning of the Copyright Act.[15]

The line drawn in the sand is the question of commercial "branding" for athletes who use their bodies as a commercial billboard for temporary tattoos. Using hats, shirts, clothing, helmets, shoes, pants, and suits for commercial branding is common with race car drivers, golfers, and tennis players adorning themselves with commercial logos. But isn't the body sacred, and where will it end? Chicago Bears quarterback Jim McMahon wore a headband with the word "Adidas" while on the sidelines during a nationally-televised NFL playoff game in 1986. As to body paint: these tattoos can be temporarily affixed to an athlete's skin so as to exhibit a commercial message or logo. It appears to be a perfect storm of our infatuation with sports and tattoos (as seen nightly on cable TV!). In March 2001, Portland Trail Blazers forward Rasheed Wallace attempted to affix a temporary tattoo advertising a candy company on his bicep. Later that year, boxer Bernard Hopkins emblazoned a temporary tattoo on his back publicizing the logo of an Internet casino. Are these tattoo billboards protected under the First Amendment? There's also the question of who owns the right to commercially brand the bodies of league athletes where there is a league corporation that controls brands, logos, and marketing. Shaquille O'Neal has a Superman tattoo on his bicep; "Superman" is a copyrighted and trademarked commercial product of D.C. Comics.[16]

First Amendment versus Intellectual Property

The First Amendment provides that "Congress shall make no law . . . abridging the freedom of speech." The First Amendment is the standard defense when an intellectual property right is asserted. But the First Amendment is not absolute; some speech, such as obscene speech, is left unprotected. But advertising speech, which is usually based on an intellectual property right, is entitled to First Amendment protection, although protection of commercial speech is accorded less protection than other constitutionally protected forms of speech.

The First Amendment is categorized as a defense to a right of publicity cause of action. There is an inherent tension between the right of publicity and First Amendment freedom of speech guarantees on the basis that the right of publicity inherently implicates the involvement of speech. It is a balancing test between an individual's right to exploit the commercial value of her intellectual property enterprise and society's value in cultivating free expression. It is a question of which right trumps the other.

Another defense is the "newsworthiness defense," where the information is newsworthy and a matter of public interest. First Amendment defenses have been used in lawsuits involving privacy claims, publicity, unfair competition, and federal Lanham Act. In *Rogers v. Grimaldi,* 875 F.2d 994 (2d. Cir. 1989), the court reviewed the conflict between protection of an artist's name and image and the First Amendment's protection of artistic expression in a commercial film. Actress Ginger Rogers alleged violation of § 43(a) of the Lanham Act, infringement of her right of publicity, and false light invasion of privacy, arising out of the distribution of Federico Fellini's motion picture *Ginger and Fred,* which was a fictionalized tale of the bittersweet reunion of two retired Italian dancers who had imitated the famous Ginger Rogers/Fred Astaire dancing team in their cabaret act. The court held that the film was a protected expression under the First Amendment. The Court narrowly construed the Lanham Act so that it would avoid intruding on First Amendment values. Generally, the statute applies to artistic works only where the public interest in avoiding consumer confusion outweighs the public interest in free expression. In the *Rogers* lawsuit, the title was artistically relevant to the film and was not misleading as to the film's content. As regards the publicity claim, the court saw the right of publicity as more expansive than the Lanham Act because it does not require a likelihood of consumer confusion. Courts more frequently recognize the need to limit publicity rights to accommodate First Amendment protections.

In *Uhlaender v. Henricksen,* 316 F. Supp. 1277 (D. Minn. 1970), the right of publicity was triggered in the defendant's production of a board game containing players' names and performance statistics of over 500 major league baseball players. The Major League Baseball Players Association filed suit alleging a violation of state misappropriation law. However, the First Amendment may still provide refuge for the fantasy industry's conduct. The inclusion of player names and statistics on a website is communicative speech rather than the less-favored commercial speech. The posting of names and statistics is no different from the box scores and sports stories found in most newspapers. In *Gionfriddo v. Major League Baseball,* 94 Cal. App. 4th 400 (2001), Major League Baseball successfully asserted a First Amendment defense against a right of publicity claim by former players. In *Gionfriddo,* a group of retired professional baseball players sued the league for its unauthorized use of the players' names, statistics, photographs, and other indicia of persona in television programs, video presentations, and on its website. The League's First Amendment rights superseded the player's right of publicity; by reporting statistics on the Internet, Major League Baseball was making historical facts available to the public through websites and video clips.[17]

CHAPTER 2

The Nature of Marketing[1]

Walter T. Champion, Kirk D. Willis,
Patrick K. Thornton, and Lawrence Ruddell

Marketing is the directing of the flow of goods and services from producers to consumers or users. There are five functions of marketing: (1) pricing; (2) product determination; (3) distribution; (4) promotion; and (5) marketing research. Product design is an integral part of marketing in sports and entertainment. When the consumer purchases a product, he receives not only the product but also the labeling, branding, and packaging. Advertising is a form of communication intended to promote the sale of a product or service ("Marketing and Merchandising," 23 Britannic Macropedia 538–551 [15th ed., 1987]). Marketing assumes a premier place in business because it is here where product or service meets customer and where payment is received. Intellectual property gives companies competitive advantages as a resource that is difficult to copy.

Marketing is tied tightly to economics. The marketing function helps business leaders determine to whom and how they can sell products or services in order to make a profit. Marketing covers several important functions in business, such as product, price, place, and promotion. Advertising is the key to marketing; however, intellectual property issues in the sports and entertainment businesses also concentrate on the *product*, misusing logos of NFL teams, for example; and *place*, for example, unauthorized broadcasts of NCAA games over the Internet.

The American Marketing Association (AMA) defines "marketing" as the performance of business activities that direct the flow of goods and services from producer to consumer to user. (*See*, http://www.marketing-power.com/aboutama/pages/definitionofmarketing.aspx).

The current definition of "marketing" presented by the AMA states: "Marketing is the activity, set of institutions, and processes for creating, communicating, delivering, and exchanging offerings that have value for customers, clients, partners, and society at large." This definition is probably the best summary of the nature of marketing in current culture. Of course, the difficult question is what "value" entails for all the stakeholders.

In translating the nature of marketing to intellectual property in sports and entertainment, we need to start with the function of intellectual property in marketing. Intellectual property is considered an "intangible asset" in that it does not have a physical existence but it still has value. Intangible assets such as trademarks, copyrights, and trade names are instrumental in building a company's brand and thus giving the company a competitive advantage. Along with building the brand, the intangible assets can prove lucrative when customers want to purchase goods and services to associate with the brand. This leads to distribution decisions on how and who will create, promote, and deliver the goods or services to customers. Companies use licensing agreements to carry out these functions. Competitive advantages can be maintained by the proper management of intellectual property assets.

Sports Marketing Generally

The marketing of both athletes and sports in general deals directly with the laws of intellectual property. Sports marketing has become a huge industry in the United States and in the international community. The business of sports has become a billion-dollar industry. The growth of sports exposes millions of people to sports every day in one form or another. Licensed sports merchandise sales totaled $13.9 billion in the United States in 2006. The National Football League has consistently been the leader in sports merchandise sales in the United States.

Sports licensing and marketing agreements are now commonplace in the business of sports and are found in many different forms. Corporate sponsorships are popular ways for a company to promote company identification and product placement through the purchasing of television time, etc. Corporations understand that sports have a universal appeal, and they attempt to use that to their advantage to assist them in expanding their presence in a global fashion. Licensing sports properties and corporate sponsorships has become commonplace in the sports world today.

The Super Bowl is the essence of sports marketing. Every year, corporate behemoths vie for the right to advertise their products on commercials during the Super Bowl (Walter Champion, *Sports Law in a Nutshell*, at 400–401 [4th ed. 2009]).

Marketing and Intellectual Property Generally

Licensing is a common means for gaining income from intellectual property such as "team-related memorabilia" (Grady, 2005). Items include sports properties, apparel companies, and memorabilia retailers, which broaden the marketplace where fans can purchase objects. These licenses need the protection of trademarks. It is difficult, however, to protect the trademark from small, "unseen" vendors who copy or otherwise use replicas of unauthorized trademarks, which hurt potential revenue from legal licensees and trademark owners. (*See* John Grady, "Univ. of Alabama Case to Test Limits of Sport Art Cases," 14 Sport Marketing Q. 251–255 [No. 4, 2005]).

In the Tiger Woods photograph art case, the question was whether a sport artist has a First Amendment right to create a work of art featuring a celebrity athlete despite the athlete's claim that this violates his right of privacy (*See ETW v. Jireh Publishing*, 332 F.3d 915 [6th Cir. 2003]).

In *University of Alabama Board of Trustees v. Daniel Moore & New Life Art, Inc.*, 677 F. Supp. 2d 1238 (N.D. Ala. 2009), artist Moore created more than 20 works of art featuring the University of Alabama athletic program since the 1980s, and the University licensed four of the works. The University says Moore used the Alabama logo, thus "infringing the University's trademarks" and thus should pay royalties for income gained from that use. Moore argues that he has a First Amendment right of free speech that should protect him. He filed a countersuit against the University, claiming violation of the U.S. Visual Artists Rights Act (17 U.S.C. § 106(A)). He also claims the University is liable for intentional interference with business relations for violation of the Alabama Deceptive Trade Practices Act.

Tiger Woods's licensing agent sued a sport artist and lost based on the artist's rendering of Woods's Master's win in 2002. The court sided with the artist and his freedom of expression. Another issue regarding the drawing was that the artist placed "Tiger Woods" in the narrative insert, thus violating his trademark (*ETW Corp. v. Jireh Pub.*, 332 F.3d 915 [6th Cir. 2003]). However, this issue appears different from the Alabama case in that the Alabama logo was not necessarily part of the artwork itself, which Moore acknowledged. It is suggested that Moore could argue that he was capturing "historic moments in sports," which might protect the work.

Promotion involves influencing potential buyers to purchase a given product or service. One aspect of promotion is the use of trademarks and social media to influence buyers' decisions to specifically choose certain consumer items. Companies pursue public relations as a way to communicate their product without paying. Public relations extend company brands through news, TV, and other media. Of course, the tradeoff is that the company loses control over the content of the message. In advertising, the company maintains tight control over the message, but at a high expense—buying 30 seconds of air time during the Super Bowl or the NCAA Final Four at some astronomical rate, for example.

One of the objectives of advertising and public relations is to elicit an emotional response to a product or service by linking the product or service with some other emotion-evoking person, place, or object from the potential buyer's past, current, or (hoped for) future experience. This approach draws from the psychoanalytical technique called *free association,* but here, the "patient" making the association is the advertiser who makes the association for the potential buyer.

Product placement has proven lucrative for movie makers as a way to show brands being used "naturally" in film and thus endorsing those brands in the minds of movie and TV viewers. A soft drink company invested in an alternative approach to product placement in a recently-released YouTube video featuring NASCAR professional driver Jeff Gordon. Drawing from a *Candid Camera* genre, Gordon disguises himself as an average car buyer and approaches a salesman about purchasing a used sports car. He then takes a test drive wherein he "morphs" into the professional sports car driver that he is. The salesman is shocked, and the video depicts his reactions. Everyone (including the dealership and those who make sure the car met Gordon's specifications) was in on the hoax except the salesman. A soft drink can that Gordon was holding and then carefully placed in the car cup holder was used as a prop for the hoax. It contained a camera that filmed the salesman's reactions during the ride but also served as a product placement for viewers. To drive viewers to the YouTube video meant using public relations efforts with, for example, ESPN, who featured the video on a segment and a "video about the video" where they also specifically mentioned the product placement. Currently, the video has received over 20 million hits. The company still had to pay to make the video but avoided expensive air time charges for normal product placement or advertising channels, since the video is distributed through YouTube. The target market of race car fans that follow Gordon should be reached through this approach, and their association between the product and a fast, exciting life is established. This example shows a growing trend of using different marketing channels to save money and still use intellectual property to impact intended target markets. It also begs the question of whether "reporting" has simply become another vehicle of consumerism for products or ideas. (*See* "Jeff Gordon Prank Video: PepsiMax Chevrolet Camaro Test Drive YouTube Video Takes Salesman for Ride.")

Fantasy sports draws from intellectual property (brand names, people, and statistics) to offer products and services to consumers. The challenge for companies and individuals who own the rights to the intellectual property is to negotiate licensing arrangements that promote their brands and provide sufficient revenue versus arguments, specifically, those regarding statistics (based on a particular player) that some information can be common knowledge so as not to be exclusive to the organization (John Grady, "Fantasy Stats Case Tests Limits of Intellectual Property Protection: Digital Age," 16 Sports Marketing Q. 220, 232 [No. 4, 2007]).

The ruling in *C.B.C. v. Major League Baseball Advanced Media*, 443 F. Supp. 2d 1077 (E.D. Mo. 2006) catalyzed the lively debate about players' rights—what belongs in the public domain and what is the scope of the First Amendment? Major League Baseball Advance Media (MLBAM) had obtained rights from the Major League Baseball Players Association (MLBPA) for players' names, statistics, and likenesses. MLBAM planned to develop online material using Major League Baseball (MLB) trademarks and license this content to seven fantasy league game providers. MLBAM denied C.B.C., a smaller marketing company that previously had access to this content, a license. C.B.C. took the legal initiative and filed suit against MLBAM on the basis that their ongoing use of player names and statistics in their fantasy leagues did not violate copyrights, trademarks, or publicity rights. MLBAM and the MLBPA filed a counterclaim that the C.B.C. misused player names and statistics because they did not have the appropriate licensing agreement. The court ruled in favor of C.B.C. in that using players' names did not constitute use of the identity of the player, particularly since C.B.C. did not use player images. The ruling equated C.B.C.'s usage of player names and statistics as the same as newspaper box scores and thus in the public domain, and, if anything, enhanced the players' livelihoods. Regarding the application of the First Amendment, the court held that statistics are part of baseball history and thus part of public interest and protected by the First Amendment. This applied to the use of statistics in that they were considered part of the public domain and thus not worthy of special protection.

From a marketing standpoint, the decision impacted fantasy league licensing agreements by removing a significant barrier to fantasy league companies that wanted to enter the market. Perhaps MLBAM and other professional organizations would be better served to focus their protests on how the player data is gathered. Fantasy leagues are based on past player statistics and, even though the statistics are in the public domain, it might prove tedious to scour public domain sources for the requisite data over a long period of time. Perhaps MLBAM and other professional organizations desiring to protect statistics might be better served to operate an official data service for a price to deliver "authorized" sets of statistics to any fantasy league company. This might lessen the licensing fees gained but might actually prove more profitable in the long run by vastly increasing the number of customers.

Sports licensing can spread to any number of products or services. NASCAR, for example, allows NASCAR burgers and barbecue sauce. In the movies, the entertainment industry pushes character replicas at fast food restaurants along with such items as shirts, video games, Lego products, and large action figures. Sometimes, the two come together, as when NASCAR and the 2007 film *Talladega Nights* combined to market replica cars, mugs, and bedding, thus building the NASCAR brand as well as reaping mutual profits. Collectibles lead to longer-term profits. For example, Lego uses licenses with major films like *Lord of the Rings*, *Star Wars*, and *Star Wars, the Clone Wars* to offer different sets and figures from the films. In the case of NASCAR, the marketing goal is to establish a "lifestyle brand," which means multi-layer selling to the target audience. Thus, NASCAR fans can find licensed products not only at the track, but in their homes, on their TVs, and on their smartphone screens, for example, in the form of wall paper and NASCAR information apps and in what they wear (Amy Johannes, "A Sporting Try: Sports Marketing, Corporate Brands Make Licensing Inroads," 19 Promo. 9–10 [No. 7, June 2006]).

The upcoming World Cup in Brazil in 2014 gives a modern example of licensing opportunities and challenges. Ralph Straus, head of strategy and brand management for FIFA, presented an outline of the issues at a licensing event in London in October 2013. Straus highlighted the magnitude of the World Cup as a sporting event and discussed the emerging trends in licensing programs for major sporting events. Straus highlighted three key marketing drivers here: the goal is to build a global brand, to have a sustainable program, which means building long-term relationships with only the best licensees and retailers, and seeing licensing as a core part of FIFA, which means they will control all aspects. This might prove difficult, since different countries have different views of licensing arrangements, like China, for example. FIFA will add an additional focus on online material generated by the World Cup, one they neglected to control in previous years. They have expanded control in the past, taking the *Fan Fest* idea, originating in Seoul in 2002, of placing large screen TVs in key metropolitan areas of teams involved and including this as a licensing offering. There is also a brand protection plan, including correct use of logos and the safety and quality of products; this will protect sponsors, rights holders, and licensees as well, which will ensure that all licensees adhere to ethical business practices, which are confirmed by signing an agreement that includes the code of conduct of The World Federation of the Sporting Goods Industry (Bob Jenkins, "FIFA's Ready to Score World Cup Goals," 15 License! 22–24 [No. 5, Sept./Oct. 2012]).

Key executives from the four major professional sports, NFL, NBA, MLB, and NHL, as well as the PGA and NASCAR, gathered several years ago to discuss licensing issues and marketing future growth opportunities. One observation was the consolidation of retailers to a smaller number, including the league's own stores, with a higher level of involvement by the leagues. The marketing involvement seems to revolve around *promotion* and *product*, with apparel being big. With fewer retailers, the leagues are giving more strategic thought to extending the product lifecycle (how long a product remains available and profitable) by better customer management (more sales) and better supply chain management (reduced costs). The NHL seems to have more of a niche market, so it distributes through "local retail levels" rather than nationally. All of the professional leagues are managing customers by extending groups in their promotion efforts, including women through apparel and children through toys and video games. NASCAR has realized a lucrative alternative to trading cards, which is, of course, historically popular in other sports (think the $1 million Honus Wagner baseball trading card), through their die-cast collector cars. The PGA is a little different in that it is a not-for-profit organization and has used its own retail stores. However, it has also increased retailers and the benefit that comes from promoting golf through non-profit means. As professional sports move into the second decade of the 21st century, there is more innovation in leveraging intellectual property for sales that make customers happy and extend brands, thus adding value (Lorri Friedfield, "Sports Licensing Roundtable," 6 License! 42–51 [No. 12, Jan. 2004]).

"Being Kind…" as a Marketing Strategy

Many of America's brands are now demanding kindness. For example, Nordstrom's opened a test store where all profits go to charity. Starbucks has a similar program. Dozens of the biggest brands have embraced socially kind deeds as an unusually effective way to sell themselves to consumers, employees, even stockholders. From there, the good news is spilling out and is being listened to as social-media chatter. The preeminent targets of marketing gurus are the Millennials, the free-spending group of about 95 million Americans who were born from 1982 to 2004, who live and breathe in the social media. Everything these millennials do is fodder for the social media, and once that synergy occurs, these companies segue into becoming charter members of the nascent "do-gooder society." This alleged epidemic of corporate kindness is grounded in one rationale: it works. Some 47 percent of consumers say they buy, every month, at least one brand that supports a good cause, according to a 2012 global survey by public relations firm Edelman. That's a 47 percent increase from 2010. What's more, 72 percent of consumers say they would recommend a brand that supports a good cause—a 38 percent increase in two years.

Just as compelling, consumers say they're more likely to discuss good deeds a company does than they are its financial performance. This trend is a powerful marketing tool for corporate brands to use to separate themselves from the competition. Not to mention the Paul Newman brands that were built on charity and kindness.

The motivation, though, must be real; if it's solely "for doing good it's just about selling more stuff or making more money, it's doomed to fail," warns Whole Foods's Mackey, who recently co-authored a best-selling book on the topic, *Conscious Capitalism*. His natural foods grocery chain runs a foundation that grants loans to aid people in poverty in 55 countries trying to start small businesses. Soon corporate kindness will be the rule, not the exception. Just the image of kindness can be an effective sales tool. This idea has even segued into the Super Bowl of marketing (Bruce Horowitz, "Be Kind and They Will Come: Millenniums Are Demanding Capitalism with a Conscience, and some of America's Biggest Brands Are Delivering," USA Today at 1A [March 26, 2013]).

NASCAR Marketing?

NASCAR is both a sport and a form of entertainment and must exude a subtle combination of both drama and predictability to successfully market its brand. "Five races into the season, and NASCAR drivers are feuding, fighting, and wrecking . . . which is *good* marketing for NASCAR." "They want to see us be human, and humans are emotional" (Jeff Gluck, "NASCAR Wins with Fighting, Wrecking, Altercations Such as the Ones in Fontana Give the Sport the Kind of Drama It has been Coveting," USA Today at 6C [March 26, 2013]).

NASCAR has seen a decline in attendance and TV ratings in recent years, a combination of the economy and changing fan tastes. Big-name drivers such as Tony Stewart, a three-time Cup chairman, and Dale Earnhardt Jr., voted NASCAR's most popular 10 years running, are among those still looking for sponsorship for some races.

If there's a question as to whether the soap opera elements are cause for hand-wringing in the NASCAR offices, there shouldn't be. Last year, NASCAR hired agency Ogilvy & Mather to relaunch its branding. The result was a series of commercials that show violent crashes (cars airborne and flipping) and fights. That's a distinct departure from NASCAR's marketing in the mid-2000s, in which crashes were never used as promotional material (Gluck at 6C).

Marketing's Effect on Berlusconi's Publicity Rights

Ford India and a British ad agency have both apologized for what they said was an unauthorized ad showing three scantily clad, gagged, and bound women in the back of a Ford Figo compact driven by a grinning caricature of Italy's Silvio Berlusconi. The ad features a grinning Berlusconi, Italy's former prime minister, with his fingers in a "V" for victory sign, with three women in the trunk of a Ford Figo driven by him. Ford said this was unauthorized and done for an ad competition. Berlusconi is, of course, a billionaire politician, some say buffoon, who controls a worldwide communications empire. He certainly is a celebrity, and as such, should control his intellectual property rights, especially his right of publicity.

The tagline is "Leave your worries behind with Figo's extra-large boot."

Another ad, on the same theme, shows a character resembling Paris Hilton hauling what looks like the Kardashian sisters in the trunk.

A third ad featured a caricature of Formula One racing driver Michael Schumacher abducting his male racing competition.

The ads, aimed at the Indian market, were produced by JWT India, a subsidiary of the British advertising and public relations giant WPP Group, who posted the Berlusconi ad online to the website Ads of the World, apparently without approval.

"We deeply regret this incident and agree with our agency partners that it should have never happened," a Ford India statement said. "Together with our partners, we are reviewing approval and oversight processes to help ensure nothing like this ever happens again."

An apology was issued.

"We deeply regret the publishing of posters that were distasteful ads contrary to the standards of professionalism and decency within WPP Group. These were never intended for paid publication and should never have been created, let alone uploaded to the Internet. This was the result of individuals acting without proper oversight, and appropriate actions have been taken within the agency where they work to deal with the situation."

Seventy-six-year-old Berlusconi is appealing a conviction for tax fraud and is on trial over accusations of paying for sex with a minor.

"The Italian newspaper *La Republica* identified two of the women depicted as Nicole Minetti, an Italian showgirl-turned-politician who has turned against Berlusconi, and former erotic pole dancer Karima El Mahroug, also known as Ruby the Heart Stealer, who is at the center of the Berlusconi sex scandal" (Doug Stanglin, "Ford Apologizes for Ad with Gagged, Bound Women. Ad Picturing Italy's Silvio Berlusconi Was Aimed at Indian Market," USA Today 3B [March 26, 2013]).

Product Placement

An essential aspect of marketing is product placement, whether it's Mel Brooks's shameless use of marketing in *Space Balls*, or sampling in rap, or branding patches for golfers and NASCAR drivers.

Product placement [is] the insertion of branded products directly into entertainment products. It is a method of marketing that has been used in varying degrees by the motion picture branch of the entertainment industry and at the beginning of television. Product placement has now become an even more important aspect of an advertiser's advertising budget and has expanded into additional branches of the industry. Product placement deals may be a straight-fee arrangement where a price is paid for the inclusion of a product or service into an entertainment project, an in-kind arrangement where expensive merchandise is provided by the manufacturer to the production company in exchange for the exposure the merchandise receives, and a promotional arrangement where the inclusion of a product or service is reciprocated with a commercial tie-in (Robert Lind *et al.*, "Product Placement," 1 Entertainment Law 3d: Legal concepts and Business Practices § 4.25 [database updated Dec. 2011]).

For example, Exxon paid $300,000 for the appearance of its trademark in *Days of Thunder*, and Cuervo Gold paid $150,000 for the placement of its products in *Tequila Sunrise*; Ford provided 100 Ford automobiles in *Diamonds Are Forever*; and of course there's the infamous tale of Mars, Inc., rejecting an offer to use M&M's during the production of *E.T. the Extra-Terrestrial*. Then Hershey stepped in, and Reese's Pieces were famously used in the film; the result was that Hershey promoted the film with $1 million of advertising and was permitted to use E.T. in its advertisements. It was a veritable marketing coup!

For decades, the discretion as to what product to use as a prop in a motion picture was given to the propmaster on a film set. On occasion, a propmaster may receive remuneration from the manufacturer of a product if the propmaster made certain that the product would be used in a scene. Later, production companies would use product placement agreements as a means to obtain needed material without increasing the film's budget. Today, product placement in the motion picture branch constitutes a revenue enhancement. Advertisers, advertising agencies, and product placement agencies review scripts to find opportunities to place a company's product into a scene and are willing to pay for that opportunity or provide promotional support for the film. Advertisers have also become involved in the financing of independent films, not as a quid-pro-quo for the placement of products as the promotion of a brand, but as the promotion of a lifestyle attractive to the consumers of their products. Although these deals are not driven by an expectation of a financial reward based solely on the success of the motion picture, they may include back-end profit participation and merchandise tie-ins (Robert Lind *et al.*, "Product placement—Motion pictures," 1 Entertainment Law 3d: Legal Concepts and Business Practices § 4.26 [database updated Dec. 2011]).

Television, along with radio, is the branch of the entertainment industry most heavily dependent on advertising for its primary revenue stream. In the early days of television, the sponsorship of entire television programs by a single advertiser was commonplace. Later, advertising time was sold to multiple advertisers that would advertise at different times during the program. Product placement in television programs was more limited than in motion pictures due to several factors. First, as a practical matter, when a television series is placed in syndication, local television stations attempt to recoup their syndication license fee with the sale of commercial time. An advertiser is not likely to be interested in supporting a television epi-sode that features the product of a competitor. Secondly, regulations by the Federal Communications Commission and the Federal Trade Commission required sponsorship identification.

As a result of increased production costs and operating expenses, at a time of decreased viewership and fractured audiences, produc-tion companies and television networks have increasingly looked to product placement as a source of revenue not dependent on the viewer sitting through commercials. Advertisers have also returned to funding the development of programming deemed advantageous to attracting consumers likely to purchase their products (Robert Lind *et al.,* "Product placement—Televisions," 1 Entertainment Law 3d: Legal Concepts and Business Practices § 4.27 [database updated Dec. 2011]).

Music has long contained references to products. In the 1970s and 1980s, many recording artists refused to allow their music in advertisements and would litigate if such use occurred. This con-cern for selling out has been a problem primarily for rock musi-cians. Brand references in music are becoming more commonplace. Hip-hop and rap artists are more comfortable with the influence brands have within pop culture. Their music often references brands that the artists use or own. Such a product reference may subsequently appear in promotional deals. Other artists are paid by brand owners to include a brand in lyrics. Some recording artists use the popularity of commercials containing their music by placing "as seen in TV commercial" stickers on their CDs. Many recording artists have diversified their interests into various companies with their own brands (Robert Lind *et al.,* "Product placement—Music," 1 Entertainment Law 3d: Legal Concepts and Business Practices § 4.28 [database updated Dec. 2011]).

Our favorite, of course, is Janis Joplin's "Mercedes Benz."

The radio branch of the entertainment industry, similar to the television branch, is highly dependent on commercial advertise-ments that accompany the creative content transmitted by radio stations. Radio first developed the episodic fictional dramatic radio programs known as soap operas in the 1920s. These programs were often sponsored by companies that advertised cleaning and laundry products. These products were often integrated into the storyline of the program. Sponsored programs eventually turned to multiple advertisers that purchased 30- or 60-second spots in which live or prerecorded commercials were aired. Federal law now requires that product placements must be disclosed (Lind at § 4.29).

The literary publishing branch of the entertainment industry has been the final frontier for product placement. Authors have long prided themselves on personally crafting story lines and dialogue without outside influence. The mention of a brand within a novel was an exercise of literary license. The age of branding innocence may be coming to an end. Currently, the largest genre of books to use product placement is children's books. However, authors of novels for adults are beginning to strike deals with companies to mention their products in the pages of the author's books (Lind, at § 4.30).

Product integration has long been an unobtrusive adjutant to the visuals in video games. The more detailed the graphics in the video game became, the higher the degree of desired realism accomplished by game designers. This heightened realism predictably included branded objects and realistic advertising (Lind, at § 4.32).

Ambush Marketing[2]

YouTube offers a special intellectual property challenge for those in the sports and entertainment industry. Since YouTube content is free, there is minimal effort to protect copyrights. For example, top European football clubs have shied away from using YouTube to reach out to fans. However, Chelsea has launched its own branded channel on YouTube. They realize that YouTube has worldwide distribution so are willing to take a risk to use this channel. Others are willing to let Chelsea be the first mover and gauge results before jumping on this opportunity. The response has been positive for Chelsea and illustrates the risk/reward potential of new brand distribution models as new technology continues to emerge (Andrew McCormick, "Top Football Clubs Snub YouTube Over Concerns about Copyright," New Media Age at 3–3 [March 8, 2007]).

"Ambush marketing" describes an effort by an advertiser to draw from the value in the form of good will and/or recognition of intellectual property owned by another organization without paying for it. The NHL sued Pepsi-Cola of Canada because Pepsi did not use NHL-registered trademarks in its promotional and advertising materials.

Instead, the company used city names that represented NHL playoff participants with game numbers printed under the bottle caps. This was all part of a "Pro Hockey Playoff Pool" promotional campaign offering hockey-related prizes around the time of the NHL playoffs, which appeared to "associate" Pepsi with the playoffs. Pepsi "covered itself" through a disclaimer that its promotion was neither associated with nor sponsored by the National Hockey League or any of its member teams. The league argued that Pepsi had engaged in unfair competition and interfered with its business associations, but the court held for Pepsi, on the grounds that Pepsi had used disclaimers sufficient to eliminate customer confusion.

Ambush marketing remains a problem for sports and entertainment organizations and their ability to capture licensing fees that normally would come with the use of images or other material associated with their teams, players, actors, and events. Is this ambush marketing? Or, from the opposing side, is it simply closer to "aggressive marketing" as opposed to the pejorative term, "parasitic marketing"? It's a "creative way" to gain an advantage in a competitive landscape. Ambush marketing, in its most egregious form, refers to a company's intentional efforts to weaken its competitor's official association with a sport organization, which has been acquired through the payment of sponsorship fees. The result is that the buying public is confused as to exactly who their direct sponsors are, or the property or event, and who are not. Ambush marketing also more generally impacts the offending company and does not directly seek to undermine the position of the trademark owners, but instead seeks to capitalize on the goodwill, reputation, and popularity of a particular sport or event by creating an association without the authorization or consent of the necessary parties. A common example is a sweepstakes where the winner receives tickets to an important event such as the Super Bowl.

It has proven difficult for intellectual property owners to overcome allusions to sports themes that might associate special events with consumers because of the wily use of disclaimers. The Lanham Act and state unfair competition statutes traditionally provide coverage, but First Amendment arguments and the care in using disclaimers and avoiding obvious associations might provide loopholes.

Two ambush marketing techniques have been addressed: use of tickets as prizes and the "use and effectiveness" of disclaimers in general. The NCAA was the first to take on the use of tickets as promotions. In January 2001, the NCAA sued Coors Brewing Co. for its offering of Final Four tickets in its "Coors Light Tourney Time Sweepstakes" promotion. It also provided a recommended approach of taking action by leagues protecting intellectual property. The NCAA based its legal argument on two legal theories: "breach of revocable licenses and unfair competition." On the first theory, they argued that Coors wrongfully induced third parties—the sweepstake winners—to breach the revocable license. Like on the back of all sporting event tickets, the NCAA had their own warning that "[U]nless specifically authorized in advance by the NCAA, this ticket may not be offered in a commercial promotion or as a prize a sweepstakes or contest." Coors essentially countered that there was no legal precedent for applying contract law to the language on the back of tickets and that they were not acting as ticket brokers.

In regard to the use of disclaimers, it appears that it is hard for the offended party to substantiate consumer options and the level of confusion. For the ambush marketer, a prominent disclaimer might minimize their intended association, and the elimination of a disclaimer might make it more difficult to be attacked legally. In any case, leagues can better operate ambushing marketing by aggressively pursuing litigation against offenders.

In 2003, the Kentucky Derby shifted its intellectual property focus from consumers to participants. Several jockeys in that event wore patches on their pants representing the Jockeys' Guild. The 3 x 5-inch patches were deemed advertising by the Churchill Downs's stewards, which violated a racing regulation against riders wearing advertisement while racing. The fine levied by the stewards was minimal (only $500), but the jockeys appealed the fine to the Kentucky Racing commission, and its appeal hinges on First Amendment issues.

Professional athletes have historically been involved in endorsements, but horse racing revolves around events—especially the Triple Crown, the Kentucky Derby, Preakness, and Belmont Stakes, of which Visa is a prominent sponsor. Jockeys do not receive any benefit from sponsors, but, like other independent contractors in professional sports such as professional golfers and tennis players, can make extra money through endorsement deals. But the sport of horse racing has shied away from allowing jockeys to wear endorsements to maintain the distinctiveness of the sport in contrast to NASCAR, where drivers' uniforms are peppered with advertising. Horse racing is regulated by state requirements, so although Kentucky does not allow advertising, New York does allow advertising on jockey outfits during races, with some limitations. Thus, in 2003, some jockeys wore advertising from Wrangler and Budweiser, which angered the overall Triple Crown sponsor, Visa.

The Kentucky legislature has given the Kentucky Racing commission power to create and enforce administrative regulations on how racing will be carried out in that state. They have prohibited jockeys from wearing any advertising, promotional, or cartoon symbols or wording that is not in keeping with local turf traditions. In the Commission's decision on the jockeys' appeal, it was deemed that the patches of the Jockeys Guild represented advertising and not a political statement. The jockeys argued that the purpose of wearing the patches was purely political in trying to increase membership in the organization and thus raise funds and not for their own commercial benefit. They also presented that being fined for wearing the patch violated their First Amendment right. The Commission ended up affirming the fines on grounds that the patches violated "the traditions of the turf" and could pose a distraction for the stewards in performing their duties to "ensure the safety and integrity of the sport."

The NCAA serves as an example of how to protect marketing interests through proactive actions on several fronts. The NCAA has worked hard to maintain control over its intellectual property rights through bundled licensing agreements. It represents over 1000 members by accruing royalties from NCAA championship television, radio, Internet, licensing, marketing, publishing, special events and equipment suppliers to distribute to NCAA members to fund scholarships, to administer NCAA championships, to assist student-athlete welfare programs, and to provide member services. The NCAA protects 40 U.S. trademarks and service marks associated with the NCAA and its championships. It also maintains worldwide registrations for its main brands. The NCAA enforces intellectual property violations of unauthorized use of championship tickets for promotions, association of products with its championships, championship broadcasts, and other copyright infringements.

In 2002, the NCAA moved from negotiating licensing and marketing rights through various media channels from varied vendors to a fewer contracting parties, believing that this shift might yield more value and counter would-be ambush marketers. CBS emerged as the winner, with ESPN maintaining some rights. Maintaining copyright control over content has been an important plank in NCAA's negotiations. This would allow royalty protection for any cable or satellite distribution.

The NCAA has approximately 35 merchandise licensees, 16 corporate marketing partners, and ten official ball licensees. These merchandisers are precluded from advancing their own company brand in producing NCAA products, but the NCAA marks also must promote the sale of the licensed products. However, NCAA corporate marketing partners may associate NCAA events with their companies.

The NCAA takes pains to communicate through educational events with the general public and letters to businesses and organizations as to the nature of unauthorized uses and why the NCAA protects its intellectual property, including trademarked phrases. The effort at distributing information can result in good will, as the NCAA relies on member organizations, the national office staff, licensing partners, and sometimes even members of the public itself to report violations, particularly those that smell of trademark ambush. The NCAA takes action to prevent companies from tying their product with an NCAA championship event by handing out free samples near a Final Four site. The NCAA also asks host cities to declare a "clean zone," which garners local law enforcement and other officials in limiting commercial activity near the venue. This includes protecting against the unauthorized sale of any counterfeit goods or apparel bearing NCAA trademarks.

Cybersquatting presents another problem for the NCAA, where users buy NCAA trademark-related website names and try to cash in on their sale. These squatters feign ignorance that they are registering something of value, but they encourage others to do so as well. The NCAA has registered and received the transfer of approximately 20 different domain names. With finite resources, the NCAA continues to face challenges protecting its domain names from a variety of groups, including sports marketing companies, gambling websites, betting pool organizers, ticket brokers, and .com retailers. The NCAA has worked with the Internet Corporation of Assigned Names and Numbers (ICANN) to ensure registration of emerging domain names such as .info and .biz, along with popular country codes. The NCAA's policy is to not pay cybersquatters for domain names but to provide some compensation commensurate with expenses incurred. The NCAA has used the Uniform Domain Name Dispute Resolution Policy, since it is more cost effective through written and electronic communication and tends to recognize the trademark owner in disputes.

CHAPTER 3

What's with the Dimples on a Golf Ball? Patents in the Sports and Entertainment Industries

Overview of Patent Law

A patent is a set of exclusive rights granted by the government to an inventor or his assignee for a fixed period of time in exchange for a disclosure of an invention. This means whoever owns a patent is the only one who has the legal right to make, use, distribute, or sell the invention that is disclosed in the patent. This exclusive right is given for a limited period of time, generally 20 years, to allow inventors a competitive advantage, by helping ensure they are the first to be able to profit from their invention.

Patents were intended to protect an invention for a set period of time to encourage the patent holder to invest the time and money into the invention. The general idea behind patents is that by giving inventors the incentive of exclusive rights for a limited period, they'll release information about their invention which will benefit the rest of society by allowing access to that information. Typically, manufacturers use the patent as a selling feature, implying that their product is unique to the market.

Patents are owned like real property. They can be bought, sold, leased, or willed by an estate. Many times, the patent owner leases the patent through a license agreement.

Acquiring a patent can be a long and expensive process. Many patents take somewhere between 2 to 3 years to issue, depending on the backlog at the United States Patent and Trademark Office (USPTO). Additionally, patents can cost between $5,000 to more than $25,000 in attorney's fees, and several hundred dollars in filing fees when filing domestically.

Anyone who desires to file internationally can easily see these costs go up exponentially depending on how many jurisdictions they are seeking protection in. The filing fees are usually several thousand dollars, and the associated fees, which may include costs like foreign attorneys and translation fees, can easily be in the excess of $25,000 per country. The most efficient way to acquire international rights is through a Patent Cooperation Treaty (PCT) application, which allows a person to file one application and designate as many of the 144 member countries as they plan on seeking patent protection. The PCT application must be filed within 12 months of the original patent application.

There are three types of patents a person may obtain. They are:

1. Utility patents, which are used to protect processes, machines, articles of manufacture, or compositions of matter.
2. Design patents, which are used to protect new, original, and ornamental design for an article of manufacture.
3. Plant patents, which are used to protect any distinct and new variety of plant.

With regards to the sports and entertainment industries, utility patents and design patents will be the primary forms of patent protection. A person is not limited to pursuing just one of these three types of patents but can pursue more than one depending on the technology. In the golf ball dimple scenario, a person could seek to protect both the functional element of a dimple pattern on the surface of a ball, through a utility patent, and at the same time seek to protect the ornamental design of that pattern through a design patent.

Through the use of patents and man-made materials such as alloys and polymers, a cycle of innovation began. The cycle of innovation replaced natural materials such as gut, rubber, twine, and wood. This progression of new materials in sports equipment that weighs less and is more durable has resulted in better performance and increased safety for its users. Equipment is not the only type of recent patents. New patents such as nutritional supplements and sports drinks add to the growing number of new patents.

For the entertainment industry, patent law is generally used for protecting equipment innovations. Equipment that continues to require patents are cameras, television equipment, and music coding. Patents for entertainment companies are essential if they plan on displaying entertainment products.[1] The Constitution of the United States grants Congress the ability to provide patent protection in legislation. A patent is essentially a grant of a property right to an inventor by the government. The patent is a detailed description of the invention and its functions. This provides protection by excluding others from reproducing or selling the invention for as long as the patent is valid. By acquiring a patent, the matter is public and open.

A patent confers on the owner the right to exclude others from selling or using the process or product. A patent owner may sue those individuals who directly infringe upon the patent by using or selling the invention without the proper authority to do so. A patent lasts approximately 20 years from the date of the filing of the patent application with the PTO. Patent law covers a variety of sports and entertainment products, including golf balls, football helmets, movie cameras, film processing, skates, rockets, trampolines, computer-generated special effects, and lawn darts.

The Patent Act defines a potential patent as any "new and useful process, machine, manufacture, or composition of matter" that includes mechanical, chemical, and electrical structures and processes. In order for an invention to be patentable, it must meet four requirements. An invention must be (1) in a subject category, (2) useful, (3) novel in relation to the prior art, and (4) not obvious from the prior art to a person of ordinary skill in the art at the time the invention was made.

Patents are an integral part of sports. In fact, the PTO issued a press release entitled "Take Me Out to the Ballgame."

> The Department of Commerce's United States Patent and Trademark Office joins in the celebration of this year's World Series by recognizing some patents and trademarks relative to baseball.
>
> Baseball is America's pastime. The thousands of patented inventions associated with the sport are testament to that. Most recently patents have been issued on a way to improve a batter's swing (patent #6,306,050); a swing speed indicator (patent #6,173,610) that measures the batter's swing using a digital readout that can be slipped onto any bat; a baseball trainer, which helps pitchers practice by indicating a "strike" or "ball" as well as the speed of the pitch by using a microcomputer (patent #5,566,964); and a glove (patent #5,113,530) with inflatable chambers which softens the impact of an incoming baseball or softball. There are also numerous patents for softball and t-ball. Design patent #418,569 is for a t-ball mat which helps children position themselves to hit the ball. Patent #4,993,708 covers a batting tee. Design patent #402,414 is for a helmet that can be used for a player to pull their ponytail through while playing softball, t-ball or little league baseball.
>
> Trademarks also play an important role in baseball and are seen on and off the field. Most professional team logos, equipment and

even mascots, have trademark registrations. The New York Yankees, which have won the most World Series Championships, have a very well-known and recognized logo, which has trademark registration #1898998 for use on baseball shirts. The Arizona Diamondbacks, a relatively new team, has several trademark applications pending, including serial #76161641 for baseball uniforms and other sports-related clothing. Trademarks for baseball equipment include Rawlings (registration #1149932) and Wilson (registration #1553005) for sporting good equipment such as baseballs, gloves, and bases.[2]

The World Intellectual Property Organization (WIPO) (http://wipo.int/ip-sport/en/technology.html) has this to say about "sport and technology":

From the sports shoe to the swimsuit and the tennis racket to the football, sports technologies have applied their ingenuity, creativity, and expertise to develop better and safer equipment in the quest for sporting excellence. The outcome has been enhanced performance, better, safer and more effective sports equipment, precision measurement of performance, a multiplicity of ways to experience sporting events anywhere and at any time.

Patents protect new inventions and facilitate the diffusion of technology. The usual life of a patent is 20 years, and it provides protection against unauthorized use of the invention. This allows inventors the opportunity to regain the financial assets they used in the creation and development of the invention.

In return for the patent's protection, the inventor must give detailed information of the product. This benefit allows the public and other inventors to use this new knowledge to make possible improvements. When the patent ends, anyone is free to use the patent's technology. Thanks to the patent system:

Manufacturers of sports equipment gain financially from innovation, which in turn boosts the strength and vitality of the industry for the benefit of the economy as a whole;

Researchers have access to a mine of technical information, which they can use to inspire innovation and improvements to existing products;

Sportsmen and women around the world benefit from innovations in sports equipment to enhance their performance, minimize injury, and promote fast recovery when injured;

The general public benefits from a wider range of high-quality sporting goods.

The British Library, in a paper entitled "Sports & Society: The Summer Olympics and Paralympics Through the Lens of Social Science," saw the importance of patented sports equipment for the disabled athlete (www.bl.uk/sportsandsociety):

Much sports equipment has been designed with the disabled athlete in mind. The disability could be the loss of a limb, or an inability to use it, or eyesight, although a huge range of possible disabilities have equipment designed especially for them. Only some, though, are patented. And only some of those that are patented are actually available as manufactured products.

Patents provide detailed descriptions and drawings of how the invention works so that it can be built from those details alone.

Many (but not all) are classified under the heading A63B-071/00H, which is defined as "games and accessories for handicapped persons". [sic] That class can be entered in the ECLA search box on the free Espacenet http:ep.espacenet.com/advancedSearch?locale=en_EP database to run a search. Keywords can also be added to the search in that database.

Some inventions involve altering the normal equipment to make the sport easier for the disabled athlete. In other cases the sport itself is modified, or entirely new sports are invented.

There is also specially adapted exercise equipment. Here are a couple of examples:

In 1992 Philip Gonzales of California applied for a "Wheelchair occupant motion stabilizer for exercise machines" patent.

http://v3.espacenet.com/publicationDetails/originalDocument?CC=US&NR=5277685A&KC=A&FT=D&date=19940111&DB=EPODOC&locale=en_EP.

The equipment is specially adapted for the restraint mechanism.

Patents and Golf Ball Dimples

In a sport like golf, where the game is won by a matter of inches, every advantage is critical. As a result, the design of a golf ball is very important to ensure that the ball will travel efficiently through the air and on course. One of the key parts of the design of a golf ball is the dimples that cover the surface of the ball.

Golf balls, like all objects that fly through the air, are subject to two major aerodynamic forces: lift and drag. A ball with dimples is able to travel farther than one without dimples, because the dimpled surface both reduces the drag and increases the lift on the ball as it flies through the air.

The dimples reduce drag by creating a turbulent layer over the upstream side of the ball. Since this layer is able to remain on the ball longer than that of a ball with a smooth surface, less of the dimpled ball is subject to the resistance in front of it, thus creating less drag.

The dimples also increase the lift when the ball has a backspin, by deforming the airflow around the ball. The backspin causes the air to move faster backward on the top of the ball, with the golf ball by way of the dimples. This creates lower air pressure above the ball than below, which creates a small amount of lift. The seams on a baseball create a similar effect.

These aerodynamic principles are not only interesting to those who love science but also to those who seek to profit from creating balls with a more efficient design than the ones currently on the market. As inventors come up with golf ball designs that allow a player the most optimal game, they can acquire patent(s) on it and for a limited time control the market with regard to that design. As a result, there are a number of patents that cover different dimple patterns on golf balls.

Since competitive advantages are so important in the sports and entertainment fields, there is a big incentive to patent the latest technology. Many athletes and entertainers will purchase a product at much higher prices than what is currently on the market if they feel it gives them the slightest advantage over the competition. By acquiring patents, a person can, for a limited time, have control over their new technology and the market that comes with it.

Wilson Sporting Goods Co. v. David Geoffrey & Associates, 904 F.2d 1942 (Fed. Cir. 1990) is a patent infringement case that discusses golf ball design. There are six major competitors in the business of golf ball design and manufacture; the competition is fierce and lucrative. Golfers have a near Homeric desire to search for the longer ball; "distance sells." Inventors have experimented with golf ball design but still must conform to the parameters of the United States Golf Association (U.S.G.A.), who has established rules that strictly control ball size, weight, and other aspects; inventors then focus their efforts on the "dimples" on the ball's surface. Apparently, new dimple designs are the only effective means that provide any real opportunity for increasing distance within the confines of U.S.G.A. rules.

So, there's now the pseudo-science for dimple technology: dimples can make the ball fly higher and farther. Dimples can be numerous or few and can vary as to shape, width, depth, and location.

The plaintiff in *Wilson* has a pattern of dimples that are arranged by dividing the cover of the ball into 80 imaginary spherical triangles and then placing the dimples in strategic locations in those triangles. The placement of the dimples is grouped into an imaginary "icosahedron," which is completely covered by 20 imaginary equilateral triangles, five of which cover each pole of the ball and ten of which surround its equator. This so-called "168 patent" basically requires that the ball possess eighty subtriangles and six great circles. The placement of dimples on triangles must be arranged so that no dimple intersects any great circle. The dimples also must be arranged so that no dimple intersects the side of any central triangle. When the dimples are arranged in this manner, the ball has six axes of symmetry, compared to prior ball design, which had only one axis of symmetry.

There are four accused products; the accused balls have dimples that are arranged in an icosahedral pattern having six great circles, but the circles are not dimple-free, as the claims literally require. Patent infringement will be found if the accused product is substantially equivalent and if the accused product performs substantially the same overall function or work, in substantially the same way, to obtain substantially the same overall result as the claimed invention. But even once the test is met, there still will be no infringement if the asserted range of equivalency encompasses the prior art, that is, what is already in the public domain. The court found that Wilson's claims were not infringed under the doctrine of equivalents.[3]

The claims of four golf ball patents were invalid for obviousness. Substantial evidence supported the jury's verdict that all elements of the asserted patent claims for a multi-layer golf ball comprising a core, an inner cover layer made of a low acid ionomer with a Shore D hardness of 60 or more, and a polyurethane outer cover layer with a Shore D hardness of 64 or less were disclosed by, or at least rendered obvious by, the prior art (*Callaway Golf Co. v. Acushnet Co.*, 2011 WL 518664 [D. Del. 2011]).

As the ABA Journal reports, golf is big business for patent lawyers:

Few areas of industry are as active in patent law as golf. There are patents for balls and putters, drivers and shafts, shoes and spikes, gloves and umbrellas—tens of thousands of patents in all. In the last five years alone [1997–2002], the U.S. Patent and Trademark Office has issued more than 3,000 golf patents. They range from the expected (Winn Grips has 20 U.S. patents for its club grips) to the unexpected (U.S. patent 5,743,809 is for a golf club with a shaft made of bamboo strips).

A golf patent begins in the factory, as engineers and designers develop ideas. Most companies have their own staffs. TaylorMade has 65 experts in-house, five of whom work solely on putters. Once the engineers formulate an idea, they complete an invention record, which explains the concept and certifies the date of initial invention. The record can be used later to sort out which company conceived of an idea first.

From there—even before the golf patent attorney begins the arduous task of drafting an application for the PTO—the search is on to determine whether anyone is sitting on the same idea. Easier said than done. . . .

That's because the hypercompetitive golf business moves faster than a Tiger Woods drive, often sending new products from idea to patent application to market in as little as six months. That leaves the lawyers scrambling for patent information anywhere they can get it. . . .

The PTO is now reviewing hundreds of these patent applications, from major manufacturers and garage inventors alike. Along with designs for new balls, cubs, gloves and bags, there is the Brush T, a plastic tee with tooth-brush-like bristles instead of the standard wooden cup; the Pop-a-Tee, a beeper-sized automatic tee dispenser; and the SoftSwipe, a toothed disk that removes the dirt and grass that get caught in a golfer's spikes. . . .

Once the patent issues—often after 15 to 18 months and multiple PTO requests for clarification—the attorneys head to the phones. Though the first call may be to the inventor, the second call often is to the marketing department. . . .

Almost as soon as the packages hit the shelves, many companies find themselves in litigation. It seems that patent infringement suits among industry competitors have become as ubiquitous in golf as the oversized metal driver. . . .

In just the last two years, Callaway sued Orlimar, Precept sued Callaway, Callaway sued Maxfli, Titleist sued TaylorMade, Ping sued Cleveland Golf, Champ sued Softspikes, Winn Grips sued two rival grip makers. Even two satellite companies, Leading Edge and Optimal Research Solutions, sued each other. Their global positioning system lets golfers know how far their carts are from the hole. . . . (Ted Curtis, "On the Green. As Golf Swings into the Stratosphere It's Big Business for Patent Lawyers," 88 A.B.A. J. 24 [May 2002]).

Patenting of Sports Techniques and Moves

Inventors have begun to obtain patents on sport techniques and moves such as methods for putting golf balls. Is this a good idea? Think about the "Fosbury flop" in high jumping. Dick Fosbury, of course, was the first person to go over the bar backward, and by doing so, revolutionized the sport. Or, to take it to something of an extreme, Tiger Woods's swing or Michael Jordan's slam dunk (How about if you add the tongue being out? Still, probably not.) A sports move or technique certainly could be patentable if it meets the requirements of utility, novelty, and non-obviousness. The problem is, what would it gain, and is it necessary? Acquiring expensive patents for the sheer thrill of acquisition makes little sense with either a cost or benefit analysis.

Nolan Ryan, the great Cy Young baseball pitcher and Texas icon and hero (who lived in Alvin, Texas) did actually receive a patent on his pitch, describing it in excruciating detail in his patent application. The biggest problem in attempting to receive a patent for a sports move or technique is the non-obviousness requirement. The "Fosbury flop" was unique, one-of-a-kind, and in fact ridiculed, in the beginning. Another problem is public use. If you practice your new "cork-screw screw ball" in front of your teammates, then that is sufficient to establish public use, which would make your move unpatentable. So, this screwy screwball patent application would have to be filed quickly, so as to not lose patentability, if that's the goal.

There are also public policy reasons to not patent: how do you enforce it, how do you get paid, and who would own the patent (athlete or team)? But the above notwithstanding, Dick Fosbury *should* have patented his patented move, the Fosbury flop.[4]

Golf, of course, is the battleground. In *Swingless Golf Club Corp. v. Taylor*, 679 F. Supp. 2d 1050 (N.D. Cal. 2009), the court discussed the patentability of a swingless, gun powder-loaded golf club. And in *In re Pelz*, 379 Fed. Appx. 975 (Fed. Cir. 2010), the court decided that a golf training mat is unpatentable. The holy grail question is whether a method for playing better golf is patentable. This scenario was discussed but not decided with any degree of certainty in *In re Lister*, 583 F.3d 1307 (Fed. Cir. 2009). It is an interesting case but sidesteps the main issue of patentability and holds that patentability is not barred on the grounds that this technique was in the public domain, since it was described in a "printed publication." For the purposes of this decision, the "printed publication must be sufficiently accessible." Here, mere registration in a copyright office buried in Internet cyberspace and US PTO gobblydegook is not enough to show sufficient accessibility.

To digress. . .

"Dr. Lister is a Ph.D. clinical psychologist and an avid sportsman. In his earlier days, he competed regularly in organized golf tournaments. However, he eventually grew tired of what he describes as the horrendously slow pace of a game of golf. Although he discontinued his participation in tournaments, he continued to play casually. During this time, he realized that casual golfers have great difficulty with the ordinary requirement that, beginning with the second stroke on each hole, the ball must be hit while lying directly on the ground. This observation led him to conclude that recreational golfers would be able to obtain better scores in a shorter time if they were permitted to tee up their balls on every shot except for those taken from designated hazard areas or the putting green.

Dr. Lister described this method of playing golf in a manuscript entitled 'Advanced Handicap Alternatives for Golf'":

It is strongly advocated that official sanctions be given to the concept of a T handicap. That is, the unrestricted use of a golf tee or peg on any golf shot. Currently, it is allowed 18 times, but only when it is the first shot of the hole being played.

The game otherwise would be played the same, including play in hazards of sand and water, where a tee would not be advocated or permitted. On the surface, this may appear to be a small and insignificant change. Ten years of careful research, by this Ph.D. clinical psychologist sports psychologist, and former professional athlete, has found that a T handicap option would make a profound, positive influence on the game of golf.

When Dr. Lister decided to use the intellectual protection plan for his method of playing golf, he did not retain a lawyer. Lister submitted the manuscript of July 5, 1994, to the United States Copyright Office. Fourteen days later, the copyright office issued a certificate of registration. Dr. Lister learned that to properly protect the invention, he needed to obtain a patent, not a copyright. Lister filed an application on August 5, 1996, to the United States Patent and Trademark office. Over the next thirteen years, Dr. Lister was rejected several times. He has had two appeals with the Board and continues his lengthy prosecution history. Dr. Lister has five claims remaining at issue; however, only claim 21, an independent claim, is representative:

> "A method for playing a game of organized golf wherein the improvement is that each participating player or group of players is permitted under the official or sanctioned rules of said game for normal play to raise or tee the ball up above turf level at any time during play, except for designated hazard areas and greens, and further comprising the step of recording the number of strokes taken by each participating player of [sic] group of players throughout said game for the purpose of comparing said number of strokes with the number of strokes of each other participating player or group of players or to an average or expected number of strokes for golf play in accordance with said game. [583 F.3d 1307, 1309-1310]"

Infringement

Successfully suing for patent infringement is the key to protecting the profitability of a sports or entertainment patent. In *Lawlor v. Nike, Inc.*, 2005 WL 1459488 (W.D. Mass.), the plaintiff claimed patent infringement by a select line of Nike shoes on two of his patents, one of which was a shock-absorbing athletic shoe with inverted cups.

Patent infringement analysis is a two-step process: the first step, claim construction, is to determine the meaning and scope of the claims, and the second step, determination of infringement, is to compare the properly-constructed claim to the product accused of infringement. The plaintiff's infringement claim centered on the design of the sole. His claim hinged upon the construction of the "bottom sole."

Both sides argued the meaning of "bottom sole." Nike argued that the terms should be constructed to mean the outsole, which is the part of the shoe that contacts the ground and is also the lowest part of the sole. The plaintiff argued that "bottom sole" means a part of the shoe attached to the upper sole, but his interpretation of "bottom sole," if believed, would likely have imputed an infringing use of Nike's shoes. If the court agreed with his interpretation, then Nike would have likely infringed. The court, however, agreed with Nike's definition. The court held that Nike's shoes did not literally infringe because none of Nike's accused shoes have the same "bottom soles," the alleged distinguishing factor, as described in plaintiff's claims. The court granted Nike's motion for summary judgment regarding the infringement claims.

The type of infringement cases in sports are myriad: athletic shoes (those with a lateral foot stabilizer), umpire chest protectors in baseball, hockey face shields, high-performance baseball bats, dual flooring surface for sports events, "dual-cushion technology" in basketballs, installation of rubberized athletic tracks, "padded inflatable" basketballs, golf bags, structural members inside softball and baseball bats, chest protectors for baseball catchers, street hockey balls, bodyboards, splayed string systems for sports racquets, softball bats with "gaps" between insert and tubular frame, double-walled aluminum softball bats, laser range-finders for sport hunting, protective athletic mouthpieces, golf putter heads, football helmet design improvement (compression-deflecting jaw pad), portable golf computer, table tennis table, football helmets again (here, one that allegedly reduces the incidence of concussions), and the life-saving, mind-boggling, game-changing "swingless golf club."

A good example of sports patent infringement can be found in a series of lawsuits initiated by Warrior Lacrosse, Inc. (*Warrior Lacrosse, Inc. v. STX, LLC*, 2005 WL 1378752, [E.D. Mich.]; *Warrior Lacrosse, Inc. v. Brine, Inc.*, 2006 WL 763190 [E.D. Mich.]; and *Warrior Sports, Inc. v. STX, L.L.C.*, 2008 WL 783768 [E.D. Mich.]). Lacrosse, although unheard of in many parts of the United States, is the prep sport, or wannabe prep sport. If you want to go to an Ivy League school, play lacrosse (or row crew or play squash or fence).

In the 2006 lawsuit, Plaintiff Warrior Lacrosse, Inc., is the proprietor of patents relating to protective sports gloves. On April 30, 2004, Warrior commenced litigation against Defendant Brine, Inc., for patent infringement.

In the 2008 lawsuit,

"[t]his controversy arises from a claim of patent infringement based on two of STX, LLC's models of protective lacrosse equipment: the "Shogun" and "Chopper." Warrior Sports, Inc. moves for preliminary injunction. . . . Warrior and STX both manufacture and sell lacrosse sports equipment. Warrior was founded between 1992 and 1993, and initially struggled to compete against STX and another established competitor until 1996. It has since made significant inroads into the market. This litigation is one of four pending patent infringement suits between the parties. However, this litigation marks the first litigation over protective gear."

Infringement lawsuits can be quite technical. For example, in Claim 1 of Warrior's 924 patent, it asserts that it was

. . .an upper body protective garment comprising:

a. a chest protector portion;
b. a back protector portion;
c. a pair of telescopic shoulder protector portions in connection between said chest protector portion and said back protector portion;
d. wherein each of said pair of telescopic shoulder protector portions includes:
e. an inner-shoulder protector portion; and
f. an outer-shoulder protector portion that is telescopically coupled to said inner-shoulder protector portion; and
g. said outer-shoulder protector portion being moveable between an extended protector and said back protection portion.

According to Warrior, it has incorporated its 924 patent into most of its protective shoulder pads products on the market today. Warrior alleges infringement through STX's manufacture and sale of two models of protective lacrosse shoulder pads: the Shogun and Chopper.

The issues presented are whether: (1) STX infringes; (2) STX raises a substantial question regarding validity or enforceability that strips Warrior of a presumption of irreparable harm; (3) STX can nonetheless rebut the presumption; (4) Warrior can demonstrate irreparable harm without the presumption; and (5) the four relevant factors for a preliminary injunction weigh towards Warrior or STX.

The point is, Warrior will win some and lose some, but it most assuredly has informed their competitors that it will zealously protect its research, intellectual property, and patent rights in the demimonde of lacrosse equipment manufacturers. The 2008 litigation was settled when certain words or claim constructions in the Warrior patents were resolved.

"The Special Master has recommended the following claim constructions with respect to the mission patents.

Table 3.1

Claim Limitation	Recommended Construction
"Adjacent"	Near
"Compliant Material"	A non-rigid material that bends, flexes, or yields when a force is applied.

"Cut-Away"	Edges having recesses forming an opening, regardless of how that opening is formed
"Hinged Sections"	Sections that are moveable in a bending or flexing manner with respect to one another.
"Lenticular"	Shaped like a double convex lens, but not shaped like a circle, an oval, or a polygon.
"Protective Hockey Glove"	A glove that is intended to shield a wearer's hand from injury.
"Proximally"	Near or approximate.

The Special Master has also recommended the following claim constructions with respect to the Morrow patents.

Table 3.2

Claim Limitation	Recommended Construction
"Adjacent"	Near
"Areas That Are Not Intended to Primarily Contact a Stick" and Like Phrases	Areas that do not ordinarily contact the stick when the stick is gripped in the hand during play
"Diagonal"	Having a generally non-horizontal and non-vertical orientation.
"Palm Portion"	Part of the glove covering the inside of the hand but not including the fingers or thumb.
"Protective Lacrosse Glove"	A glove that is intended to shield a wearer's hand from injury.

Additionally, the Special Master recommends that Warrior's motion to preclude Brine from contesting the validity and enforceability of the mission patents be granted on the basis of contractual estoppel" (2008 WL 783768).

There are many lawsuits about digital technology and the implications with gaming, sports entertainment, and patent law. New patent infringement lawsuits in the mobile entertainment industry seem to occur every day.[5] For example, a company that argues that it developed the technology used in handheld viewers that allow NASCAR fans to receive audio and video information during races has settled its patent infringement suit for $4 million.[6]

In *Fantasy Sports Properties, Inc. v. SportsLine.com, Inc.*, 287 F.3d 1108 (Fed Cir. 2002), it was held that competing computer football games by SportsLine.com, Yahoo, and ESPN did not infringe Fantasy Sports Properties's patented "fantasy" football because none of the competitors had adopted Fantasy Sports's unique "bonus points" system.

Fantasy Sports patented its computer football game under U.S. Patent No. 4,918,603. The game allowed people to act as "managers" or "owners" and use their personal computer to pick players and call plays for simulated football games. Bonus points were awarded based on the difficulty of the play called. Cable television network ESPN and Internet websites Yahoo and SportsLine.com released similar football games. Fantasy sports sued for patent infringement in U.S. District court for the Eastern District of Virginia, but the court granted summary judgment in favor of the three defendants. According to the court, the defendants had not infringed the '603 patent because their games did not give bonus points for difficulty of a play. Fantasy Sports appealed.

In its ruling, the U.S. Court of Appeals for the Federal Circuit affirmed the Virginia federal court's summary judgment for ESPN and Yahoo. Although extra points were given in their computer games, the points were based on actual scores and not on the difficulty of a particular football play, the appellate court said. Two of SportsLine's games also fell under the court's interpretation of bonus points, but a third did not. The court held that, in the third game, Commissioner.com had the ability to be customized to offer bonus points based on the difficulty of a play. Because Commissioner.com could be modified to infringe the '603 patent, the appellate court said triable issues of material fact existed and remanded that part of the case to the lower court for further proceedings (See also, "Yahoo, ESPN, SportsLine Win E. Patent Case on "Bonus Points," 3 No. 9 Andrews E. Bus. L. Bull. 3 [June 2002]).

In *Harrah's Entertainment, Inc. v. Station Casinos, Inc.,* 2004 WL 1237500 (D. Nev.), a federal court has ruled that patents for a customer-tracking system held by Harrah's Entertainment, Inc., and challenged by its competitors are invalid because they are indefinite and do not have an adequate written description, two essential requirements of patents that describe and claim methods and systems for rewarding customer patronage, tracking customers, and making customer data available to affiliated casino properties.

The patents are based on a concept called the "theoretical win profile," which is a measure of a customer's value to the affiliated properties. Together, they work to implement a system that awards points to customers based on the customers' tracked activity at all casino properties. Customers can then redeem the points for gifts or services. Harrah's filed suit in the U.S. District court for the District of Nevada against several other casinos for infringement of the patents. The defendants challenged the suit and moved for partial summary judgment on the grounds that the patents are invalid due to indefiniteness and are unsupported by an adequate written description. They focused on the term "theoretical win profile." The court explained that a claim is considered to be indefinite if its legal scope is not clear enough that a person of ordinary skill in the art could determine whether a particular composition infringes or not. The claim must be capable of being construed, no matter how difficult the task may be.

The court concluded that the defendants established that the customer-tracking patent claims were indefinite because of the ill-defined method for determining a theoretical win profile. The profile is based on a customer's estimated winnings from betting activity at the plurality of casino properties for a period of time. Harrah's assertion that the specific means for calculating the theoretical win profile did not have to be provided because the term could be calculated by using a number of different methods. The court disagreed (See also "Casinos Win Big Over Customer-Tracking Patents," 1 No. 1 Andrews Patent Litig. Rep. 3 [June 28, 2004]).

CHAPTER 4

Who Is the King of the Road? Copyright in the Music Business

Roger Miller, singer-songwriter, savant, wrote many pithy songs, including "King of the Road." As the song goes, "Trailer for sale or rent, rooms to let 50 cents. I'm a man of means by no means king of the road." Not to mention such classic lines as "dang me, dang me, they ought to take a rope and hang me, high from the highest tree. Woman, would you weep for me?" A true icon and the one individual who introduced "Bangor, Maine" to the greater population. But he died, and his wife wanted some money. An interesting case and a salient point in which to observe the importance of copyright in the music business. The *Miller* case involves renewal copyrights; there is a distinct difference between original and renewal copyright. Roger Miller also wrote, "You Can't Roller Skate in a Buffalo Herd" and "Chug-a-Lug"—certainly intellectual property such as that must be protected.

The United States Constitution, Article I, Section 8, Clause 8 provides that Congress shall have the power "[t]o promote the progress of science and useful arts, by securing for limited time to authors . . . the exclusive right to their respective writings . . . Congress thus provides the framework for copyright protection. The first Copyright Act was passed on May 13, 1790 (Ch. 15, 1 Stat. 124). Essential to the current copyright protection are the Copyright Revision Act of 1909 and of 1976 (17 U.S.C. § 101 *et seq.,* which was a complete revision of the copyright laws; for example, works copyrighted prior to 1978 operate under special rules of duration (28 years for the first term), renewal (the work must be registered for renewal within one year prior to the expiration of the original term), and an extended renewal term, so that the work is protected for a total of 75 years, but with termination with respect to the extension of 19 years that allows termination by the grantor, authors, or beneficiaries. All transfers, assignments infringements, and registration requirements occurring prior to 1978 are governed by the 1909 Act. So even though most works are created under the 1976 Act, a new work may be based on a prior work protected under the 1909 Act.

For an author's work to be considered copyrightable, the Copyright Act of 1976 requires that the work be "an original work of authorship." Although a copyrightable work must be original, the required creativity for originality is not high. All that is required is that the author contribute "something recognizably 'his own'" and that the author not merely copy another's work in its entirety.

The Copyright Act also requires that a copyrightable work must be fixed in a "tangible medium of expression." A work is deemed to meet this fixation requirement "when its embodiment . . . is sufficiently permanent . . . to permit it to be perceived, reproduced or otherwise communicated for a period of more than transitory duration." Recorded television events are copyrightable because they fulfill the Copyright Act's requirements for originality and fixation.

The Supreme Court has held that while copyright law may protect an author's expression of ideas, it does not protect the author's ideas themselves. This differentiation is commonly known as "the idea expression dichotomy" and is noted in the Copyright Act's prohibition against protection for an author's "idea, procedure, process, system, method of operation . . . regardless of the form in which it is described, explained, illustrated, or embodied in such work." Judicial application of this dichotomy occurred in *Baker v. Selden*, where the Supreme Court asserted that, while an author may copyright a mathematics textbook, the author may not copyright the specific formulas and methods utilized within the textbook. The dichotomy exists because one of the copyright laws' primary purposes is "to promote the Progress of Science and the useful Arts" rather than to reward authors' labor and creativity. The *Baker* Court reasoned that extending copyright protection to the mathematical formulas would prevent an engineer from legally applying the formulas whenever necessary, frustrating the copyright laws' primary purpose to further scientific progress.

Generally, copyright protection lasts from the moment of creation through the life of the author plus 70 years. While the copyright subsists, the author is granted certain exclusive rights. After the copyright is terminated, the work is released into the public domain.

Copyright Generally

A basic tenet of copyright law is that copyright protects only the expression of ideas, not the ideas themselves. (See *Meshwerks, Inc. v. Toyota*

Motor Sales U.S.A., Inc., 528 F.3d 1258, 1265, 87 U.S.P.Q.2d 1055 (10th Cir. 2008), cert. denied, 129 S.Ct. 1006 (2009) ("Facts and ideas are the public's domain and open to exploitation to ensure the progress of science and the useful arts.") Forms of intellectual property other than copyright may protect the use of ideas. The application of ideas may be protected by patent law, the disclosure of ideas may be protected by contract, and ideas may be claimed as a trade secret. This is known as the idea/expression dichotomy and is often difficult to apply to concrete situations. The line between an idea and protected expression is often unclear (*Oravec v. Sunny Isles Luxury Ventures, L.C.*, 527 F.3d 1218, 1225, 86 U.S.P.Q.2d 1661 (11th Cir. 2008) ("The idea/expression dichotomy seeks to achieve a proper balance between competing societal interests: that of encouraging the creation of original works on the one hand, and that of promoting the free flow of ideas and information on the other.") See *Suntrust Bank v. Houghton Mifflin Co.*, 268 F.3d 1257, 1266, 60 U.S.P.Q.2d 1225 (11th Cir. 2001) ("as plots become more intricately detailed and characters become more idiosyncratic, they at some point cross the line into 'expression.'"); Abrams, Law of Copyright § 3:1. "Obviously, no principle can be stated as to when an imitator has gone beyond copying the 'idea,' and has borrowed its 'expression.' Decisions must therefore inevitably be *ad hoc*." *Peter Pan Fabrics, Inc. v. Martin Weiner Corp.*, 274 F.2d 487, 489, 124 U.S.P.Q. 154 (2d Cir. 1960). See *Peter Letterese and Associates, Inc. v. World Institute of Scientology Enterprises*, 533 F.3d 1287, 1305, 87 U.S.P.Q.2 1563 (11th Cir. 2008) (in many copyright cases, the line between idea and expression is not easily drawn). (See *Ivory v. Holme*, 209 WL 513720 (M.D. Fla. 2009) ("As a general principle, simply because a work is copyrighted does not mean every element of that work is protected.") (See *Baker v. Selden*, 101 U.S. 99, 1879 WL 16689 (1879); *Nash v. CBS, Inc.*, 899 F.2d 1537, 1542, 17 Media L. Rep. (BNA) 1798, 14 U.S.P.Q.2d 1755 (7th Cir. 1990); *Satava v. Lowry*, 323 .3d 805, 813, 66 U.S.P.Q.2d 1206 (9th Cir. 2003) "Only by vigorously policing the line between idea and expression can we ensure both that artists receive the reward for their original creations and that proper latitude is granted other artists to make use of ideas that properly belong to us all." *Curtin v. Star Editorial, Inc.*, 2 F. Supp. 2d 670, 674, 47 U.S.P.Q.2d 1051 (E.D. Pa. 1998) (plaintiff could not claim copyright protection for his "idea" to display photographs of Elvis Presley with celebrities). But, see *American Dental Ass'n v. Delta Dental Plans Ass'n*, 126 F.3d 977, 979, 44 U.S.P.Q.2d 1296 (7th Cir. 1997) (Taxonomy of dental procedures held to be protected expression: "Classification is a creative endeavor"). Basic story ideas are not protectable, no matter how novel or distinctive. (See *Berkic v. Crichton*, 761 F.2d 1289, 1293, 11 Media L. Rep. (BNA) 2450, 26 U.S.P.Q. 787 (9th Cir. 1985)).

Copyright law does not preclude others from using the ideas revealed by an author's work. Once an expression is fixed, any ideas contained in the expression are given to the public. A literary work that is fixed and original will be protected by copyright. The copyright protects the expression contained in the work, not the ideas that are being expressed. *West Side Story* is a musical play protected by copyright. Its copyright protection, however, does not include the idea of two young lovers, each from different groups engaged in a deadly feud, falling in love and the subsequent death of one of the lovers (See *Walker v. Time Life Films, Inc.,* 784 F.2d 44, 50, 12 Media L. Rep. [BNA] 1634, 228 U.S.P.Q 505 [2d Cir. 1986]). "Foot chases and the morale problems of policemen, not to mention the familiar figure of the Irish cop, are venerable and often-recurring themes of police fiction."

The distinction between protectable expression and nonprotectible ideas is codified in section 102(b) of the Copyright Act. Descriptions of a process or system are copyrightable, but the underlying process or system itself is not. Pursuant to this statutory rule, words and short phrases such as names, titles, and slogans, the rules of a game, or the mere listing of ingredients or contents are not protected by copyright. "In no case does copyright protection for an original work of authorship extend to any idea, procedure, system, method of operation, concept, principle, or discovery, regardless of the form in which it is described, explained, illustrated, or embodied in such work." (17 U.S.C. § 102[b]).

After the 1976 Copyright Act, the length of copyright protection was set at the life of the author plus 50 years (17 U.S.C. § 302[a]). Under the recently enacted Sonny Bono Copyright Term Extension Act, the length of copyright protection has extended copyright terms by an additional twenty years (P.L. No. 105–278, 112 Stat. 2827, codified at 15 U.S.C. §§ 1031–1127). Any length of protection that survives beyond the life of the author seems innately unfair. If Congress's rationale was to focus on protecting the author's expression, copyright protection should be granted for only the life of the author. Death should be considered the ultimate abandonment of will.

By granting protection for a longer period, the current copyright system provides an author's heirs with the right to control the author's works. When the author dies, he can no longer exert his will on the work—he cannot add to it or subtract from it. In effect, the current system permits authors to control their works from the grave. Further, by making subsequent authors wait seventy-five years until the work goes into the public domain, society loses out on the creativity of those secondary authors. Therefore, at the very least, copyright protection should be reduced to last only through the life of the author.

Another possibility with respect to the length of protection could be to add a use requirement similar to the requirement in trademark law. Under trademark law, the mark's owner must submit an affidavit stating that they will continue to use the mark to renew protection. If the owner discontinues use of the mark, the mark is considered abandoned and falls back into the public domain. A similar requirement should be implemented under Copyright law. By forcing authors to submit proof that they plan to use their works again, it forces authors to stay in tune with the market and react as the market demands. If they do not wish to participate, they have the options of selling, licensing, or losing their copyrights.

As technology has progressed, Congress has periodically developed compulsory licenses to "(1) ensure public dissemination and authors compensation; (2) avoid market failure-high transaction costs; and (3) enforcement problems due to free riders. These compulsory licenses have allowed the re-recording of music onto new media (17 U.S.C. § 115), retransmission of broadcast signals through cable wires and satellite carriers (17 U.S.C. § 111[c]), and public performance of music through public broadcasting (17 U.S.C. § 118[b]), and jukeboxes (17 U.S.C. § 116).

The Audio Home Recording Act of 1992 permits unauthorized audio recording for noncommercial use. (17 U.S.C. § 1008.) The reproduction and distribution of musical recordings with the use of a computer do not fall within the protection of section 1008. See *Recording Industry Ass'n of America v. Diamond Multimedia Systems, Inc.* 180 F.3d 1072, 1078, 51 U.S.P.Q.2d 115, 178 A.L.R. Fed. 689 (9th Cir. 1999) (computers do not constitute "digital audio recording devices" under AHRA). To combat piracy, all digital audio recording devices must include SCMS technology that precludes serial copying (See *Recording Industry Ass'n of America v. Diamond Multimedia Systems, Inc.,* 180 F.3d 1072, 51 U.S.P.Q.2d 1115, 178 A.L.R. Fed. 689 (9th Cir. 1999) (Rio portable music player held not required to employ a Serial Copyright Management System because player, which is not able to reproduce a digital music recording "directly" or "from a transmission," was not a digital audio recording device).

Copyright and the Music Business

A brief history of relevant portions of 17 U.S.C. § 101, *et seq.,* The Copyright Law of the United States, should be helpful to an understanding of the issues. Section 301(a) preempts state law with respect to any provision that is equivalent to provisions of Title 17. It states as follows:

On and after January 1, 1978, all legal or equitable rights that are equivalent to any of the exclusive rights within the general scope of copyright as specified by section 106 in works of authorship . . . are governed exclusively by this title . . .
(17 U.S.C. § 301[a]).

Section 106 sets out the enumerated exclusive rights an owner of copyright enjoys under Title 17.

. . . [t]he owner of copyright under this title has the exclusive rights to do and to authorize any of the following:

1. To reproduce the copyrighted work in copies or phonorecords;
2. To prepare derivative works based upon the copyrighted work;
3. To distribute copies or phonorecords of the copyrighted work to the public . . . ;
4. in the case of . . . musical . . . works . . . to perform the copyrighted work publicly;
5. in the case of . . . musical . . . works . . . to display the copyrighted work publicly;
6. in the case of sound recordings, to perform the copyrighted work publicly. . .

(17 U.S.C. § 106).

Section 203(a)(5) provides conditions under which any transfer or license granted by an author after January 1, 1978, can be terminated. This right is absolute and inalienable:

Termination of the grant may be effected notwithstanding any *AGREEMENT* to the contrary, including an agreement to make a will or to make any future grant.

Section 304 sets forth both the original 28-year term of copyright and the 67-year renewal period, together with a statutory expression that the author, or his heirs, shall enjoy the renewal term, if the statutory conditions are met (17 U.S.C. § 304). Additionally, 304(c)(3) provides for the termination of transfers and licenses covering the 67-year renewal term with respect to transfers or licenses executed prior to 1978 by either an author or his heirs; if applicable (17 U.S.C. § 304). This right of termination is also inalienable.

Both sections 203 and 304 are recapture sections, which demonstrate the express congressional intention to give authors and their heirs a second chance to enjoy the economic benefits of the author's creative work.

A brief review of the history of the renewal clauses is as follows:

1790 – 14-year original term. . . . An additional 14-year renewal term was available if prescribed formalities were complied with, ... provided the author was alive on the first day of the renewal term. If the author was not alive on the first day of the renewal term, the work went into the public domain, regardless of whether the author had a surviving spouse or children.

1831 – The original term was doubled to 28 years, for a potential total term of 42 years . . . Where the author was not alive on the first day of the renewal term, the renewal term vested in his or her spouse and children. If the author had no surviving spouse or children, however, the work went into the public domain at the expiration of the first term.

1909 – The renewal term was doubled to 28 years, for a potential term of 56 years . . .

1976 – . . . Works that were in their renewal term on January 1, 1978 (the effective date of the new law) had that term extended for an extra 19 years, for a total of 47 years, coupled with a termination of transfer provision for the extended 19 years in § 304(c)(6). Works in either their original term or renewal term on January 1, 1978, were granted a 47-year renewal term if a timely renewal was made.

1992 – The renewal term was extended from 47 years to 67 years by amendment to the Copyright Act in 1992. The same amendment provided for automatic renewal and established standards for vesting of the copyright renewal estate.

A previously distributed musical composition may be reproduced without the consent of the copyright owner pursuant to a compulsory mechanical license (17 U.S.C. § 115). Under this compulsory license, the composition can be recorded, manufactured in phonorecords, and sold to the public for its private use, as long as the statutory royalty of 9.1 cents per unit is paid to the copyright owner. Stylistic changes to the composition are permitted as long as the composition is not perverted or distorted, nor the fundamental character of the work changed.

The Digital Performance Right in Sound Recordings Act of 1995 has created a compulsory mechanical for "digital phonorecord delivery," the distribution of recorded musical compositions by digital transmissions. The Copyright Office has defined "digital phonorecord delivery" as

A "digital phonorecord delivery" is each individual delivery of a phonorecord by digital transmission of a sound recording which results in a specifically identifiable reproduction by or for any transmission recipient of a phonorecord of that sound recording, regardless of whether the digital transmission is also a public performance of the sound recording or any nondramatic musical work embodied therein. The reproduction of the phonorecord must be sufficiently permanent or stable to permit it to be perceived, reproduced, or otherwise communicated for a period of more than transitory duration. Such a phonorecord may be permanent or it may be made available to the transmission recipient for a limited period of time or for a specified number of performances. A digital phonorecord delivery includes all phonorecords that are made for the purpose of making the digital phonorecord delivery (37 C.F.R. § 255.4). Currently, the amount of the license is the same as the traditional section 115 compulsory mechanical license. Unlike the traditional section 115 compulsory mechanical license, the compulsory mechanical license for "digital phonorecord delivery" may include controlled compositions.

In 2009, the Copyright Office interpreted "digital phonorecord delivery" to include the interactive streaming and limited or tethered digital downloads of musical works. As a result, compulsory licenses are available for the use of musical works by Web sites and digital music services. The compulsory license fee for interactive streaming is 10.5 percent of revenue, the definition of which varies according to the business model employed, such as subscription-based or advertising supported. In either case, a minimum payment is required. In the case of limited digital downloads, the compulsory license fee is 10 percent of revenue, with a required minimum payment.

The Sound Recording Industry Generally

The recording industry and the music publishing industry are closely intertwined. The recording industry produces income from the exploitation of music but makes most of its income on the sale of the recordings.

The key question is who maintains copyright ownership among the artist, producer, or recording company. In *Systems XIX, Inc. v. Parker,* 30 F. Supp. 2d 1225 (N.D. Cal. 1998), the court discussed the ownership of the two live recordings at a venue. The venue, a combined amphitheater and recording studio, claimed joint copyright ownership of the sound recordings. Defendants argued that the venue was not a joint author of the sound recordings because the artist and his recording company lacked the requisite intent to create a joint work and never authorized the venue to use the underlying musical corporation to make the sound recording. Section 101 of the Copyright Act of 1976 defines a "joint work" as "a work prepared by two or more authors with the intention that their contributions be merged into inseparable or interdependent parts of a unitary whole." Therefore, a party claiming joint authorship must establish that the authors (1) intended to merge their contributions into a unitary whole and (2) contributed copyrightable subject matter to the joint work. In *Systems XIX, Inc.,* the court held that the jury could reasonably conclude that the artist/recording company and the venue shared an implied agreement to jointly create a sound recording. Additionally, a jury could reasonably infer that the artist, vested with his recording company's authority to perform the copyrighted compositions, acted as the recording company's agent when he asked the venue to record the concert. The recording company's commercial exploitation of the sound recordings creates a question of fact as to whether the artist's request to record the performance constituted an implied license for the venue to use the underlying compositions to produce the sound recording.[1]

The integrity of the sound recording industry was revisited in this chapter's lead case, *Roger Miller Music, Inc. v. Sony/ATV Publ'g, LLC,* 2012 WL 555485 (6th Cir. 2012), which struck a blow against songwriters (and their widow brides) by asserting that the music publisher successfully secured renewal copyrights in some of Roger Miller's most famous songs. The federal Court of Appeals held that Mary Miller, the widow of country music legend Roger Miller, does not own the rights to some of his biggest hits, including "King of the Road." The court reasoned that Sony/ATV Music Publishing owns the renewal copyrights to the songs the artist published in 1964. Other courts have already ruled that Sony owns the rights to Miller's songs published from 1958 to 1963.

Roger Miller was 56 when he died in 1992 after a battle with cancer. The singer willed his widow the entitlement to the rights to his work. But before his death, he assigned copyrights to Sony, who applied to renew the copyrights. Mary Miller was in a drawn-out legal battle with Sony and argued that she was entitled to the rights to the songs because her husband died before the copyrights were renewed. But the appeals court asserts Sony's ownership since Roger Miller assigned rights to the company at the time applications were made to renew the copyrights.

Roger Miller, "King of the Road," and the Loss of Renewal Copyrights

Roger was an American icon. He was Nashville's resident jester and wit. He saw America's underbelly and made us smile. With no disrespect, he was the Country & Western standup version of Woody Guthrie. He helped to bring Country & Western music into America's mainstream. He was literally "the King of the Road."

He evoked Robert Service in a way that was hummable.

The loss of renewal copyright that was presumably bequeathed to his widow was lost to giant Sony. This is a big deal and a tremor in the force to all singer/songwriters, who feel that they are losing ground in maintaining their royalties from the incursion of the Internet, downloading, iTunes, sampling, piracy, and now bullying music-publishing mega-corporations.

Artists Attempt to Reclaim Rights after 30 Years

Since the release of their songs in 1978, artists like Bruce Springsteen, Billy Joel, the Doobie Brothers, and Funkadelic have generated hundreds of millions of dollars for record companies. However, due to a lesser known provision in U.S. copyright law, these artists have a new sense of control over their music. Thousands of artists now have the right to retain ownership of their recordings, potentially leaving their labels stranded.

Copyright law was pivotal to musicians and creators of works of art, where given "termination rights." These termination rights allow them to regain control of the work under the stipulation agreement after 35 years. These creators of art, however, must apply at least 2 years in advance. The recordings occurring in 1978 were the first to fall under this new law.

The provision also allows artists the ability to reclaim ownership of qualifying songs. Artists such as Bob Dylan, Tom Petty, Charlie Daniels, and other artists have utilized this provision. Although the artists themselves make the music, the recording industry profits greatly from the masters. Don Henley is the founder of the Eagles and Recording Artists Coalition, an organization that seeks to protect performers' legal rights. The consensus belief from the Henley organization is that this disparity in profits will only increase in the future.

When the industry reeled from plummeting sales at the turn of the millennium, termination rights also acted as another blow. At the end of 2009, sales went from 14.6 billion to 6.3 billion. These losses are accredited to unauthorized music downloads of new music from artists. This left the majority of record labels to rely heavily on past releases in their inventory. Presently, the fight to maintain the masters of artists is a heated debate. Record companies' perspective is that because of perpetuity, the records are classified as "works for hire." They believe that the music artists are employees and the record label formed a compilation to produce the music created. A large portion of independent copyright experts disagree with this argument. Recording artists usually pay for records, and music companies usually advance the money to them. This money that is advanced is also charged with royalties. This practice has been around for multiple decades. Experts point to the fact that since artists usually do not pay social security or have taxes withheld from their paychecks, they are not employees but instead independent contractors.

Performing Rights Societies & Copyright Enforcement

The right of copyright owners to control the public performance of their music was first established by Congress in the late nineteenth century. But since music use in non-dramatic settings was exclusively live and often spontaneous, performance rights were difficult to enforce, unauthorized performances were frequent, and music users found it difficult, if not impossible, to obtain performance rights in a timely manner. Thus the stage was set for a "performing rights society." The first such society in the U.S., the American Society of Composers, Authors and Publishers (ASCAP), was founded by composer Victor Herbert on February 13, 1914. Its initial purpose was to protect the copyrighted musical compositions of its members, who were songwriters, performers, lyricists, and publishers.

ASCAP is the largest performing rights society, but it's not the only game in town. The second oldest performing rights organization, the Society of European Stage Authors and Composers (SESAC), was founded in 1930 to provide European songwriters with a US presence. SESAC is smaller in number of members because of its unique practice of choosing its clients rather than just accepting anyone who applies. Although initially formed for the benefit of European authors and composers, in later years, SESAC distanced itself from its original name in favor of a more global reach.

With its broader membership base, as ASCAP grew in membership, so did its leverage in fee negotiations with restaurants, theatres, movie houses, and other venues. More leverage brought greater success. And as often happens with great success, greed crept in. As expiration of then-current broadcast licenses approached, ASCAP announced in 1939 that it would increase its license fees. Broadcasters began looking at alternatives.[2] In response, Broadcast Music, Inc. (BMI) formed that year and quickly became a serious ASCAP competitor, securing agreements from nearly 250 radio stations by offering annual fees that were about 40 percent of total fees they paid to ASCAP just two years prior.[3] By late 1940, BMI signed long-term contracts with several major clients.[4]

On the flip side, the Recording Industry Association of America (RIAA) represents U.S. recording industry distributors such as the "Big Four," EMI, Sony Music Entertainment, Universal Music Group, and Warner Music Group. Formed in 1952, RIAA claims over 1,600 member labels that create, manufacture or distribute 85 to 90 percent of all legally-sold recorded music in the United States.[5] Although RIAA, BMI, SESAC, and ASCAP existed long before, it wasn't until 1976 that copyright law included the definition of a "performing rights society" as "an association, corporation, or other entity that licenses and collects fees for the use of music written or published by its members, the copyright owners."[6]

Generally, these performing rights associations provide intermediary functions between its members and parties who wish to use copyrighted works *publicly* in locations such as shopping and dining venues. The members grant the association a nonexclusive right to license for public use nondramatic performances of their works. ASCAP takes in substantial revenues from these use licenses, and the revenues, less deductions for operating expenses, are distributed to the members as royalties.

A performing rights society also serves as an enforcer of the copyrights that apply to the works of its members. As an agent for member songwriters, performers, lyricists, publishers, musicians, and others, it therefore stands in the shoes of its members. It protects its members' musical copyrights by monitoring public performances of their music, whether via a broadcast or live performance. Prior to enactment of the Copyright Act of 1976, copyright protection attached to original works only when they were (a) published and (b) had a notice of copyright affixed. The 1976 Act effectuated major change, recognizing dramatic advances in technology and U.S. participation in the Universal Copyright Convention. Under Section 106 of the 1976 Act, copyright law afforded greatly expanded exclusive rights, separate and distinct from those under patent and trademark laws, to do and to authorize any of the following:

1. to *reproduce* the copyrighted work;
2. to *prepare derivative works* based on the copyrighted work;
3. to *distribute copies* of the copyrighted work;
4. to *perform* copyrighted literary, musical, dramatic, and choreographic works, pantomimes, and motion pictures and other audiovisual works publicly; and
5. to *display* the copyrighted work publicly. The Act was amended in 1995 to include a sixth exclusive right:
6. in the case of sound recordings, to *perform* the copyrighted work publicly by means of digital audio transmission.

Clearly, it is impossible for a member to monitor the thousands of entities that might perform his composition, so the performing rights societies become the eyes and ears of the member in the marketplace, ensuring that all users of his compositions have paid the right to do so. This is uniformly accomplished by the use of the blanket license. ASCAP, SESAC, BMI, RIAA, and a myriad of other similar organizations have immense tools to investigate and collect data on business practices related to those licenses. Other types of licenses include per-program, which differs from a blanket license in that per-program license limits use of the covered music to specific radio or television programs.

Radio stations and the Internet are easily monitored targets.[7] Any business that plays music is vulnerable. Such businesses, for example, include background music services, colleges and universities, bars, hotels, theme parks, and skating rinks. If any entities play music, they have to have a license and pay royalties. This process includes proving the artist name, broadcast time, and what type of music is performed. After the investigator logs the evidence and reports it to ASCAP, the evidence is compared to songs played to ASCAP's repertory. In the event that stations' songs are part of ASCAP's repertory and that station has no license, there will be repercussions for the violation.

Although SESAC, BMI, RIAA, and others monitor their members' creations similarly, mass violation of members' rights dictate investigation on a larger scale. Unauthorized copying of records, tapes, and live performances likely have occurred from the time copying mechanisms were available. However, because the technology of duplicating CDs developed rapidly, making CDs a quicker, easier, and cheaper duplicate than most other forms of sound recording, compact disc piracy[8] became a global problem in the 1990s. Counterfeit recordings are shipped for sale around the world through complicated distribution channels, making the place of origin difficult to determine. By 1998, the sale of pirated recordings comprised fully one third of global music sales. These sales not only infringe upon the rights of the artists involved but they also create unfair competition at every level of the industry supply chain.

The advent of the Internet served as a major springboard for the problem. Many cases based on such piracy are well known, especially those involving Napster. Founded in 1999, Napster initially was envisioned as an independent peer-to-peer file sharing service that allowed people to easily share their MP3 files with other participants, but its ease of use led to massive copyright violations of music and film media, as well as other intellectual property. At its peak, there were 25 million Napster users and 80 million songs, yet the system never once crashed.

Although *A&M Records v. Napster, Inc.*, no longer reflects state-of-the-art for peer-to-peer file sharing, the case captures the technological and social trends critical to understanding the revolution taking place in music distribution. It also anticipated changes in legal doctrines of fair use and reveals the impact of computer software on the music industry.[9] Napster's original operation ceased because of this and other legal difficulties over copyright infringement, and Roxio eventually acquired it. Thereafter, Napster was an online music store; it merged with Rhapsody in December 2011.

In another bold move against digital piracy, RIAA announced in December 2003 that it had hired big guns to head its anti-piracy division. Bradley A. Buckles, then director of the U.S. Bureau of Alcohol, Tobacco, Firearms, and Explosives, was slated to lead industry efforts against the digital piracy that, according to the industry, resulted in slumping sales and lost profits. This announcement, following in the wake of 261 lawsuits RIAA had filed that September against people who allegedly downloaded its members' music illegally, was followed by the arrest of three flea market vendors and 16 other vendors from a St. Louis County, Missouri, flea market. The arrests followed an investigation of the defendants for purportedly manufacturing and selling nearly 30,000 counterfeit and pirated CDs. On December 4, 2003, the RIAA filed an additional 41 lawsuits and sent 99 warning letters to people it alleged illegally shared music via the Internet.

Despite wide public knowledge of the possible consequences of file-sharing, it continues nevertheless. In the first case to be tried before a jury for file-sharing copyright infringement, a federal district court in Duluth, MN, held a woman liable for willfully infringing upon copyrights of 24 works.[10] The jury awarded the music companies $9,250 for each of the works that she uploaded.[11] A new trial was granted because of an error in jury instructions. In this second trial, the defendant, Jammie Thomas-Rasset, was found liable for the uploading recordings and "making [them] available" to others, but the jury's award of $1.92 million was reduced to $54,000 under the common-law doctrine of remittitur.[12] The Plaintiff refused the remittur and was granted a new trial to determine damages. An award of $1.5 million was found, and in July 2011, it was again reduced to $54,000,[13] and the music labels appealed. The Eighth Circuit Court of Appeals reversed the district court's reduction and reinstated the original award of $222,000 on September 11, 2012.[14]

While many suits have been filed alleging copyright violations, not all suits concerning activities in the music industry were filed for the benefit of the associations' members. As the only significant source of music since 1914, ASCAP's aggressive use of this tremendous leverage led the United States Department of Justice to commence antitrust actions against ASCAP, the first of which was filed in 1934. In that action, the Department contended that ASCAP dominated the radio industry and due to this should no longer function.

The department sued both ASCAP and BMI in 1941 in separate suits alleging that their blanket licenses constituted restraint of trade. In the consent decrees that resulted from settlement of those cases, ongoing federal jurisdiction over many of the organization's activities was vested in the Southern District of New York.[15] Amended several times since then, most notably in 1950, the consent decrees impose a variety of restrictions and obligations on ASCAP and BMI related to the collective licensing of its members' works as well as its relationship with its members. Another case, filed in 1947, relates to ASCAP's relationships with certain foreign performance rights organizations.[16]

The modified Consent Decree served ASCAP well in 1967; the organization brought suit that contended ASCAP's blanket license was an unlawful combination in violation of the Sherman Act. This case went to the district court and was upheld and affirmed in the Ninth Circut. These courts were in agreement that the blanket licenses were non-exclusive and the license fees were under surveillance of the district court. The Supreme Court denied certiorari after the U.S. Solicitor General supported the decision of the lower courts.

Given the dramatic changes in the music industry over the last half of the 20th century, the Consent Decree was modified in 2001, when the Department and ASCAP concluded that changes were necessary to improve competition in music licensing.[17] The modifications expand and clarify ASCAP's obligation to offer certain types of music users, including background music providers and Internet companies, a genuine alternative to a blanket license. Yet, the blanket license remains a subject of litigation. In *United States v. American Society of Composers, Authors and Publishers*,[18] the court affirmed that the downloading of a digital music file over the Internet does not constitute a "public performance" of the work embodied in that file (compare with "upload" of works in *Capitol Records v. Thomas-Rasset, supra*) but vacated the lower court's assessment of fees for the blanket ASCAP licenses.

ASCAP in that case argued that downloading of music falls within the meaning of a performance because downloads "transmit or otherwise communicate a performance"; that is, the initial performance of the copyrighted work is transmitted to the public. The Court found this argument to be flawed because it separates the "transmission" of the music from its simultaneous "performance" and treats the transmission itself as a performance. Transmission of a performance refers to the performance created by the act of transmission and not the other way around.[19]

A stream transmission, on the other hand, is a public performance, and the distinction illustrates why a download is not a public performance. In a streaming transmission, the musical work is audible as the user's computer receives it in much the same way as a television or radio broadcast. The playing of the song is perceived simultaneously with the transmission. Downloading, in contrast, produces no sound; in fact, the user must perform additional action in order to hear the transmission. Unlike television and radio broadcasts and stream transmissions, downloaded music is transmitted at one point in time while the actual performance occurs at another. Transmittal without a performance does not constitute a "public performance."[20]

Infringement

In the music world, there are many examples of copyright infringement examples. In one of the most famous cases, former Beatle George Harrison released "My Sweet Lord" as his first solo. It hit the charts just one week later and enjoyed the number one spot originally for five weeks then, in 2002, again for one week. It remained on the charts for a total of 27 weeks. After the song had left the charts, Bright Tunes Music Corporation filed a suit against Harrison for plagiarism of a song called "He's So Fine" by the Chiffons, written in 1962.

It is apparent from casually listening to the two songs that their lyrics are quite different. In making its determination, the court looked at the structure of the two songs. "He's So Fine" consists of four repetitions of a short musical phrase, followed by four repetitions of another phrase, the second of which includes a unique grace note. "My Sweet Lord" has a very similar structure. Particularly telling, however, is that the fourth repetition of phrases that, like "He's So Fine," also includes the grace note.

Harrison was unable to show that the song was substantially different from the Chiffons' song, and in February 1976, the court ruled against him. Although the court did not believe Harrison purposefully plagiarized the song, it did find that the two songs were essentially the same, displaying only minor differences to note and chord. The court found that "[h]is subconscious knew it already had worked in a song his conscious did not remember. . . That is, under the law, infringement of copyright, and is no less so even though subconsciously accomplished."

Although a money judgment of $587,000.00 was entered against him, Harrison maintained copyright of "My Sweet Lord."[21]

The decision was unique in that the court acknowledged that Harrison may have unconsciously copied the tune.

The other side of the coin is found in *Steele v. Turner Broadcasting System, Inc.*[22] Here, Steele wrote a love anthem about the Boston Red Sox entitled "Man I Really Love This Team," which caught on around Fenway Park in the fall of 2004, when the team played toward its first World Series Championship in 86 years. Steele alleged that Turner Broadcasting, the popular band Bon Jovi, the Boston Red Sox, and others infringed his copyright when they created an advertisement promoting post-season telecasts in 2007. The ad featured a song performed by Bon Jovi entitled "I Love This Town" synchronized to baseball video footage. The court found there was no substantial similarity between Steele's song and the song from the advertisement, a finding supported by experts.

Copyright infringement occurs when another person's software, music, or any other media is downloaded without their permission. This usually occurs on the Internet and is done in a purposeful manner. One such case is the well-known *A&M Records v Napster*, one of the most famous cases of copyright infringement related to the music industry. As peer-to-peer file sharing increased, Napster established a website where it offered downloads of songs of all genres—new and old. A&M Records brought in a joint copyright infringement case that accused Napster of stealing music and making it available to people worldwide. Before closing the site in 2002, Napster settled for $26 million to different recording companies and songwriters, and its apology and agreement to shut down the site likely saved it millions more.[23]

The court found a commercial use in the "repeated and exploitative copying" of the works, even if they are not offered for sale.[24] In particular, the court found a commercial purpose in the repeated copying "made to save the expense of purchasing authorized copies."[25] It seems that making copies to save money may not necessarily prejudice the claim of fair use, but if the copying is "repeated" and "exploitative" and "unauthorized," the court might infer a net substantial economic advantage to the user and hence resolve that the activity has a "commercial" purpose.

To conclude that the users were committing infringements can result in legal liability imposed on millions of Napster users. Litigation against vast numbers of individuals is obviously problematic; a lawsuit against the Napster Corporation itself is a vastly more efficient means of either shutting down the system or restructuring it to include payment of royalties. The court found that the users were committing the infringements when they uploaded and downloaded files. The company is liable for the misdeeds of the users, if the court can find that Napster committed "contributory infringement" or "vicarious infringement." The court found that Napster was liable on both counts.[26]

Of central importance in the ruling—and of great importance to the Digital Music Library (project based at Indiana University and supported by a grant from the National Science Foundation)—was the court's analysis of whether the actions of Napster and its users fit into any of the exceptions in the law from copyright liability. Most notably, the court ruled that file sharing by individual users was not a "fair use" of the copyrighted sound recordings, which would have exempted the activities from infringement liability. The court also ruled that Napster's role in facilitating the dissemination of recordings was not within the four various "safe harbors" created by either the Audio Home Recording Act or the Digital Millennium Copyright Act.[27]

At an absolute minimum, the *Napster* decision is a firm reminder that copyright law clearly applies to sound recordings, that courts will look critically at large-scale services that copy and distribute works, and that the applicable law is multilayered and subject to potentially complex definitions and interpretations.

Even though *Napster* is an example of the consequences of infringement, it still does not act as a deterrent for other music websites that offer free music downloads. In its 2007 decision, the court in *Metro-Goldwyn-Mayer Studios, Inc. v. Grokster, Ltd.*, also established that it had the power to issue a permanent injunction prohibiting this distributor of peer-to-peer file sharing software from inducing infringement by end users of its software to require the distributor to undertake sufficient efforts to minimize end user infringement.[28]

Infringement actions are not limited to huge corporations. In *London-Sire Records v. Armstrong*, seven music and entertainment corporations sued a Connecticut resident, alleging that he "used, and continues to use, an online media distribution system" to download plaintiffs' copyrighted recordings that he made available to the public for distribution.[29] In a default judgment, the court awarded damages of $7,907.05 plus costs.

CHAPTER 5

Mickey Mouse and Copyrights

Mickey Mouse is America's icon. From Steamboat Willie to pornographic replications of Mickey with Snow White, Minnie, and the Seven Dwarfs, Mickey Mouse is America. Mickey Mouse is emblematic of America's dance macabre with Intellectual Property. Just think of how many patents, copyrights, and trademarks are associated with Mickey and the Disney empire. Forget the light bulb; it's Mickey that coalesces the many rationales associated with the protections established by Intellectual Property. The Sony Bono Copyright Extension Act could just as easily be designated as the Mickey Mouse Copyright Extension Act because that was the animus for its unprecedented extension. It extended copyright protection by an additional seven years, which coincidentally began when Mickey's copyright protection was expiring. The question is how long Congress will extend Mickey's copyright. Walt Disney, *et al.,* have vigorously pursued any perceived infringement or weakening of the copyright of all things Mickey. The Disney Co. is especially vigilant in protecting Mickey from scandalous and lewd characterizations and associations that, in their minds, besmirch Mickey's alleged family values (and, ultimately, the keys to the kingdom, literally).

Mickey and Walt started out humbly enough. But at least by 1939 and *Fantasia,* which featured Mickey's bravura performance in Dukas's Sorcerer's Apprentice, Mickey's brand was conspicuously, purposefully, and specifically attached to Walt's burgeoning empire. Those of us of a certain age remember Mickey's Playhouse—those ears, Mickey's ears, that hat, Mickey's lunchbox, the religious pilgrimages to California and then later to Florida, and, of course, "who's the leader of the gang that's made for you and me, Mickey Mouse . . ." This was revisited 30 years later in an eerie rendition in Stanley Kubrick's *Full Metal Jacket.* It is difficult to imagine anything, anybody, or any idea that pervades American society like Mickey. Presidents and cars go out of fashion, but Mickey prevails. Outsiders think of Mickey Mouse as representative of our culture. It's no wonder that Premier Nikita Khrushchev had a fit when he was told he couldn't visit Disney World because of security concerns. But is there anything even remotely comparable to Disney World in the U.S.S.R. of the Cold War Era? Nyet.

Mickey Mouse, of course, is only a cartoon character. In fact, he's only a cartoon representation of a lowly mouse (he looks like a rat, though), albeit with anthropomorphic implications. But, yet, he's still a mouse. Why a mouse? Why should a mouse be our "leader?" Is it the mouse that roared, or something comparable to Teddy Roosevelt's "speak softly and carry a big stick?" Mickey was used by the Allied Forces as a morale booster; he was even enlisted at one time. And certainly, he was America's number one bond salesman. He reminded us that a "slip of the lips sink ships" and urged us to save tin and obey blackouts, etc. Did Mickey win the War? Yes, but not single-handedly. Maybe the extension of Mickey's copyright was a recompense for his meritorious wartime service. It certainly is food for thought. No, it's not suggested that Ike Eisenhower and Walt Disney indulged in some Machiavellian connivance, but, in truth, no other cartoon character has been afforded such an honor.

Although Mickey Mouse began as a celluloid cartoon character, he, of course, has morphed into every conceivable medium: TV, newspaper, film, video games, marketing, cyberspace, clay figures, stop-action, radio, comic books, amusement parks, animatronics, Internet, ring tones, etc. He is ubiquitous and, seemingly, never ending. Three-year-olds born today are obsessed with Mickey. Is it in our DNA? Is that the reason for the copyright extension?

If Mickey is one of a kind in many conceivable and inconceivable ways, is it then only appropriate that we celebrate his uniqueness by stretching, and maybe breaking, the copyright laws? Although he is undoubtedly unique, he doesn't appear to be legally unique. Perhaps there should be a new type of intellectual property right that protects this wily military veteran/entrepreneur/movie star/cultural icon. The more interesting question is whether the copyright extension begins with Steamboat Willie or if copyright extension should attach to the year of each incantation and morphing of "Willie" in different roles and mediums: Mickey the movie star, Mickey the TV star, Mickey the newspaper cartoon, Mickey the iTune, Mickey the Internet warrior, Mickey the board game, Mickey the video game, Mickey the amusement park,

Mickey the marketing icon, etc. Is Mickey Mickey for everything, or are there discernible specific representations or medium collages that also merit particular copyright protection for the maximum length of time allowable by law? It is an interesting question and one unique to American jurisprudence; something is definitely going on. One wonders if the H-bomb would merit such protection.

Copyright Law Generally

Copyright law not only affords protection and fully expanded rights to the owners of copyrights, but it also limits the powers of non-holders regarding copyrighted instruments. The reason it is important to have an understanding of copyright law is not necessarily because you want to get something copyrighted; it is more so because you need to know what privileges and restrictions you have regarding currently copyrighted material.

Copyright literally means "the right to copy."[1] Article I of the United States Constitution introduces the idea of copyright by mandating that Congress shall have the power to promote the progress of science and useful arts by securing for limited times to authors and investors the exclusive right to their respective writings and discoveries.[2] Copyright protection exists in the original works of authorship fixed in a tangible medium of expression, now known or later developed, from which they can be perceived, reproduced, or otherwise communicated, either directly or with the aid of a machine or device.[3] Copyright law exists to protect works of authorship including literary works; musical works, including accompanying words; dramatic works, including accompanying words; pantomimes and choreographic works; pictorial, graphic, and sculptural works; motion picture and other audio visual works; sound recordings; and architectural works.[4] Though the protections afforded by copyright laws are extensive, such protections are not designed to extend to any idea, procedure, process, system, method of operation, concept, principle, or discovery that is in any way described, explained, illustrated, or embodied in such work.[5] Essentially, the laws are designed to protect the actual work itself, not any byproducts that may be a result of that which is contained in it.

The ability to copyright one's material is best identified as an intangible property right.[6] In distinguishing the right to the intangible property from the actual physical property itself, the original Copyright Act of 1976 explained: "Ownership of a copyright, or of any of the exclusive rights under a copyright, is distinct from ownership of any material object in which the work is embodied. Transfer of ownership of any material object, including the copy or phonorecord in which the work is first fixed, does not of itself convey any rights in the copyrighted work embodied in the object."[7] The right to copyright something is an authorship right, and it exists separately and independently from its ultimate physical expression.[8] Congress has granted exclusive rights to such authors upon acquiring ownership of a copyright.[9] Congress has explicitly exercised its Article I power to identify the scope and application of copyright protection and to designate the rights granted to those who carry them.

The first discussion of the Constitution's copyright clause was at the Constitutional Convention on September 5, 1787.[10] The clause was unanimously approved.[11] The first federal copyright laws were adopted in 1790.[12] Congress passed the Copyright Act of 1790, which provided copyright protection against only the copying of certain types of printed material.[13] It was not until 1889 that performance rights were granted statutory protection.[14] It took an additional 20 years for the right of mechanical reproduction of phonograph records to be added in 1909; this occurred at a time when piano rolls were prominent.

Works which are not fixed in sheet music, song folios, phonorecords, or any tangible medium of expression do not qualify for statutory protection under the federal copyright laws.[15] When these particular forms of unpublished works exist and they have not been submitted for federal copyright registration and protection,[16] they are protected by state common law.[17] The protections of common law copyright are applicable without any sort of formalities, registration, or notice.[18] This copyright system affords an artist, composer, or author complete protection against any unauthorized commercialization of his or her work.[19] However, it remains a requirement, before common law copyright is triggered, that the author's work is not in "a fixed tangible form sufficiently permanent or stable to permit it to be perceived, heard, or otherwise communicated for a period of more than transitory duration."[20] However, common law copyright extends to protect "live" television, or radio presentation of a song, as long as it is not recorded simultaneously with transmission. Federal copyright laws create a uniform method for establishing, protecting, and owning rights to one's work. The common law copyright protection acts as a safety net, catching all forms which may have fallen through the federal spider web.

By the middle of the 1950s, the Copyright Act of 1909 appeared to be completely outdated. The tremendous amount of technological innovations and industrial advancements that occurred in the years following the establishment of the Copyright Act in 1909, until the mid-1950s, provided the courts with very little knowledge on how to cope with the vast changes. Certain innovations such as television, cable television, transcripts, synchronization with film, offset printing, Xerox reprography, and long-playing records were not contemplated in the Copyright Act of 1909; for that reason, as was the case several times before then, the Act was in desperate need of a revision. During this period of innovation, in 1955, the United States Copyright Office initiated and conducted a series of valuable studies specifically designed in preparation for necessary revisions to the antiquated Copyright Act. Additionally, the United States Copyright Office distributed 34 reports on a multitude of problems to an established panel of consultants on the matter; these reports were also disseminated to the general public. Following the distribution of the reports, the United States Copyright Office circulated preliminary drafts of the new copyright statute for review. After circulating the many preliminary drafts, the United States Copyright Office submitted a general revision of the Copyright Act of 1909 to Congress in 1964. There were several groups who opposed certain provisions of the revised copyright act, and the opposition led to an extended deliberation period referencing the proposed revisions to the statute. However, after twelve long years of discussions, hearings, and compromises in the industry, Congress passed the Copyright Act of 1976.

The Copyright Act of 1790 provided for a copyright duration of 14 years. This duration allowed for an additional 14-year period if, in the fourteenth year of the original copyright, the owner exercised the right to renew it. The Copyright Act of 1909 allowed for a total copyright term of 56 years. In the early 1960s, Congress extended the renewal term by one year each year during that time period. This, however, was not the only revision; the Copyright Act of 1976 distinguished between pre-1978 and post-1977 copyrights. Since the Act went into effect on January 1, 1978, the year separating the applicable rules for copyright was set at 1978. This Act differed from its predecessors by listing the renewal term for pre-1978 works at 47 years. This created a total of 75 years of copyright protection tacked onto the original protection of 28 years. This version of the Act completely abolished the requirements of renewal for works after 1977 and instead imposed a copyright duration for the length of the life of the author plus an additional 50 years. This Act also listed a 75-year copyright term for works created for hire. Included in the Copyright Renewal Act of 1992 was an automatic extension for works whose copyrights were filed between January 1, 1964, and December 31, 1977. This automatic extension increased the term to

67 years. In 1998, the Copyright Term Extension Act (CTEA) increased the term by an additional 20 years and provided for copyright duration for the life of the author plus 70 years.[21]

The Supreme Court Protects Mickey in *Eldred v. Ashcroft*

This 20-year increase under CTEA came under fire in *Eldred v. Ashcroft*.[22] It was alleged that CTEA was unconstitutional under the Copyright Clause's "limited times" prescription and First Amendment free speech. The district court found that the CTEA did not violate the "limited times" restriction because the CTEA's terms, though longer than the 1976 Act's terms, were still limited and not perpetual. The Court of Appeals affirmed the district court's ruling. The Appeals Court found that the case of *Harper & Row, Publishers, Inc. v. National Enterprises*[23] foreclosed the petitioners' First Amendment challenge. The Appeals Court reasoned that copyright does not impermissibly restrict free speech because it grants the author an exclusive right to only the specified form of expression. The court further held that that copyright does not shield any idea or fact contained in the copyrighted work and allows for "fair use" even of the expression itself. The Court of Appeals also found that Congress did not exceed the scope of its Constitutional powers.

In *Eldred*, the Supreme Court of the United States affirmed the decision of the Appeals Court and the district court and found for respondents. The issue was whether to extend the protection of an already existing copyright. The court emphasized that the copyright's goal should be the promotion of scientific progress. Congress should have the say on the way in which the objectives of the Copyright Clause in the Constitution are pursued. The court noted that the term "limited," as found in the Copyright Clause of the Constitution, did not mean "inalterable" or "fixed."[24] Following this case, the standard duration for copyright has been set as the life of the author plus 70 years. However, if the actual works are anonymous, pseudonymous, or works for hire, the copyright duration will be determined by looking at the date of publication or the date of creation. The copyright duration for these works is either 95 years from the first publication or 120 years from creation, whichever occurs first.[25]

The Origin and Evolution of Mickey Mouse

Mickey Mouse is highly regarded as an international personality. Walt Disney built the majority of his creative organization on the success and foundation established by the character of Mickey Mouse. As an international icon, Mickey Mouse's face is recognized around the world. This character has endured as a unique and specific personality. The character of Mickey Mouse was first imagined by Walt Disney early in 1928. It is noted that Walt Disney thought of the character on a long train ride going from New York to Los Angeles. Walt Disney had already experienced his first issue with copyrights before leaving New York. The purpose of his New York trip was to persuade his financial backers to expend more money to assist him in improving the quality of his "Oswald the Lucky Rabbit" pictures. These financial backers had copyright ownership of the pictures since the character was copyrighted in their name. The backers declined to assist Walt with additional funds, and, because they had ownership of the copyrights, they took control of "Oswald." After this experience, but prior to arriving back in Los Angeles, Walt Disney created the Mickey Mouse character, named him "Mortimer" for the majority of the train ride, and began to visualize a cartoon in his mind.

After the ride, when he returned to his studio, he immediately began working on the first Mickey Mouse cartoon. This cartoon was entitled "Plane Crazy." Unfortunately, no distributor wanted to pick up this film, and the enthusiasm of the studio began to fade. After this temporary defeat, Walt Disney dived head first into production on another silent Mickey Mouse cartoon; this second cartoon was entitled "The Gallopin' Gaucho." However, after seeing a Warner Brothers production involving sound films, Walt Disney dropped his work on the second silent production to begin a third Mickey Mouse cartoon film. This was entitled "Steamboat Willie" and included music and sound effects. Walt Disney had to complete the film in New York because the West Coast had not yet caught up to the technological advances of the East Coast. Once the film was completed, Walt Disney got his lucky break when the manager of Colony Theatre decided to give the film an opportunity. The film was an overnight success.

Mickey Mouse quickly became popular throughout the nation and grew in popularity as time progressed. The popularity of the character of Mickey Mouse spawned a national Mickey Mouse Club. The Mickey Mouse Club was established in 1929, and it met every Saturday afternoon. At these gatherings, the members would watch cartoons and play games at the local theaters. They were consistently referred to as "Mouse Clubbers," and the club included several million members. The club had a secret handshake, a special member greeting, a code of behavior, and a special club song. The club song, "Minnie's Yoo-Hoo," eventually became Mickey and Minnie Mouse's early theme song. This song was composed by Carl Stalling, and the lyrics were created by Walt Disney. Mickey Mouse's first "words" were spoken in the 1929 film, *The Karnival Kid*. His first words were "Hot Dog!" In fact, Walt Disney himself originally supplied the voice of Mickey Mouse.

Many artists have noted the character has one of the most powerful and innately attractive graphic designs ever created. This particular graphic design, the three-circle symbol that represents Mickey Mouse's head and ears, has over the years become an instantly recognized and internationally recognized icon. The success of Mickey Mouse spawned the creation of a host of other Disney animated characters, including Minnie Mouse, Goofy, Pluto, Donald Duck, Clarabelle Cow, Horace Horsecollar, and many others. In the 1930s, Mickey was ubiquitous: he played everything from fireman to giant killer, cowboy to inventor, detective to plumber. Mickey Mouse's fame, however, did not stop on the animated screen.

Mickey Mouse appeared on several different types of merchandise including watches and T-shirts. There was even a doll created in the likeness of the character. Not limited to film and merchandise, Mickey Mouse was also featured in a long-running newspaper comic strip. Mickey Mouse continued to expand to touch all facets of media, including comic books, magazines, and books. Mickey remained heavily shown on the screen as an animated cartoon through the 1940s and into the early 1950s. Mickey's next success was in television. In 1954, Walt Disney introduced the "Disneyland" television series on ABC. This series traced Mickey Mouse's career as well as his many accomplishments. After this primetime success, an afternoon program was created for ABC entitled "The Mickey Mouse Club." In fact, Mickey Mouse actually appeared on the Academy Awards telecast presenting an envelope to an actor.[26]

Mickey Mouse and Copyright

Walt Disney Co. v. Powell

In *Powell*, the defendant conducted a wholesale souvenir business that sold items to tourists through street vendors. Included in his inventory were shirts with mouse faces. These faces resembled Mickey and Minnie Mouse. During the period in which the defendant was selling the mouse-face shirts, representatives of the Hard Rock Café, whose mark the defendant was also infringing, executed a search and seizure order at defendant's trading premises. The defendant claims that after the raid, he stopped selling the shirts and confined his sales to only authorized merchandise. The district court found that the defendant's infringements were willful. Relying on Mickey and Minnie's six copyrights, the district court found the defendant guilty of six infringements and awarded damages. The district court also awarded Disney attorney's fees and permanently enjoined defendants from infringing Disney's copyrights.

In his appeal, the defendant argued that the district court abused its discretion in granting a permanent injunction and awarding attorney's fees and statutory damages. The court found that the abuse of discretion claim, as it relates to the permanent injunction remedy, was without merit. The court found that when a copyright plaintiff has established a threat of continuing infringements, he is entitled to an injunction. The court noted that it would generally be an abuse of discretion to deny a permanent injunction where liability has been established and there is a threat of continuing infringement. Furthermore, the defendant's voluntary cession was insufficient to ensure future non-infringement. Instead, the court found that the defendant "simply took the action that best suited him at the time." The court also stated that where there has been a history of continuing infringement and a significant threat of future infringements, it is appropriate to permanently enjoin the future infringement of works owned by the plaintiff but not in this suit.[27]

Walt Disney Prods. v. Air Pirates

The *Air Pirates* case involves the admitted copying of Walt Disney Productions' cartoon characters in the defendants' adult "counter-culture" comic books. Walt Disney Productions's complaint alleges that the defendants infringed Disney copyrights, a Disney trademark, and engaged in unfair competition, trade disparagement, and interference with Disney's business. The works that are protected by valid copyrights are a series of cartoon drawings ranging anywhere from a single page to "book length." The cartoon drawings depict the antics of characters created by Walt Disney Productions with speech bubbles over each of the characters' heads with the character's dialog in each bubble. The cartoons are drawn in such a sequence as to form a narrative. According to Walt Disney Productions, the defendants infringed on owned copyrights by copying the graphic depiction of over 17 of its characters. Two characters were represented as insects, and the remaining majority as animals endowed with human qualities; each of the copied characters had a recognizable image.

The individual defendants participated in the preparation and publishing of two cartoon magazines entitled "Air Pirates Funnies." The characters in the defendants' magazines bore a marked similarity to those for which Walt Disney Productions had obtained copyrights. The names given to the defendants' characters were the same names used in Walt Disney's copyrighted works. The difference, however, was that the themes of the defendants' publications differed markedly from those of Walt Disney Productions. While Walt Disney sought only "to foster an image of innocent delightfulness," the defendants supposedly sought to convey an "allegorical message of significance."

The district court awarded Walt Disney Productions a temporary restraining order and subsequently granted its motion for a preliminary injunction. In awarding Walt Disney Productions a preliminary injunction, the district court held that Disney's graphic depictions were, in fact, protectable under the Copyright Act as component parts of Disney's copyrighted work. The defendants attempted to defend against the claims by arguing "fair use," but their defense was rejected because it was found that the defendants had copied the "substance" of the Disney products. The court also held that after balancing the competing interests of freedom of speech and the press versus "encouraging creation by protection expression" of ideas as indicated in the Copyright Clause of the Constitution, the First Amendment did not bar the district court's issuance of a preliminary injunction.

The Court of Appeals found that there was a copyright violation and affirmed the decision of the district court. In supporting the lower court's decision, the Court of Appeals considered it immaterial that, in certain instances, the defendants used the challenged cartoon figures in different plots than Walt Disney Productions or that they portrayed them with different personalities. The court stated that "the test is whether the figures drawn by Defendants are substantial copies of the work of Plaintiff." The court noted that in some instances Disney's copyrights may cover a book and others may cover an entire strip of several cartoon panels. The court also noted that the fact that Walt Disney Productions' characters are not the separate subject of a copyright does not preclude their protection, because Section 3 of the applicable Copyright Act provides that Disney's copyrights included protection for "all the copyrightable component parts of the work copyrighted." In addressing the defendants' assertion that characters are never copyrightable and therefore cannot in any way constitute a copyrightable component part, the court responded that the argument "flies in the face of a series of cases dating back to 1914 that have held comic strip characters protectable under the old Copyright Act."

In distinguishing the concept of a literary character, which is not afforded the same protection, from a comic book character, the court noted that a comic book character which has physical as well as conceptual qualities is more likely to contain some unique elements of expression.

The court also addressed the attempted fair use defense offered by the defendants. In rejecting that defense, the court averred that while "evaluating how much of a taking was necessary to recall . . . the original, it is first important to recognize that given the widespread public recognition . . . Mickey Mouse and Donald Duck [possess], in comparison with other characters [then] very little would have been necessary to place Mickey Mouse and his image in the minds of the readers." The court further reasoned that when the medium involved is a comic book, a recognizable caricature is not difficult to draw, so that an alternative that involves less copying is more likely to be available than, for example, when speech is parodied. Additionally, the court indicated that the essence of parody does not focus on how the characters look but rather distorts "their personalities, their wholesomeness and their innocence." The court noted that any other interpretation would substantially justify verbatim copying. The court held that when persons are parodying a copyrighted work, the constraints of the existing precedent do not permit them to take as much of a component part as they need to make the "best parody"; instead, their desire to make the "best parody" is balanced against the rights of the copyright owner in his original expression.[28]

Walt Disney Prods. v. Mature Pictures Corp.

The *Mature Pictures* case involved an action for preliminary injunction brought by Walt Disney Productions as owners of the copyright of "Mickey Mouse March." Walt Disney Productions sought to prevent the defendants' use of that music in a movie entitled *The Life and Times of the Happy Hooker*. The "Mickey Mouse March" was an original song written by Jimmie Dodd and used generally in connection with the Mickey Mouse Club television series.

The court viewed, at the request of the parties, major segments of the taped Mickey Mouse Club and came to the conclusion that the target audience for the Mickey Mouse Club was "youngsters." The "Mickey Mouse March" is the theme song for the Mickey Mouse Club television series. In a portion of the defendants' movie, three male actors sang some of the words of the "Mickey Mouse March" for a period of approximately four to five minutes. The "Mickey Mouse March" was played as background music while the female protagonist of the film appeared to "simultaneously gratify the sexual drive of the three other actors while the group of them is located on or near a billiards table." Supposedly, the three male actors were teenagers "whose father had arranged for her (the female protagonist) to be present as a birthday surprise to them." The cast was naked except that the male actors were wearing "Mouseketeer" hats. The background music was the copyrighted "Mickey Mouse March." The court found that the only real question presented was whether the use of the copyrighted material by defendants constituted "fair use" as a parody.

The court issued a preliminary injunction against the defendants. The court noted that the permissible parody of the copyright article is not a complete copy of the original. It highlighted that parody of copyright can be permitted only where the parodist does not appropriate a greater amount of the original work than is necessary to "recall or conjure up" the object of his satire. In this instance, the court held that the use was far from the parody and there was a complete copy of the copyrighted material. The court noted that the original song lasted only two minutes while the defendants used the work over and over again for substantially more time than was required to "conjure up the original." The court also noted the distinction that "while defendants may have been seeking in their display of bestiality to parody life, they did not parody the 'Mickey Mouse March' but sought only to improperly use the copyrighted material." In response to the defendants' contention that no injunctive relief should be granted because there was no danger of irreparable damage being done through their use of the copyrighted material, the court found that they were "totally wrong." It said that their use of the copyrighted material in the setting provided was such as to immediately compromise the work.[29]

Conclusion

Some critics of the copyright laws take the position that Congress's continued alteration and extension of copyright protection is correlated to Mickey Mouse and the Disney Corporation. The Walt Disney Company cites the "Steamboat Willie" cartoon as having established its copyright ownership in Mickey Mouse. The Copyright Reform Act of 1909 permitted the extension of protection in "Steamboat Willie" that otherwise would have fallen into the public domain. Some scholars claim that because the formalities of the 1909 Copyright Act were not satisfied, the

"Steamboat Willie" film is now in the public domain. The response of the Walt Disney Company to such allegations has been threats of suit for "slander of title."

The copyright term of "Steamboat Willie" has twice approached extinction. In both instances in which the copyright was to expire, the federal lawmakers in Congress amended the Copyright Act to extend the duration of the copyrights that were in existence prior to the date on the amendments. In each circumstance, "Steamboat Willie" benefited from the amendments and revisions to the Copyright Act. Specifically, the copyright term of "Steamboat Willie" increased the effective date of the Copyright Act of 1976 (January 1, 1978) and then again on the effective date of the Sonny Bono Copyright Term Extension Act (October 27, 1998). However, "Steamboat Willie" did not receive the maximum possible copyright duration under either of the extensions because of complications arising from the film's status as a work in its second term under the 1909 Copyright Act. "It does not take a great deal of skepticism, however, to predict that federal lawmakers will extend copyrights again before 2023, at which time *Steamboat Willie* will once more risk sailing beyond the limits of copyright's duration."[30] Many critics believe that this trend is designed to prevent Mickey Mouse from sliding into the public domain. While it has not been stated with any degree of certainty that the Walt Disney Company has in fact lobbied, or even advocated, for the extensions, it stands to reason that they have benefited from the timely extensions.

CHAPTER 6

Broadcasting and Licensing Rights

The developing technology in sports and entertainment broadcasting such as satellite networks, Internet copying, and retransmission has raised many questions that, when answered, will have repercussions in the licensing of copyrighted materials.[1] Taverns now use NASA technology to intercept cable programming for unauthorized reception of copyrighted boxing matches. In situations such as this, the bar owner must first pay a licensing fee to transmit or retransmit boxing matches (or live opera) to cable and satellite affiliates.

In the case titled *In re NCAA Student Athlete Name and Likeness,* former college athletes sued the NCAA and its licensing arm, the Collegiate Licensing Company (CLC), and the popular and wildly lucrative video game maker Electronic Arts, Inc. (EA). Former college quarterbacks sued EA, alleging violations of their right of publicity by using their likenesses and images (for money) in a series of video games based on "NCAA football." In these games they mirrored their college images by including the same jersey number, height, and weight, which the court held went beyond the mere reporting of relevant information. And for defendant Sam Keller, at least, the game setting was identical to the iconic football field at Arizona State where he played his collegiate career.

Matt Leinart was the best college quarterback of his era: six feet 5 inches, 225 pounds, number 11 quarterback at U.S.C., etc. Coincidentally, the best player in the wildly popular video game called "NCAA Football 06" also happens to be a U.S.C. quarterback, six feet 5 inches, 225 pounds, and wears number 11; his name, however, is "QB#11." The digitized analogue of Leinart has a mop of dark hair. Yet another coincidence? The NCAA prohibits companies from profiting from an athlete's likeness. However, the NCAA gets a cut from video game revenues, and in return, the NCAA grants the game manufacturers the right to reproduce the stadiums, uniforms, and mascots of NCAA schools. The video game cannot use the specific athlete's name and recognizable facial features (mops of dark hair notwithstanding), but that's it![2]

Licensing Generally

The F.C.C. (Federal Communications Commission) is a quasi-autonomous commission that controls, among other things, licensing in TV, radio, and cable television. But there are other regulations. For example, companies cannot import distant signals to circumvent local blackouts. The NFL blackouts games in a certain geographical area if the game is not sold out, and the Cable Act of 1984 makes it illegal to attract and lure unauthorized signals, that is, blacked out football games, by way of "black box" devices.[3]

In *C.B.C. Distribution and Marketing, Inc. v. Major League Baseball Advanced Media, L.P.,* 2006 WL 2263993 (E.D. Mo.), aff'd, 505 F.3d 818 (8th Cir. 2007), the court held that public domain lists of major league baseball players and statistics lacked the element of originality that is necessary for copyright protection. Consequently, players were precluded from claiming that a fantasy baseball game producer violated the players' copyrights by using particular names with their accompanying specific data in their video games.

CBC was one of the few companies that held a license from the Major League Baseball Players' Association (MLBPA) before 2005. During that period, CBC licensed MLB players' likenesses and team logos to produce fantasy baseball leagues for major media companies. On the other hand, another competing company, Major Media, before 2005, did not take licenses from the MLBPA. But in early 2005, just a month after CBC's license expired, Advanced Media secured an exclusive license to recreate players' likenesses for fantasy video games concerning baseball. CBC was forced out.[4]

Parrish v. NFLPA, Inc., is a putative class action suit dealing with video game licensing revenue for retired football players, including Bernard Parrish, Herb Adderly, and Walter Roberts. Defendant National Football League Players' Association (NFLPA) is a union that represents active NFL players. Co-defendant Players, Inc., is the marketing and group licensing arm for active and some retired NFL players; it is 79 percent owned by the NFLPA. The retired football players allege that Players, Inc., breached a fiduciary duty by failing to provide adequate licensing disclosure and not diligently pursuing marketing and licensing rights. The NFLPA reached a $26.25 million settlement with the retired players, who sued for a fairer share of lucrative marketing deals. The amount was close to the $28.1 million a federal jury ordered the NFLPA to pay for their failure to include NFL retired players in deals with Electronic Arts, Inc., the maker of the immensely popular and lucrative "Madden NFL" video game.[5]

World-renowned golf course architect Robert Trent Jones II and his design firm, Robert Trent Jones II, Inc., and Robert Trent Jones Licensing Group, LLC, as licensors, filed suit against the licensee, pursuant to the intellectual property licensing agreement, providing that the licensee would manufacture and distribute apparel bearing the licensor's trademarks. The plaintiff asserts claims for fraudulent misrepresentation, negligent misrepresentation, breach of contract, unfair competition, and trademark infringement. The court denied the plaintiff's motion for a preliminary injunction on the basis that the licensors did not have the likelihood of success on their trademark infringement claim and that they would not suffer irreparable harm.[6]

The key to success in trademark infringement suits is to prove the likelihood of consumer confusion about the source of the goods. However, in licensee-licensor disputes, the inquiry is much different. "Where a licensee persists in the unauthorized use of a licensor's trademark, courts found that the continued use alone establishes a likelihood of consumer confusion" (*Sun Microsystems v. Microsoft Corp.*, 999 F. Supp. 1301, 1311 (N. D. Cal. 1998) (footnotes omitted)). In the *Robert Trent Jones* case, the plaintiff sought injunctive relief before the termination of the license agreement. Jones lost his request for injunctive relief, basically, because he failed to adequately and accurately define the meanings of "discount store" and "retail store" as specified in the licensing agreement, and thus would not succeed on the merits of the case or suffer irreparable harm, both mandatory requirements for injunctions.[7]

American Needle, NFL Licensing, and the Antitrust Laws

Remember, it's the logo that drives the market! In *American Needle, Inc. v. NFL*,[8] the company that sold headwear carrying trademarked names or logos of various professional sports teams sued in antitrust NFL Properties (NFLP), which is a corporation that licenses NFL trademarks. The NFLP, however, gave sports shoe manufacturer Reebok the exclusive licensing agreement for trademarked headwear and apparel. Prior to this "back door" agreement, American Needle had a license to manufacture apparel with NFL logos. The U.S. Supreme Court held that the licensing activities for individual teams' intellectual property, conducted through a corporation that is separate from the teams, with its own management, was an antitrust violation and constitute an illegal concerted action. Therefore, all teams' trademarks are not interchangeable for licensing purposes. That is, the Dallas Cowboys' logo may be more marketable and lucrative than, say, the Green Bay Packers' logo (with personal apologies to appropriate fans if applicable).

In *NFLP, Inc. v. Wichita Falls Sportswear,*[9] there was a controversy concerning Wichita Falls Sportswear's manufacture of replica football jerseys complete with numerals, NFL team sleeve design, and player's name (e.g., Jim Zorn). Plaintiffs sought to stop Wichita from manufacturing and selling replica jerseys on the basis of infringement, unfair competition, deceptive business practices, misappropriation of the teams' publicity rights, and tortious interference of the NFLP's business relationships between its licensees and the consumer/fan, among many other charges. The court concluded that Wichita *intended* to create confusion, so it enlarged the scope of the injunction to include any jerseys that use the dominant team color of any NFL club.[10] Of course, this was a federal district court in 1982, as opposed to the Supreme Court's 2010 opinion in *American Needle,* which might allow Wichita to work their own deals with individual teams, such as the Seattle Seahawks, who were their primary marketing target in the *Wichita Falls Sportswear* case, but that was not the case in 1982 of this particular suit.

Federal Communications Commission

A key player in licensing and the broadcasting and rebroadcasting of sports and entertainment programming is the Federal Communications Commission (FCC), which is an independent regulatory agency that has regulatory control of radio, television and Cable TV, and interstate telephone and telegraph communication. The FCC's primary functions are licensing and registration, adjudication, rulemaking, and enforcement. Broadcast licenses must be renewed every five to ten years; cable systems need not be licensed, but they have to register with the FCC. The FCC has the power to impose penalties, which can range from revocation of licenses to simple fines. Remember Janet Jackson's Super Bowl wardrobe malfunction, where the question of penalties, fines, and even possible license revocation was hotly debated for many years.[11]

Betty Boop and Character Licensing

Betty Boop is, of course, a cultural icon and the first cartoon pinup (with cleavage!). She was a sex symbol that symbolized flappers and the jazz age. She had a "baby" singing voice who cooed "boop-boop-a-doop." She was created by famed cartoonist Max Fleischer in 1930 as an anthropomorphic black poodle that morphed into a 16-year-old flapper with the poodle ears transforming into hoop earrings, etc. In May 1932, famed "baby voice" singer/actress Helen Kane filed a $250,000 infringement lawsuit against Max Fleischer and his Paramount Public Corp. She alleged deliberate caricature and exploitation of her image as the "Boop-Oop-A-Doop girl." But in actuality, the Betty Boop character and Helen Kane's persona both more closely resembled Clara Bow, the "It girl." But Kane's major failing was that she could not prove a unique singing style and, in fact, admitted that the "baby" singing technique did not originate with her but was purloined from African American performer Baby Esther.

Fast forward about 80 years, and the "Betty Boop" character is currently owned by Fleischer Studios with its merchandising rights licensed to King Features Studios. In 2010, she became the official fantasy cheerleader of the upstart United Football League.

Character licensing for sports logos, team names, and mascots has become a huge business. In the case of *Fleischer Studios, Inc. v. AVELA, Inc.*, the court first held that BETTY BOOP on defendants' t-shirts and handbags was not protected under trademark law; however, the court withdrew that opinion, and although it affirmed the court's decision in favor of the defendant on its copyright and image trademark claims, it reversed on defendant's trademark claim in the words "Betty Boop." Fleischer proved that it possessed registered trademarks in the words "Betty Boop," and evidence was insufficient to show that defendants did not infringe the trademark. The court also held that there was no secondary meaning or evidence of confusion in the marketplace.[12] In short, "Betty Boop" was the trademark!

Who Owns the Copyright in the Broadcast?

Broadcast network television is still the major player in the television industry; the three original networks plus Fox. Each network owns and operates affiliates, which also operate as separate companies. Cable TV, or community antennae television (CATV), creates a boost to reception in areas where broadcast TV signals are blocked or weakened.

The seminal case of *NBA v. Motorola, Inc.,* 105 F.3d 841 (2d Cir. 1997), discusses the question of who owns the copyright of real time NBA game statistics. The case is one of copyright infringement against the manufacturer and promoter of hand-held pagers that provide real-time information on professional basketball games. The court reasoned that professional basketball games are not "original works of authorship" as protected by the Copyright Act. Also, the NBA's misappropriation claims were preempted by the Copyright Act. The court compared real-time statistics to "hot news," which is not worthy of copyright protection.

Since copyright protects fixed events, such as broadcasted, finished games, it is vital to determine the owner of such copyright. Basic copyright law states that the author of the work holds rights in the work. However, in the professional sports world, complications arise, spawning litigation over who owns the rights to every part of the broadcast, whether it is the original broadcast, a replay of it, or the highlights cut from it. For example, restrictions imposed by the NBA include the use of their game highlights such that stations wishing to show them may only use clips totaling less than two minutes, and exorbitant fees ranging anywhere from $1000 to $5000 *per minute* of footage must be paid for such use.

Radio and TV Broadcasts

In *NBA v. Motorola,* 105 F.3d 841, 845–847 (2d Cir. 1997), the NBA asserted copyright infringement claims of both the games and the accompanying broadcasts. The games themselves are not copyrightable; the broadcasts, however, merit copyright protection. But Motorola and STATS did not infringe on the NBA's copyright since they reproduced only the facts from the broadcasts and not incidental comments masquerading as "color commentary." TV and radio broadcast reception on home-style receivers that may be seen or heard by the public is exempt from the payment of public performance fees as long as there is no direct charge. The factors that will determine the availability of the exception include the physical size of the business, the type of receiver used, whether the receiving apparatus was augmented, the number of speakers in the system, and whether the system was professionally installed. However, the unlicensed use of a music-on-hold device by a service station will constitute an infringement outside of the small business exception.

Cable and Satellite Transmission

In *Sports Productions v. Pay Per View Network, Inc.,* 1998 WL 19998 (S.D. N.Y. 1998), the defendant PPV entered into an Event License

Agreement with a licensor known as M. sports, pursuant to which PPV was granted a license to transmit to its cable and satellite network affiliates a boxing event, scheduled to air live on February 13, 1997. On the day of the telecast, the plaintiff delivered his television signal to a satellite transmission facility operated by Group W. However, as a result of technical difficulties, there was a freeze of the telecast for about 70 minutes, and as a result, some of the event subscribers asked for and received their money back. The plaintiff alleged that PPV and Group W violated the agreement by failing to telecast the event.

Under New York law, consequential damages are recoverable only if they were reasonably within the contemplation of the parties at the time the contract was made. Here, the uplink agreement provided that under no circumstances shall Group W be liable to any third parties for any loss of revenue, claims of service interruption, or any other consequential damages. Thus, the plaintiff could not be considered a third-party beneficiary, and accordingly, plaintiff's first cause of action against Group W was dismissed.

Infringement

Dastar Corp. v. Twentieth Century Fox Film Corp., 539 U.S. 23 (2003), involves the scenario where a film producer incorporates a pre-existing film, which has fallen into the public domain in a current production; the question is what are the legal responsibilities of the producer regarding the previous copyright owners of the public domain footage. In *Dastar,* the U.S Supreme Court basically said, "not much." In other words, there is no infringement.

In *NBA v. Motorola,* the court held that the hand-held pagers that provided real time information on NBA basketball games results and statistics did not infringe on the NBA's copyright. The bottom line was that there was no infringement since the NBA's professional basketball games were not "original works of authorship" that would have been protected by the Copyright Act.

In *Sportvision, Inc. v. SportsMEDIA Technology Corp.*, 2006 WL 408634 (N.D. Cal. 2006), plaintiff Sportvision, Inc. initiated a lawsuit against defendant SportsMEDIA Technology corporation for patent infringement, trademark infringement, and unfair competition. Sportvision provides sports broadcasters' first-down marker technology, as well as the manufacture and sale of video graphics effects equipment and software. SportsMEDIA provides real-time graphics and interface services and products to the live sports television production industry. At issue are the rights to a virtual yellow line first-down marker used in football game broadcasts.

In the fall of 2003, Sportvision became aware that SportsMEDIA was providing a virtual yellow first-down indicator to certain college football broadcasts. Sportvision advised SportsMEDIA of its intellectual property rights and requested that SportsMEDIA not infringe those rights. Sportvision then learned in June of 2004 that SportsMEDIA had offered an allegedly infringing service for the 2004 ABC Monday Night Football schedule.

Unlawful Interception and Retransmission of Signals

Garden City Boxing Cub, Inc. v. De Jesus, 2006 WL1155166 (E.D. N.Y. 206) is a classic case of taverns using NASA-like satellite dishes to illegally intercept pirated boxing matches. The plaintiff alleged N.Y.C.-area taverns and restaurants knowingly and willfully violated the Communications Act of 1934 (47 U.S.C. § 605) by unlawfully intercepting and exhibiting the Barerra/Morales pay-per-view boxing event on November 27, 2004. The court declined to vacate its default judgment against defendants because they had not demonstrated that their default was not willful.

In *NFL v. Insight Telecommunications Corp*, 158 F. Supp. 2d 124 (D. Mass. 2001), a professional sports league, the NFL, sued for infringement against the retransmission of their copyrighted television broadcasts. The court allowed summary judgment against the NFL on the grounds that the defendant comes within the "passive carrier" exception. The NFL sued defendant Insight Communications Corporation for violating its copyright in copyrighted materials by retransmitting its copyrighted materials in interstate commerce on a number of occasions in 1999. On account of that, the plaintiff sought statutory damages and injunctive relief under the copyright laws (17 U.S.C. §§ 502[a] and 504[c][2]). As part of its answer, Insight averred that they were a passive carrier within the meaning of 17 U.S.C. § 111(a)(3) and thus exempt from liability for direct or indirect infringement. The court allowed Insight's motion for summary judgment.

CHAPTER 7

March Madness® and Trademarks

In recent years, the use of trademarks has become a dominant theme in professional sports as clubs and players vie for marketing channels in attempts to attract fans to their products and services. Trademarks dominate the American landscape. Companies use a variety of trademarks to assist customers in identifying their goods and services. Sporting clubs and professional athletes are no different. In professional sports, clubs use trademarks to identify their brand. NFL fans quickly recognize the star on the side of an NFL helmet to represent the Dallas Cowboys football team. "March Madness" is a valued trademark that the NCAA wields like a knife to protect the annual NCAA basketball tournament. The NCAA paid $40 million for this mark!

Clubs use a variety of colors, logos, and catch phrases to attract fans to the clubs. Trademarks are a mainstay of American society and are ubiquitous in the American marketplace. Trademarks can be extremely valuable for a business and can establish the "good will" and reputation of a company. The golden arches, the Nike Swoosh, and the Coca-Cola trademark are all well-known trademarks worth billions of dollars.

A trademark can be a word, name, symbol, or device used by a manufacturer or merchant to identify their goods. The basis of trademark law lies in the concept of unfair competition between merchants.[1] In 1946, Congress passed the Lanham Act, which governs trademark use and provides for their protection and registration. Trademark law deals with the balancing of rights between trademark owners and others who want to use the same trademark or one similar to another merchant. One of the primary purposes behind trademarks is to prevent "consumer confusion." Because consumers are not always able to examine the goods or services before purchasing them to determine the quality and source of those goods, the consumer must rely on trademarks to ensure quality. Trademarks protect the exclusivity of a good or service. The same is true for sports organizations and players. If an owner of a business has established name recognition and goodwill through the use and subsequent recognition of trademarks, they certainly have a stake in ensuring that the trademark is protected. The owner will do everything possible to make sure no one steals the mark, infringes upon it, or uses it in an obscene way.

The theft or illegal infringement of a trademark or a player's identity can mean a loss of millions of dollars and, for a player, possibly tarnishing of the athlete's reputation.[2] Trademark counterfeiting is rampant and is the most egregious form of trademark infringement. A counterfeiter intentionally uses a trademark that is identical or "substantially undistinguishable" from a registered trademark in order to illegally profit from the goodwill of a business. In essence, the intentional infringer is taking money out of the pockets of the trademark owner by loss of sales and also by harming the reputation of the owner of the mark. "Knock off" goods are typically not of the same quality of the "real" goods. Those goods can tarnish the actual mark and cause a business to lose customers through the placing of "sub-par goods" in the marketplace. Counterfeiters can sometimes be deterred by fines, civil lawsuits, criminal sanctions, and court orders for the seizure of the counterfeit goods, but not always. There can be extensive criminal penalties for the manufacturer of counterfeit or "knock-off" goods.

Consumers purchase goods and services produced by companies sometimes lured by an entity or famous trademark. Companies spend millions of dollars attempting to find the right saying, jingle, or picture (or combination) to attract customers to their product or to use their service. When they find a successful mark, others may try to copy or steal the mark to draw customers away or use the famous mark to generate a revenue stream of their own.

The purpose of trademark law is to prevent customer confusion. Consumers need to be able to rely on trademarks to assist them in purchasing goods in the marketplace and to have confidence in the quality of the goods they purchase and use. Consumers benefit greatly when they are able to identify the origin of goods. Trademark law additionally assists business owners, helping them create and protect the "goodwill" for the business they have built up over time. Trademarks serve as labels "that identif[y] and distinguish a particular product"[3] and thereby create certainty in the marketplace for both the consumer and the business owner.

The Lanham Act, 15 U.S.C. § 1051, *et seq.*, is the federal statute dealing with trademarks in the United States. The U.S. Patent and

Trademark Office (PTO) is the agency that governs trademarks in the United States. Once a trademark has been registered with the PTO, parties are on notice that the registrant of that mark owns the exclusive rights to that mark. The registrant is allowed to use the symbol ® to give notice to others that the mark is a registered mark. However, a trademark does not have to be registered for a party to sue for trademark infringement. Trademarks can be registered at either the federal or state level.

The law does not recognize every possible symbol for trademark protection. The more distinctive a mark is, the more likely it is to receive trademark protection under the law. The law states that only certain marks are allowed trademark protection. Many corporations use slogans or phrases that also qualify as trademarks, such as Nike's "Just Do It," and American Express's "Don't leave home without it." These slogans have become well known to the consuming public.

The Lanham Act defines a trademark as follows:

> The term "trademark" includes any word, name, symbol, or device, or any combination thereof —
>
> 1. used by a person, or
> 2. which a person has a bona fide intention to use in commerce and applies to register on the principal register established by this Act, to identify and distinguish his or her goods, including a unique product, from those manufactured or sold by others and to indicate the source of the goods, even if that source is unknown.[4]

A service mark performs the same function as a trademark but is used to identify services rather than goods. Colors, fragrances, and even sounds can constitute trademarks.[5]

Whether a mark is entitled to protection depends upon the classification or strength of the trademark. The initial issue in any action for trademark protection is whether the word, name, symbol, or device is protected by trademark law. Courts have generally divided trademarks into four categories: 1. Arbitrary or fanciful, 2. Suggestive, 3. Descriptive, or 4. Generic.[6]

In *Major League Baseball Properties, Inc. v. Opening Day Productions, Inc.*, 385 F. Supp. 2d 256, 272 (S.D.N.Y. 2005), the court described the relevant categories as follows:

> . . . Whether a mark qualifies for § 43(a) protection depends on its classification within the system established by Judge Friendly in

Abercrombie & Fitch Co. v. Hunting World, Inc., 537 F.2d 4, 9 (2d Cir. 1976). That system incorporates four classes of marks, in ascending order of strength: (1) generic, (2) descriptive, (3) suggestive, and (4) arbitrary or fanciful. Suggestive and arbitrary marks are considered "inherently distinctive and entitled to protection" due to the fact that "their intrinsic nature serves to identify a particular source of a product." *Two Pesos, Inc. v. Taco Cabana, Inc.,* 505 U.S. 763, 768, 112 S. Ct. 2753, 120 L. Ed. 2d 615 (1992). Therefore, they are "automatically protected" without a showing of secondary meaning. A generic mark can never be protected, but a descriptive mark is eligible for protection if it has acquired secondary meaning. Therefore, a descriptive mark must have become distinctive of the particular producer's goods in commerce. Secondary meaning attaches to a mark when a significant number of prospective purchasers understand the term when used in connection with the particular kinds of goods involved . . . as indicative of an association with a specific entity. *Bernard v. Commerce Drug Co.,* 964 F.2d 1338, 1343 (2d Cir. 1992).

A "fanciful" mark is a newly coined word that is created for the sole purpose of functioning as a trademark. Fanciful terms can include invented words such as "Xerox."[7] "Kodak" has been classified as a fanciful term for photographic supplies.[8] "Exxon" is also a fanciful trademark. An "arbitrary" mark has a common meaning, but that meaning is unrelated to the product itself. An arbitrary mark in no way describes the product or service it is meant to identify. "Ivory" has been held to be an arbitrary term referring to soap, but it is generic when referring to elephant tusks.[9] "Apple" would be an arbitrary term when referring to computers.[10] "Bicycle" could be considered arbitrary when referring to playing cards. Both arbitrary and fanciful marks are completely unrelated to the goods with which they are associated.

"Suggestive" marks allude to the nature of the product but take some effort and imagination on the part of the public to make the connection between the product and its source. These types of marks indirectly describe the service or product they identify. The names "Coppertone" for tanning products, "Greyhound" for bus services, and "Mustang" for automobiles are all examples of suggestive marks. "Roach Motel" may be a suggestive mark as well.[11]

"Descriptive" marks usually describe some element of the product, such as size, the provider of the goods, or some particular characteristic of the goods. "Tender Vittles" as applied to cat food is descriptive.[12] An example of this type of mark is "barbeque beans." The term "half price books" is categorized as either generic or descriptive.[13]

Section 1052 of the Lanham Act states that five years of continuous and substantial use serves as prima facie evidence that the mark has acquired secondary meaning under the Act. The Lanham Act indicates that certain items cannot acquire trademark protection. Some of these are as follows: generic marks, scandalous or immoral marks, marks that are descriptive, marks that are primarily a surname, or marks in prior use.

Trademark Infringement Factors

For a trademark owner to prevail in a trademark infringement lawsuit, the owner of the mark must show (1) ownership of a protectable mark and (2) likelihood of consumer confusion.[14] A plaintiff must meet five requirements in a trademark infringement action to have an actual claim: (1) there must have been either a reproduction or counterfeit of the mark; (2) the reproduction must have occurred without the authority of the registrant; (3) the reproduction has been used in the stream of commerce; (4) the use must have been in the sale, distribution, or offering of goods and services; and (5) the use of the reproduction must be likely to cause confusion.

Trademark Dilution

The legal concept of dilution is that such a use tarnishes or dilutes the original mark because the viewing public will associate the original manufacturer's product with an unsavory product. Infringement under a dilution theory is a recent development in trademark law. The Federal Trademark Dilution Act (FTDA) (15 U.S.C. § 1127) was passed in 1995, giving owners of famous trademarks some protection against those parties diluting or tarnishing their trademark. Many states have also passed dilution laws protecting "distinctive" or "famous" trademarks from unauthorized use. In effect, dilution laws protect the goodwill associated with a famous mark.

Dilution is available only to the holder of a "famous" mark.[15] Under dilution analysis, the mark holder is not required to prove that "likelihood of confusion" exists. Infringement by way of dilution can occur in two ways: tarnishment or blurring.[16] Tarnishment involves harm to the goodwill of the plaintiff caused by the defendant's conduct, creating a link in people's minds between the plaintiff's mark and the poor quality of the defendant's goods. Under a "blurring" theory, the plaintiff's trademark loses some distinctiveness because of its association with the defendant's mark.[17] The law also protects the owner when a party uses a mark in an attempt at parody that has the effect of tarnishing the mark.[18]

The NBA's famous logo was the subject of litigation in *NBA Properties v. Untertainment Records, LLC,* 1999 WL 335147 (S.D.N.Y. 1999). In that case, NBA Properties sought an injunction against Untertainment Records for its use of an altered NBA logo. Instead of NBA Hall of Famer Jerry West bouncing a ball, a silhouetted player was shown holding a gun alongside a message containing the words "Drugs." The NBA alleged that the defendant was diluting its famous mark and infringing upon its goodwill.

The court stated that,

> [b]ased on a consideration of these factors, it appears indisputable that the NBA Logo is a famous mark. The NBA Logo is registered on the Principal Trademark Register of the United States in a variety of forms. It is a recognized symbol of the NBA and NBA Properties (NBAP) among consumers located both in the United States and around the world. Accordingly, the NBA Logo is a famous mark entitled to protection under the Dilution Act.

Dilution is "the lessening of the capacity of a famous mark to identify and distinguish goods or services, regardless of the presence or absence of (1) competition between the owner of the famous mark and other parties or (2) likelihood of confusion, mistake, or deception." Dilution under federal law can occur in two forms: blurring or tarnishment. Blurring occurs when a party uses or modifies the plaintiff's mark and creates the possibility that the mark will lose the ability to serve as a unique identifier. Tarnishment occurs where the defendant uses the plaintiff's mark in association with unwholesome or shoddy goods or services.

Further, the Second Circuit affirmed a preliminary injunction based on dilution by tarnishment and stated in part:

> "Tarnishment" generally arises when the plaintiff's trademark . . . is portrayed in an unwholesome or unsavory context likely to evoke unflattering thoughts about the owner's product. In such situations, the trademark's reputation and commercial value might be diminished because . . . the defendant's use reduces the trademark's reputation and standing in the eyes of consumers as a wholesome identifier of the owner's products or services.

The NBAP claims that linking the NBA Logo with violence and drugs will adversely color the public's impressions of the NBA. The NBA is bound to suffer negative associations from the juxtaposition of the distorted NBA Logo containing the basketball player with a gun in his right hand and the words "SPORTS, DRUGS, & ENTERTAINMENT." Indeed, the outrage generated in response to the banner indicates that the advertisement placed the NBA Logo in an unwholesome and unsavory context in the eyes of the public. Any suggestion that the NBAP or the NBA endorses violence, gunplay, or drug use, or that they have chosen to associate themselves with those who do, will likely tarnish their reputation with their corporate customers and partners, as well as the public at large.

The plaintiff has made a clear showing that the defendant's publication will create negative associations with the NBA Logo and that there is a likelihood of confusion under the tarnishment theory of dilution. Thus, the plaintiff is entitled to injunctive relief based on its claims of trademark dilution.

Trademark Parody

Many parties have chosen to make fun of a mark or to parody a mark. Noted professor J. Thomas McCarthy writes, "[N]o one likes to be the butt of a joke, not even a trademark. But the requirement of trademark law is that a likely confusion of source, sponsorship or affiliation must be proven, which is not the same thing as a 'right' not to be made fun of."[19]

Many parties have asserted that their use of a mark was actually a parody of the mark and therefore not an infringement and defended the use of the mark on First Amendment grounds. The purpose of a parody is "to create a comic or satiric contrast to a serious work." A parody does not intend to confuse the public but makes its humorous point by association with the original work. Its actual point is to amuse the public, not to confuse. Courts have found a viable parody "only when there was a discernable direct comment on the original."[20] A parody or satire can also be provided First Amendment protection. In *Cardtoons, L.C. v. Major League Baseball Players' Ass'n*, 182 F.3d 1132, 1134 (10th Cir. 1999), the court found in favor of a plaintiff who was manufacturing baseball cards featuring caricatures of players on the basis of the First Amendment.

There have been many sports-related lawsuits dealing with the use of parody under trademark law. For a serious look at the character Barney, see *Lyons Partnership v. Giannoulas*, 179 F.3d 384 (5th Cir. 1999). In that case, the best-known mascot in sports history, the San Diego Chicken, used a Barney look-alike in his act and proceeded to assault Barney. When the Chicken's owner was sued for trademark infringement, the "Chicken" was granted summary judgment on his defense that his use of a Barney look-alike was a parody under trademark law. The court summarized the defense as follows:

> Giannoulas offers a slightly different perspective on what happened. True, he argues, Barney, depicted with his large, rounded body, never changing grin, giddy chuckles, and exclamations like Super-dee-Dooper!, may represent a simplistic ideal of goodness. Giannoulas, however, also considers Barney to be a symbol of what is wrong with our society—homage, if you will, to all the inane, banal platitudes that we readily accept and thrust unthinkingly upon our children. Apparently, he is not alone in criticizing society's acceptance of a children's icon with such insipid and corny qualities. Quoting from an article in The New Yorker, he argues that at least some perceive Barney as a potbellied, sloppily fat dinosaur who giggle[s] compulsively in a tone of unequaled feeble-mindedness and jiggles his lumpish body like an overripe eggplant. The Internet also contains numerous web sites devoted to delivering an anti-Barney message. Giannoulas further notes that he is not the only satirist to take shots at Barney. Saturday Night Live, Jay Leno, and a movie starring Tom Arnold have all engaged in parodies at the ungainly dinosaur's expense. One Internet search service provides a list of links to anti-Barney websites, many of which contain warnings like the following: "If you're offended by material that suggests the killing of Barney, or like him in any way, please don't come here."
>
> Perhaps the most insightful criticism regarding Barney is that his shows do not assist children in learning to deal with negative feelings and emotions. As one commentator puts it, the real danger from Barney is denial: the refusal to recognize the existence of unpleasant realities. For along with his steady diet of giggles and unconditional love, Barney offers our children a one-dimensional world where everyone must be happy and everything must be resolved right away. Giannoulas claims that, through careful use of parody, he sought to highlight the differences between Barney and the Chicken. Giannoulas was not merely profiting from the spectacle of a Barney look-alike making an appearance in his show.

Instead, he was engaged in a sophisticated critique of society's acceptance of this ubiquitous and insipid creature. Furthermore, Giannoulas argues that he performed the sketch only at evening sporting events. The sketch would begin with the Chicken disco dancing. The Barney character would join the Chicken on the field and dance too, but in an ungainly manner that mimicked the real Barney's dance. The Chicken would then indicate that Barney should try to follow the Chicken's dance steps (albeit, by slapping the bewildered dinosaur across the face). At this point, Barney would break character and out-dance the Chicken, to the crowd's surprise. The Chicken would then resort to violence, tackling Barney and generally assaulting Barney. Barney would ultimately submit to the Chicken and they would walk off the field apparently friends, only for the Chicken to play one last gag on the back-in-character naive and trusting Barney. The Chicken would flip Barney over a nearby obstacle, such as a railing.[21]

In a case involving both trademark and copyright infringement, *Dallas Cowboys Cheerleaders, Inc. v. Pussycat Cinema, Ltd.*, 467 F. Supp. 366 (D.C.N.Y. 1979), the famous cheerleaders sued when the defendant made a 90-minute film entitled *Debbie Does Dallas*. The defendant asserted that the film was a parody or satire and therefore entitled to the "fair use" defense under trademark law. The court found that a preliminary injunction should be issued against the defendant on various legal grounds. In discussing the fair use defense in the context of parody or satire, the court stated:

A parody is a work in which the language or style or another work is closely imitated or mimicked for comic effect or ridicule. A satire is a work which holds up the vices or shortcomings of an individual or institution to ridicule or derision, usually with an intent to stimulate change; the use of wit, irony or sarcasm for the purpose of exposing and discrediting vice or folly.

In the present case, there is no content, by way of story line or otherwise, which could conceivably place the movie Debbie Does Dallas within any definition of parody or satire. The purpose of the movie has nothing to do with humor; it has nothing to do with a commentary, either by ridicule or otherwise, upon the Dallas Cowboys Cheerleaders. There is basically nothing to the movie Debbie Does Dallas, except a series of depictions of sex acts. The other phases of the movie the dialogue and the "narrative" are simply momentary and artificial settings for the depiction of the sex acts. The associations with the Dallas Cowboys Cheerleaders obviously play an important role in the film and in the advertising; but this is a role that has nothing to do with parody or satire. The purpose is simply to use the attracting power and fame of the Dallas Cowboys Cheerleaders to draw customers for the sexual "performances" in the film. The obvious intent of defendant Zaffarano and the others responsible for this film is to cash in upon the favorable public image of the Dallas Cheerleaders, including the image of a particular quality of feminine beauty and character.

Defendant argues that there is, at most, only a minor association with the Dallas Cheerleaders in the movie, since the scene with Debbie performing sex acts partly clothed in the Dallas Cheerleaders uniform is only a small part of the film. This is unrealistic. Debbie's "performance" is the culmination of the film. It is Debbie and her selection to be a cheerleader in Dallas (obviously a Dallas Cowboys Cheerleader) which gives rise to the title, and the opportunity to display the uniform prominently in the advertising as well as to use the various slogans associating the film with the Dallas Cheerleaders.

In this connection, it is apparent that the movie and the advertising are intended to be closely connected, and are in fact closely connected. If injunctive relief is merited, it is not appropriate to limit such relief solely to the advertising, as defendant Zaffarano suggests. The use of the associations with the Dallas Cheerleaders both in the film and in the advertising, all have the single purpose of exploiting the Dallas Cheerleaders' popularity in order to attract customers to view the sex acts in the movie. . . . [22]

Trademarks and Domain Names

What happens when a famous trademark is being used as a domain name by another party? Congress has initiated legislation in an attempt to determine how to best resolve disputes between those who own domain names and trademarks.[23] The most important tool for fighting cybersquatters has become the Anticybersquatting Consumer Protection Act of 1999 (ACPA).

When the domain name system first became available, many people were able to acquire otherwise protected trademarks of companies through the domain name registration process, an activity labeled *cybersquatting.* Cybersquatting was defined by the Second Circuit Court of Appeals in *Sporty's Farm v. Sportsman's Mkt., Inc.,* 202 F.3d 489, 493 (2nd Cir. 2000), as "involv[ing] the registration as domain names of well-known trademarks by non-trademark holders who then try to sell the names back to the trademark holder." Courts have described cybersquatting in many different ways, including "the Internet version of a land grab."[24] There are many different types of cybersquatting. For example, many cybersquatters rely on the fact that people often make spelling or typing mistakes; these cybersquatters are known as "typosquatters."[25]

The evolution of cybersquatting has included such legal concepts as trademark infringement, unfair competition, First Amendment issues, and property ownership rights. In *People for Ethical Treatment of Animals v. Doughney,* 263 F.3d 359 (4th Cir. 2001), the plaintiffs brought claims of trademark infringement and unfair competition under the Lanham Act, whereas the defendant asserted that he was entitled to keep the domain name "peta.org" because his website was a constitutionally protected parody. The court found that the unauthorized use of the PETA trademark in a domain name was infringement.

Athletes have had conflicts with individuals who have taken the athlete's name in the form of a domain name. Courts have had to decide whether such an action is a violation of the athlete's right of publicity, violation of trademark law, or both. Does an athlete have trademark protection in his or her name? Some athletes and celebrities have argued that their famous name is equal to a common law trademark. Individuals may attempt to register an athlete's name as a domain name and use it as a fan website. Many cybersquatters have purchased the domain names of athletes and entertainers in hopes of making a profit by selling the name back to them. Some cybersquatters have successfully defended their use of such a domain name on First Amendment grounds.

Barry Zito, a star pitcher for the San Francisco Giants, had his name registered as a domain name by another party. He sought return of his domain name through the dispute resolution process of the Internet Corporation for Assigned Names and Numbers (ICANN). Effective December 1, 1999, ICANN initiated the Uniform Domain Name Resolution Policy. Zito was able to wrestle away his domain name, barryzito.com, from the registrant. In an arbitration decision (Claim Number: FA0207000114773 [2002]), the panel found that Zito had built up "commercial value" in his name and was entitled to the return of the domain name.

In *Woods v. Whitford,* Claim Number: FA09050012633-52, National Arbitration Forum Decision, Tiger Woods, the world's most famous golfer, sought to retrieve the domain name of his second child, Charlie Axel Woods, through the dispute resolution process of the World Intellectual Property Organization. The domain name at issue is <charlieaxelwoods .com>, which was registered with Godaddy.com, Inc.

Complainant Eldrick "Tiger" Woods is one of the world's best-known sports personalities. Charlie Axel Woods was born on February 8, 2009, which event was announced and widely reported around the world in all forms of media. The disputed domain name, <charlieaxelwoods.com>, was registered on February 9, 2009; the day after Charlie Axel Woods was born.

Tiger Woods asserted that the disputed domain name was confusingly similar to the registered and common law trademarks in which the complainant has rights. The complainant asserts that TIGER WOODS had acquired distinctiveness and secondary association with Complainant in the mind of the public that even if the name was not trademarked, common law trademark rights certainly existed. Tiger further alleged that the disputed domain name, less the ".com" extension, is identical to his minor child's name and common law trademark, CHARLIE AXEL WOODS.

There is no question but that the <charlieaxelwoods.com> domain name is, for all intents and purposes, identical to the term "Charlie Axel Woods." The key issue to be decided, however, is whether the personal name "Charlie Axel Woods" is protectable as a common law trademark or service mark. The panel concluded that it was not.

Tiger baldly asserted that "Charlie Axel Woods" is a common law trademark but presented no evidence that "Charlie Axel Woods" had been used in connection with the commercial offering of goods or services or that the personal name in question had acquired secondary meaning as the source of such goods or services. Accordingly, the panel found that Tiger has no trademark or service mark rights in the name "Charlie Axel Woods."

In *Hart v. New York Yankees Partnership,* 184 Fed. Appx. 972 (C.A. Fed. 2006), the New York Yankees claimed the term "Baby Bombers" was an infringement of their trademark rights. Leon P. Hart filed an intent-to-use application with the United States Patent and Trademark Office to register the mark BABY BOMBERS for clothing and athletic wear. The New York Yankees Partnership and Staten Island Minor League Holdings, L.L.C. (collectively, the "New York Yankees") filed an opposition, which the Trademark Trial and Appeal Board sustained and was affirmed.

The New York Yankees opposed Hart's mark on the basis of their use of the common law mark BABY BOMBERS in association with the New York Yankees major league baseball club and with the Yankees' minor league affiliate, the Staten Island Yankees baseball club. In order to establish their ground of opposition under section 2(d) of the Lanham Act, 15 U.S.C. § 1052(d), the Yankees must show that they have priority of use in the mark and that Hart's mark, when used on the goods set forth in the application, would create a likelihood of confusion with the Yankees' mark. Because the Yankees' BABY BOMBERS mark was unregistered, the Yankees must also show that their mark was distinctive in order to establish priority. Hart's priority date is July 23, 2001, the date he filed his intent-to-use application. The Board found that the New York Yankees had used the term BABY BOMBERS in promotional materials to refer to their Staten Island minor league affiliate since its inception in 1999. The Board also found that the term had been used by the press to refer to both the minor league and major league Yankees teams for several years before Hart's priority date. Contrary to Hart's argument on appeal, the Board's finding that the Yankees have priority in the mark did not rely on uses of the term subsequent to July 23, 2001. The Board determined that the mark BABY BOMBERS for clothing and athletic wear would be confusingly similar to the Yankees' identical mark when used in association with entertainment services involving baseball games.

In *Major League Baseball Properties v. Opening Day Productions, Inc.,* 385 F. Supp. 2d 256 (S.D.N.Y. 2005), Major League Baseball brought a declaratory judgment action asking the court to find that the league was not an infringer of the term "Opening Day." The defendant, Opening Day Productions, argued that the term "opening day" was "arbitrary" and not a descriptive mark. If the mark was descriptive, the defendant would have to show "secondary meaning" under trademark law to garner trademark protection.[26] Consider the term "Super Bowl." How should that be classified? What about a trademark for using "Super Bowl" in greeting cards?[27]

In *Lemon v. Harlem Globetrotters International, Inc.,* 437 F. Supp. 2d 1089 (D. Ariz. 2006), the plaintiffs alleged that their names "when combined with their nicknames and player numbers are 'fanciful' marks and are therefore inherently strong" and that no secondary meaning was needed to establish protection under the Lanham Act.[28]

Many celebrities and athletes have fought for their control of their domain names and won. Courts and arbitration panels have found that a person may acquire common law trademark rights in his or her name.[29]

However, trademark rights must be established by secondary meaning. In *Yao Ming v. Evergreen Sports, Inc.*, FA 030400015140 (2003), the well-known former NBA center was seeking return of the domain name yaoming.com. The panel refused to transfer the domain name to Yao; however, the panel seemed to be encouraging Yao to present evidence of his rights to the common law trademark use of his name. Why was Barry Zito entitled to the return of his domain name when Yao Ming was denied?

Bruce Springsteen was not able to persuade a World Intellectual Property Organization panel that he was entitled to brucespringsteen .com, notwithstanding the fact that he is "the Boss" (WIPO No. D2000-15). Gordon Sumner, better known as Sting, is a world-famous musician who has been recording songs for more than 25 years. He alleged he was entitled to sting.com because of his use of the nickname. Although the WIPO panel ordered that the name be transferred to Sumner or be canceled, it did not find that he had a common law right to the nickname.

A party has a duty to protect and police its trademark to ensure no one else is using the mark. In 2006, Texas A&M University filed a lawsuit over the Seattle Seahawks' use of what the university believed to be an infringement of its noted "12th Man" trademark. What likelihood-of-confusion factors would be considered in this trademark litigation? Does it make a difference that the Seahawks are a professional team and the Aggies are collegiate? Is the "12th Man" mark suggestive, arbitrary, fanciful, descriptive, or generic? The matter was eventually settled between the parties.

In recent years, sports stars have tried to trademark certain phrases to establish their public image and for marketing purposes. For example, former New York Giants defensive end Michael Strahan ("Stomp you out"), baseball player ("Manny being Manny"—later dropped by Manny Ramirez), and Minnesota Vikings player Jared Allan ("Got Strange").[30]

In 2007, the Colorado Rockies filed an application with the patent and trademark office for "Rocktober," shorthand for the Rockies playoff run; they sought exclusive rights for "Rocktober" for use on stuffed animals, bobblehead dolls, and similar items (Associated Press, *Rockies Seek Trademark Protection for 'Rocktober'*, ESPN.com, October 19, 2007).

The NFL shot down the sales of t-shirts that said "Yes, We Did" with a picture of the Lombardi trophy and a black and gold "Six Burgh" T-Shirt after the Steelers' 6th Super Bowl win. A cease-and-desist order stated that the picture of the NFL's Lombardi Trophy violated the NFL trademark and copyright rights (*NFL Orders Cease-and-Desist to Pittsburgh Retailer Over SB Gear,* Sports Business Daily, February 6, 2009).

The NFL wanted to trademark "The Big Game," but Cal and Stanford objected, saying they had played in "The Big Game" since 1897 (FitzGerald, *NFL Marketers Want 'Big Game' Trademark,* San Francisco Gate, March 1, 2007; Mendle, Craig, *On Watching 'The Big Game,'* Forbes.com, February 1, 2008).

The New England Patriots filed for trademark protection for the terms "19-0" and "19-0 The Perfect Season." The Patriots lost the 2008 Super Bowl to the New York Giants. The *New York Post* was so confident that the Giants would beat the Pats that they applied for their own trademark, "18-1," application number 77385477 (Fargen, *Pats Try to Trademark Perfection,* Boston Herald, February 1, 2008).

Trademarks that are considered scandalous or immoral cannot be registered if they give offense to the conscience or moral feelings or are "shocking" to the sense of decency or propriety. For example, a trademark "Old Glory Condom Corp.," along with a pictorial representation of a condom decorated with stars and stripes suggesting the American flag, was not considered either "scandalous" or "immoral." A design for a defecating dog on the word "bullshit" for handbags was considered scandalous and immoral. Who should decide what is scandalous or immoral? (*In re old Glory Condom Corp.,* Trademark Trial and Appeals Board, March 3, 1992)

In *Stop Olympic Prison v. United States Olympic Committee,* 489 F. Supp. 1112 (S.D.N.Y. 1980), the defendant used the five interlocking rings symbol of the Olympic games in its "stop the Olympic prison" poster as part of their protest to convert the Olympic village in Lake Placid into a prison after the Olympic games. The court held the use was not a dilution of the Olympic mark.

A trademark can be held for as long as the owner desires as long as they don't abandon the mark. What are the ethical concerns to be able to hold intellectual property in perpetuity? Should there be limitations on the length that intellectual property can be held? In *Indianapolis Colts, Inc. v. Metropolitan Baltimore Baseball Club Ltd. Partnership.,* 34 F.3d 410, 31 U.S.P.Q.2d (BNA) 1811 (7th Cir. 1994), the court found a team trying to call itself the "Baltimore CFL Colts" was likely to confuse a substantial number of consumers and therefore granted a preliminary injunction.

Entertainers' Trademarks

Tom Waits, he of the unusually raspy, gravelly voice, was awarded $2.5 million for the use of a Waits sound-alike in a Salsa Rio Dorito chips commercial (*Waits v. Frito-Lay, Inc.,* 978 F.2d 1093 [9th Cir. 1992]). He sued for voice misappropriation and false endorsement. The commercial was based on a 1976 Tom Waits song "Step Right Up" and sung by Stephen Carter in a near perfect imitation of Waits. A false endorsement claim based on the unauthorized imitation of an entertainer's distinctive vocal identity is actionable since it is a type of a false association claim since it alleges the misuse of a trademark. Like Waits, Bette Midler, noted chanteuse (the "Divine Miss M"), sued to protect her voice from commercial exploitation without consent (*Midler v. Ford Motor Co.,* 849 F.2d 460 [9th Cir. 1988]). Ford's "Yuppie Campaign" included a former member of her backup singers, "the Harlettes," impersonating Midler's version of "Do You Want to Dance." Ford, for its own profit in selling its product, appropriated part of her identity, since she had a distinctive voice as a well-known singer.

However, Nancy Sinatra was not able to prove unfair competition for the commercial use of her song "These Boots Are Made for Walkin'" in a tire commercial (*Sinatra v. Goodyear Tire & Robber Co.,* 435 F.2d 711 [9th Cir. 1970]). The imitation of a performer absent public deception does not constitute unfair competition. But the imitation of Bert Lahr, a famous comedian/entertainer, constituted unfair competition since his voice was so well-known that a TV commercial deceives the public into believing that Lahr's imitated voice is actually performed by Bert Lahr himself (*Lahr v. Adell Chemical Co.,* 300 F.2d 256 [1st Cir. 1962]). The court stated that Bert Lahr had achieved stardom in substantial measure because of his particular "style of vocal comic delivery which, by reason of its distinctive and original combination of pitch, inflection, accent, and comic sounds" caused him to be "widely known and readily recognized as a unique and extraordinary comic character." [Hint: He was the cowardly lion in the *Wizard of Oz.*]

"March Madness" Mayhem

The National Collegiate Athletic Association (NCAA) owns and protects approximately 40 U.S. trademarks and service marks that are associated with the Association and their Championships. The NCAA uses various preventive and enforcement measures to combat "ambush marketing" and attempts to misuse the NCAA's intellectual property. There was much litigation associated with the ownership of the "March Madness" trademark (*See Illinois High School Association v. GTE Vantage, Inc.,* 99 F.3d 244 [7th Cir. 1996]; *March Madness Athletic Association, LLC v. Netfire, Inc.,* 310 F. Supp. 2d 786 [N.D. Tex. 2003], corrected final j. 2003 WL 22173199 [N.D. Tex.], aff'd 120 Fed. Appx. 540 [5th Cir. 2005] and *Intersport, Inc. v. NCAA,* 381 Ill. App. 3d 312 [Ill. App. 2008]).

The NCAA is an unincorporated membership association of more than 1,000 colleges, universities, athletic conferences, and sports and academic organizations, supporting approximately 300,000 student-athletes participating in 22 men's and women's sports. The NCAA administers 87 championships annually in their three membership divisions, including the Men's and Women's Division I Basketball Championship, with more common nom de guerres, such as the Final Four, March Madness, or the Big Dance. The television, radio, Internet, licensing, marketing, and publicity revenues emanating from the tournament easily reach into the billions—not bad for a non-profit organization. The NCAA vigorously protects its intellectual property rights associated with March Madness (See generally Bearby, "Marketing Protection and Enforcement of NCAA marks," 12 Marq. Sports L. Rev. 543 [Spr. 2002]).

The March Madness Athletic Association was created in February 2000 to pool the respective trademark rights to the "March Madness" name claimed by both the NCAA and the Illinois High School Association (IHSA). Since 1908, the IHSA has organized a boy's high school basketball tournament in Illinois every year. It has used the term "March Madness" as descriptive of its tournament since the 1940s. However, the term "March Madness" is much more widely associated (and some say synonymous) with the NCAA's annual college basketball tournament, which is a yearly icon of office pools, "bracket" browsing, and sports broadcasting. CBS broadcaster Brent Musberger used the term in 1982 to describe the tournament that year; the term subsequently gained popularity as a catchy and alliterative nickname for the three-week event in March (or mostly so; in 2012 the championship game occurred on April 2).

There was a legal fight in which the IHSA nationally claimed that it had exclusive rights to the commercial use of the phrase "March Madness." Although the court ultimately ruled that the IHSA had no right over the term in connection with the NCAA tournament following the litigation, the NCAA and IHSA negotiated for several years, ultimately agreeing to form the "March Madness Athletic Association" (MMAA) (See generally Gan, "March Madness: An Examination of Dual-use Trademark Terms and Reverse Confusion," 50 Hastings L.J. 223 [Nov. 1998]). From that point on, each group assigned its rights to the phrase, and each received an exclusive perpetual license from the MMAA to use the term for their respective basketball tournaments. In a related lawsuit, the MMAA won its trademark infringement suit against a company that attempted to use "March Madness" on its commercial website.

In the original lawsuit, IHSA sued GE Vantage, which was a licensee of the "March Madness" mark. The key to the decision was the dual-use aspects of the mark and that IHSA's long-time use of "March Madness" in connection with its basketball tournament did not extend to the NCAA's basketball tournament and the merchandise associated with it. In the second lawsuit against Netfire, the MMAA sought to police its marks against websites, claiming trademark infringement and cybersquatting. The court held that there was a likelihood of confusion between the registered phrase "March Madness" and the identical domain name (marchmadness.com). The court did not buy the defendant's argument that the use of the phrase was fair use. In short, "March Madness" was a descriptive term which had acquired secondary meaning and was therefore protected as a trademark. The recent case of *Intersport, Inc. v. NCAA,* 885 N.E.2d 532 (Ill. App. 2008), involved Intersport, which is a producer of sport-related programming that includes basketball coaches discussing the annual NCAA basketball tournament, generally called Intersport Coaches shows, which then are broadcasted on ESPN, Fox Sports Network, and elsewhere.

Intersport has been using the term "March Madness" in connection with its programming since 1986. In 1989, Intersport registered the term "March Madness" as a service mark with the United States Patent and Trademark Office.

In 1990, however, IHSA sought to register the mark, claiming that it had used it in connection with its state high school basketball championships since the 1940s. IHSA and Intersport ultimately agreed to resolve any dispute regarding the ownership of the mark by pooling their trademark rights into a new entity, March Madness, L.L.C. This arrangement continued until 1995, when the IHSA became involved in a dispute with the NCAA over the use of the term. At that time, Intersport assigned its rights in the March Madness mark to the IHSA in exchange for, *inter alia,* royalties and an exclusive, perpetual license to use the mark in connection with its Coaches Shows.

The day after Intersport and Sprint announced their agreement, the NCAA sent Intersport and Sprint a letter asserting that if Intersport were to provide the Coaches Shows to Sprint for distribution to mobile communications subscribers, Intersport will have violated the license agreement. The court held that the agreement allowed distribution of content with the March Madness mark to the wireless media even though that technology did not exist at the time the agreement was created.

CHAPTER 8

Trade Dress and Boutique Golf Clubs

Walter T. Champion and Tina Y. Burleson

Golf is the sport that epitomizes American conspicuous consumption. It is a phenomenon that establishes our relative status and success: What country club do you belong to? How expensive are your golf clubs? Anything that is offered to the golfing masses that appears to have the slightest chance of improving one's golf game is devoured as bread by a starving man. These gimmicks include energized golf balls, special gloves, weighted shoulder pads, and golf clubs with "sweet spots" or enlarged heads that promise to add 20 yards or so to the length of your drive, or long-iron, and accuracy to your short-iron and wedge. The biggest offender is the boutique golf club. One would think that the science and technology that "improves" the game of golf is reserved for NASA. But golf is a billion-dollar industry, and these "improvements" are extremely expensive to the avaricious golfer–consumer. Exorbitant price tags on golf clubs do not deter golfers when they are convinced of the advanced technology that these clubs promise. Golfers, like most professional players, gain notice for possessing the newest, flashiest, and priciest golf gear that is available.

In reality, technology of a golf club can enhance a golfer's ability only so far. The basic factors that produce a device that can hit a ball are length and feasibility. Although it is advertised that "new technology" is a complex procedure, that information is misleading. Most new technology has minimal enhancements and can be readily duplicated. Due to this easy reproduction, golf club manufacturers sternly defend and champion their technology as superior to remain profitable. The difference in price between top-name brands and look-alikes can be a difference of hundreds of dollars. The only way to defend their mercantile victories is through the traditional bastions of intellectual property: copyright, patents, and trademarks. However, the most efficacious line of defense is intellectual property's newest penumbra: trade dress. "Trade dress protection is available for non-functional features if they distinguish the goods' origin."[1] "Trade dress originally meant a products' packaging, but more recent court decisions have extended trade dress to include the configuration and ornamentation of the product."[2]

Golf is a conundrum.[3] As an example of how high-tech the golf industry has become, NASA scientists now work for golf club manufacturers. Titanium, the preferred material for a golf club's head, is considered to be key in achieving success as a golfer. Titanium allows the club head to be made larger; Titanium is 40 percent lighter and stronger than steel. Larger club heads tend to be more forgiving than smaller heads.[4] Another technological innovation in the industry is golf club manufacturer Callaway's computerized, cart-mounted swing-analysis and club-design system. "The system will utilize a radar gun and an IBM notebook computer to record golfers' swing data."[5]

Ely Callaway, founder of Callaway Golf, was the man behind the high-tech nature of golf clubs and the corresponding need to protect them from knock-offs through trade dress protection. The backbone of Callaway Golf's success is the Big Bertha driver. Developed in 1991, the Big Bertha "allowed even mediocre players to get the ball airborne more quickly and with more distance." Mr. Callaway predicted from his own experience that the new driver would revolutionize the golf industry. It did. "One of Mr. Callaway's slogans was that his new product should be 'demonstrably superior and pleasingly different.'" The fact that his clubs were "pleasingly different" necessitated the forceful use of trade dress as a vital part of doing business as Callaway Golf.[6]

Intellectual Property: Generally

Intellectual property law encompasses ideas and subjects such as patents, trademarks, copyrights, trade secrets, and trade dress as well as other subjects that relate to topics such as publicity rights, misappropriation, false advertising, and unfair competition.[7] "No legal topic places more emphasis on relativity than the area of intellectual property."[8] Justice Story called intellectual property "legal metaphysics," saying "[p]atents and copyrights approach, nearer than any other class of cases belonging . . . to what may be called the metaphysics of the laws, where the distinctions are, or at least may be, very subtle and refined, and sometimes, almost effervescent."[9] "Surely, the products of a person's intellect is personal and thus can be viewed as property. However, a problem arises when we move to give legal protection from the proprietary interest to the ideas generated from the use of that intellect. Generally, one's [mere] ideas are not protectable under the law."[10]

Patents

Patent law is governed by the Federal Patent Act. The patent act defines a potential patent as any "new and useful process, machine, manufacture, or composition of matter" which includes mechanical, chemical, and electrical structures and processes. In order for an invention to be patentable, it must meet four requirements: it must be (1) in a subject matter category, (2) useful, (3) novel in relation to the prior art, and (4) nonobvious at the time the invention was made to a person of ordinary skill in the art to which the subject matter pertains. A patent confers on the owner the right to exclude others from selling or using the process or product. The owner may sue those individuals who directly infringe upon the patent by using or selling the invention without proper authority. A patent lasts 20 years from the date of the issuance from the Patent and Trademark Office ("PTO").[11]

Copyrights

Copyright law protects original works of authorship embodied in a tangible medium of expression.[12] There are three basic conditions: (1) a work must be within the constitutional and statutory definitions of a work of authorship, (2) the work must be in a tangible medium of expression, and (3) it must be original. Subject matter that may be copyrighted includes music, drama, computer programs, sound recordings, and the visual arts. Copyright protects the original expression of ideas, not the ideas themselves. Copyright law gives exclusive rights to produce the work, to prepare derivative works based on the work, to distribute copies or photo records of the work, and to publicly display or perform such work. A copyright term extends for the life of the author plus 70 years after the author's death.[13]

Trademarks

A trademark is a type of symbol used to identify a particular set of goods and to distinguish them from similar goods. A trademark owner can prevent others from using the same or similar marks that create a likelihood of confusion or deception. Trademark law distinguishes between the following: (1) the right to use a mark, (2) the right to exclude others from using a mark, and (3) the right to register the mark.[14]

The Federal Trademark Act of 1946, commonly referred to as the Lanham Act, governs the registration, enforcement, procedure, and remedies for infringement of trademarks. Under the Lanham Act, a trademark is defined as including "any word, name, symbol, or device or any combination thereof adopted and used by manufacturer or merchant to identify his or her goods and also to distinguish from those manufactured or sold by others." The Lanham Act provides for the registration of service marks, certification marks, and trademarks.[15]

In a trademark infringement action, the plaintiff must meet five requirements: (1) there must have been either a reproduction or counterfeit of the mark; (2) the reproduction must have occurred without the authority of the registrant; (3) the reproduction has been used in the stream of commerce; (4) the use must have been in the sale, distribution or offering of goods or services; and (5) the use of the reproduction must be likely to cause confusion.[16]

Intellectual Property and Sports

The marketing of both athletes and sports in general deal directly with the laws of intellectual property. Sports marketing became a billion-dollar industry in the United States and the international community in the 1990s. The growth of sports in the last decade has exposed millions of people to sports every day in one form or another. Sports licensing and marketing agreements are now commonplace in the business of sports and are found in a variety of forms. Corporate sponsorships are popular ways for a company to promote company and product identification. Corporations understand that sports have universal appeal, and they attempt to use that to their advantage to assist them in expanding their global presence. Sports have become part of the huge entertainment landscape in America. Athletes have always been associated with the entertainment industry and are now appearing in movies and television on a regular basis as endorsers for major corporations.[17]

Patent law's ambit in the sports industry comes in many different guises, from golfing gizmos to football helmets to skates to rackets to lawn darts. There are many copyright concerns that entangle the sporting world, from autobiographies to instructional videos to television broadcasts and re-broadcasts.[18] Copyright law even protects against the unauthorized reception of "blacked-out"[19] or cable[20] television sports programming by way of a satellite dish antenna.

The biggest trademark issue in the arena of sports is whether the use of the reproduction is likely to cause confusion.[21] "There are many recent explosions in the trademark and trade dress jihad that is festering in the sports cosmos. The battle between golf club manufacturers against knock-off artists is . . . one example." To most consumers, the Nike Swoosh or golfer Greg "the Shark" Norman's Shark or the Dallas Cowboys' logo is the product itself. Therefore, "the trademark holders must enforce their property as vigorously as Coca-Cola® or any other business would, since their identity is so intricately and completely associated with the trademark."[22]

Intellectual Property Defines the Parameters of the Golf Club War

A manufacturer of a boutique golf club will attempt to protect its product by alleging patent, copyright, trademark, and trade dress infringement.[23] The most effective tool appears to be seeking an injunction on the basis of an allegation of a trade dress violation,[24] as long as the trade dress of the manufacturer's golf clubs was inherently distinctive.[25]

Protection of Golf Club Design

Trade dress protection could be essential as it relates to the golfing industry. If we look at it from the perspective of the large manufacturers, such as Callaway Golf,[26] there exist two preeminent issues: (1) they need to know that their investment in design, technology, and creative product design will not be decreased by greedy pirates who inundate the market with knock-off clubs, misleading the confused but gullible consumer; and (2) the behemoth manufacturers must constantly guard against the unauthorized use to avoid claims of abandonment and genericism which are defenses to trade dress claims.[27]

From the point of view of golf manufacturers such as Turin Golf,[28] which is smaller than the giants such as Callaway Golf, equally compelling but distinctly different concerns exist. Companies like Turin tend to spend less money on R&D and, correspondingly, borrow some design features from their more prosperous brethren. Thus, it will be the Turin-type companies that delineate the boundaries of infringement. Consumers respond to the familiarity of trade designs. These popular designs establish barriers to entry for golf manufacturers that would offer newly developed products. In order to compete, these new manufacturers might need to add common but non-protectable designs to help complement features that are uniquely attributable to their product. For example, assume that black is the color of choice among male golfers. Perhaps, many male golfers will base their buying decisions on this preference. A new manufacturer should be able to use that color so as to effectively compete. "However, the use of that color may not be abused in order to create an unauthorized association with clubs offered by other manufacturers."[29] The smaller manufacturers then must know the limits and difference between the authorized and unauthorized use of trade accouterments.

Intellectual Property Protects Golf Accessories and Instruction Programs

Obviously, patents will protect devices such as golf carts or ball-striking practice mechanisms. Just as obviously, copyright will protect instruction tapes, manuals, and books. Trademarks will protect those marks that tend to be associated with a particular product such as the Nike Swoosh on Tiger's cap or the Shark on Greg Norman's golf shirt. Trade dress will cover the rest: the particular coloring, bands, bubble shapes, shaft width, etc.[30]

Intellectual Property Fails to Protect the "Perfect Swing"

As formidable as the protection of intellectual property is as it relates to the golfing industry, it will still not afford protection for the "perfect swing." The grooved swing is to a duffer what the Fountain of Youth was to Ponce de León or what the Holy Grail was to King Arthur. However, unlike all other protectable aspects of golf, there is no tangible manifestation of the swing; therefore, it is more akin to pure knowledge. Similarly, Einstein was unable to patent $E = mc^2$ because it was a mental process. A perfect example of a tangible, and thus protectable, manifestation of the perfect swing is the patented Digitized Computer-Video Swing Coaching System.[31]

Intellectual Property Protects Golf Club Design

Legal warfare will continue between competitors when one competitor attempts to protect its intricately designed and adorned golf clubs from pirate manufacturers. An example of this is the case of *Callaway Golf Co. v. Turin Golf Corp.*[32] The plaintiff develops, manufactures, and markets golf clubs, including its line of Big Bertha® metal woods and Big Bertha® Blade Putter. Defendant Turin Golf distributes golf components and assembled clubs throughout the United States; it sells over 46 different makes of clubs, including the Warrior and the Toad putter.

In early 1995, Callaway Golf learned that Turin Golf had distributed advertising brochures offering clubs nearly identical to Callaway's clubs.[33] Turin was copying Callaway's clubs. The companies negotiated and tried to reach an agreement, but Turin continued copying and in a Christmas catalog touted a "NEW PRODUCT" called the "Warrior Professional Putter," which was a blatant copy of the newly developed Callaway® Big Bertha® Blade Putter.[34] Callaway brought suit for trade dress and trademark infringement under the Lanham Act[35] and design patent infringement.[36] Callaway was granted a temporary restraining order enjoining Turin Golf from "further manufacturing, selling or importing" the Callaway knock-offs.[37]

A product's trade dress "involves the total image of a product and may include features such as size, shape, color or color combinations, texture, graphics, or even particular sales techniques."[38] A plaintiff must satisfy the following elements in order to show likelihood of success on the merits: (1) that its trade dress is inherently distinctive, or (2) that it has attained acquired distinctiveness or "secondary meaning," (3) that its trade dress is nonfunctional, and (4) that defendant's use of the same or similar trade dress is likely to cause consumer confusion.[39]

Trade Dress as Intellectual Property's Step-Child

Trade dress protection is available for non-functional features if they distinguish the goods' origin. The Lanham Act provides protection against the creation of confusion by the simulation of a product or services' "trade dress." Trade dress was once confined to a product's packaging, but now it includes the product's configuration and ornamentation.[40]

The preeminent U.S. Supreme Court case that defines trade dress infringement is *Two Pesos, Inc. v. Taco Cabana, Inc.*[41] In *Two Pesos,* one operator of a Mexican food chain sued another chain for trade dress infringement under Section 43(a) of the Lanham Act. The defendant adopted a design motif nearly identical to that of Two Pesos's. Also, the defendant operated their chain in a market that adjoined one targeted by plaintiff for expansion.[42] The issue was whether plaintiff had to show that the trade dress was inherently distinctive. Since the plaintiff, at the time of the suit, had not actually expanded into the Taco Cabana market, a showing of secondary meaning would have been difficult.[43] The Supreme Court held that a showing of secondary meaning was not required for a trade dress violation if it was determined to be inherently distinctive. This type of determination was unnecessary since the trade dress itself could identify a product or service as emanating from a common source.[44] The Supreme Court proclaimed that a product's trade dress "involves the total image of a product and may include features such as size, shape, color or color combinations, texture, graphics, or even particular sales techniques."[45] Also, if a party can satisfy the Section 43(a) inherently distinctive requirement, the burden of proof will decrease slightly for those who seek trade dress protection.[46]

The seminal trade dress case for golf is *Pebble Beach Co. v. Tour 18, Ltd.* Tour 18 is a golf course outside of Houston that has purposefully attempted to emulate the most famous golf holes from some of America's most prestigious golf courses. The plaintiffs, owners of three of the copied holes, filed a complaint alleging that Tour 18 violated their design proprietary rights, including infringement of their trademarks, trade dress, copyrights, and goodwill. Judge Hittner found trade dress infringement only with respect to the reproduction of the "lighthouse" hole (#18) at Harbour Town. Tour 18 was enjoined from any use of it in its promotions and had to disclaim any association with the replicated holes.[47] In short, only the truly distinctive signature holes, like Harbour Town's 18th hole, deserve trade dress protection.[48]

Trade Dress: Protection against "Knock-offs"

The entire concept of "knocking-off" a golf club is, at best, subtle. Regardless of the accouterments and color schemes, a golf club is still, at its functional best, a golf club—that is, it is a tapered stick with a solid block at its end. Copyright, patent, and trademark law are not legally sufficient to protect the "aura" and the "look" of a boutique golf club. Trade dress is just subtle enough to detect, evaluate, and protect the nuances that differentiate a popular, plume-like golf club from a crass imitation. Unlike the more traditional property rights, trade dress is a safety net that protects the total image of a product.[49]

In *Taylor Made Golf Co., Inc. v. Carsten Sports, Ltd.,*[50] the plaintiffs vigorously asserted their trademark privilege and patent rights against "knock-offs" of their clubs. Among their protected registrations is the trade dress of its "Burner Bubble" metal wood. The plaintiffs' motion for summary judgment was granted, along with a monetary award based on the infringer's profits. However, in *Taylor Made Golf Co. v. Trend Precision Golf, Inc.,* a trade dress infringement case to protect Taylor Made Golf's Big Bertha Irons, the Court held that the plaintiff manufacturer failed to show that the placement of the copper and black colors on its golf club was inherently distinctive or had acquired secondary meaning as required for preliminary injunctive relief.[51]

The crux of Taylor Made's concern was Trend Precision's introduction, at a January 1995 PGA merchandise show, of a Player's Edition line of metal woods using the same copper and black colors Taylor Made employed.[52] A party may seek trade dress protection for color combinations, provided the combination meets the inherent distinctiveness requirements for Section 43 protection. Taylor Made could also have satisfied the "inherently distinctive" requirement by showing that the Burner Bubble's copper and black trade dress had acquired secondary meaning,[53] which they failed to do.[54]

In another "Big Bertha" irons infringement case,[55] the Court granted a preliminary injunction and held that: (1) the trade dress of manufacturer's clubs was inherently distinctive, (2) the trade dress had acquired secondary meaning (3) the trade dress was nonfunctional; (4) the manufacturer demonstrated likelihood of confusion, and (5) the balance of equities favored the grant of preliminary injunctive relief.[56] Elements that must be considered to determine the likelihood of confusion in trade dress infringement cases are strength of trade dress, similarity of design, similarity of product, similarity of retail outlets and purchases, similarity of advertising media used, defendant's intent, and actual confusion.[57] In this case, evidence was sufficient to establish that the trade dress of the manufacturer's "Big Bertha" golf clubs was likely to be confused with the competitor's "Big Bursar" clubs. This threat of confusion was established on a showing that Callaway's trade dress was fairly strong, the competitor's clubs were nearly identical, both clubs were sold in similar retail outlets, the competitor affirmatively intended to misrepresent its product as materially the same as Callaway's product, and there was some indication of actual confusion.[58]

Callaway Golf Co. v. Turin Golf Corp.[59] enjoins the knock-off of Big Bertha® War Bird® metal clubs by the defendant's rote imitation, the Tuttle Putter; Judge Stotler discussed the deciding factors in her decision:

> [T]he four-faceted soleplate with concave, recessed heel and toe facets on either side of the center facet; the brand name in arched and stylized Old English script on the soleplate toe; the block, capital letters on the center facet; the black dot on the soleplate center facet; the polished metal soleplate and tumbled, gray finish on the remainder of the head; the chevron [or ball alignment mark] on the crown; the particular pattern and painting of scorelines on the clubface

(angled vertical lines and horizontal lines having the bottom most scoreline shortened and centered and the bottom scorelines painted a contrasting color; and the low-hosel, bore through configuration— [where the club shaft enters the club head]). . .

[T]he straight, wide, substantially flat top line; the semi-circular relief facet on the sole; the large straight-cut rear cavity; and the particular pattern and painting of scorelines on the clubface (horizontal lines having the bottom most scoreline shortened and centered and the bottom scorelines painted a contrasting color; and the distinctive, escutcheon-shaped, black, silver and red medallion [name plate inset on the back of the club]).[60]

The court apparently accepted Callaway's argument that the specific design was developed primarily for aesthetic reasons and was chosen to distinguish the Big Bertha® line from other golf clubs that were available on the market.[61] The court failed to contrast the plaintiff's club with other designs in order to support the conclusion that the Big Bertha® line was inherently distinctive. "However, Judge Stotler's laundry list of design elements implies that the particular combination of features was sufficient to create a distinctive impression and that no one element was dispositive to a finding of inherent distinctiveness."

Legal Components of, and Remedies for, a Successful Trade Dress Attack

There is a dearth of relevant cases that espouse a successful strategy to thwart golf club "knock-off" artists. However, there are two cases, which when combined, establish the paradigm for a successful suit. *Callaway Golf Co. v. Golf Clean, Inc.*[62] established a legal background for assessing components of a trade dress infringement action, and *Taylor Made Golf Club Co., Inc. v. Carsten Sports, Ltd.*[63] created a realistic basis for attaining significant monetary damages for trade dress infringement.

Legal Components

In *Callaway Golf Co. v. Golf Clean, Inc.*, the court found that the defendant's "knock-offs" infringed the trade dress rights of Callaway's Big Bertha® irons.[64] This case delineated the legal components necessary to successfully protect the plaintiff's trade dress from "knock-off" infringement.[65] It is truly the paradigm trade dress case since defendant questioned the very existence of the cause of action, asserting that "Callaway cannot claim trade dress protection for the overall appearance of the Callaway Big Bertha irons. . ."[66] The Court took exception in its discussion of the marketing campaigns of the two parties. First Callaway: "Callaway's marketing strategy is to design clubs that are 'Demonstrably Superior and Pleasingly Different.'" Their advertisements emphasized shape and design. The Court then discussed Callaway's prior legal battles, noting "[t]he success of Callaway's clubs, both woods and irons, has resulted in a cottage industry of 'knock-off' clubs, and the company has vigorously attempted to protect her interest." The Court felt that the similarity was not an accident. Indeed, a Callaway investigator masquerading as a customer was told by defendant's salesperson that "the Big Bursar irons were made from the same molds used by Callaway." The Court said that the "[d]efendant's effort to copy Callaway's club includes matching the shape, script, color, and size of Callaway's Big Bertha medallion."

The key to the awarding of a preliminary injunction was for Callaway to show a substantial likelihood of success on the merits; that is, that defendants have infringed on Callaway's trade dress and trademarks. Trade dress infringement is an implied federal cause of action based upon that portion of the Lanham Act, which provides that "[a]ny person who shall . . . use in connection with any goods or services . . . any false description or representation, including words or other symbols tending falsely to describe or represent the same . . . shall be liable to a civil action by . . . any person who believes that he is or likely to be damaged by the use of any such false description or representation."[67] If a product is inherently distinctive, secondary meaning need not be demonstrated.[68] Callaway's irons are inherently distinctive; therefore, secondary meaning need not be shown.[69] However, the evidence indicates that the Callaway Big Bertha® Irons have nonetheless established secondary meaning.[70]

Callaway's trade dress is strong; it has spent millions on advertising and placing the image in the golfing public's eye. Accordingly, for the same reasons that the Court determined that the trade dress is inherently distinctive and has acquired secondary meaning, the Callaway Big Bertha also has a strong trade dress.[71] The similarity of design test is nothing more than a subjective eyeball test.[72] After eyeballing the clubs, the Callaway Big Bertha and the Canterbury Big Bursar look almost exactly alike. The Professional Big Brother's design copies Callaway's club, even with the defendants' change in logo. Hence, this factor weighs heavily in Callaway's favor.[73]

If a plaintiff can show that a defendant adopted a mark with the intent of deriving benefit from the reputation of the plaintiff, that fact alone may be sufficient to justify an inference that there is confusing similarity.[74] Golf Clean "marketed the Big Bursars clubs as Callaway copies even to the extent as to suggest they were manufactured from the same molds. In this case, imitation is the sincerest form of flattery."[75] "Although evidence of actual confusion is not necessary to a finding of likelihood of confusion, it is nevertheless the best evidence of likelihood of confusion."[76] There was ample evidence here of actual confusion.[77]

Legal Remedies

While only a default judgment, *Taylor Made Golf Co., Inc. v. Carsten Sports, Ltd.*,[78] allowed for proof of actual damages in trade dress infringement actions, even though the proof was problematic at best. In trademark and trade dress infringement cases, if there is no evidence of actual damage or actual profit in dollars and cents, no monetary award may be made, and the mark owner then must be content with injunctive relief.[79] Taylor Made's $200,000 claim was derived from a series of estimates from a Department of Commerce calculation that Taiwan exports $100 million worth of golf clubs each year.[80] The Court did not feel it could verify Taylor Made's bold assumptions. When faced with such a situation, "[D]oubts about the actual assessment of damages will be resolved against the party who frustrates proof of such, and the fact finder may calculate damages at the highest reasonably ascertainable value."[81]

The Lanham Act permits collection of attorney's fees in some exceptional cases.[82] A trademark or trade dress suit may qualify for attorney's fees if "the infringement made is malicious, fraudulent, deliberate or willful."[83] In *Carsten,* the court awarded attorney's fees in the amount of $7,910.00. The court noted that the Lanham Act did not define "exceptional" but reasoned that disregard for the judicial process could be deemed exceptional. Thus, "[b]ecause the defendant has failed to appear, Plaintiff may request an award of reasonable attorney fees in this case."[84]

Conclusion

The image and the look of an expensive boutique golf club can be quite spectacular. It is all design—sleekness personified. You must have it in your golf bag! The trade dress is the lure that calls you to shell out $500. In this particular case, you know that the trade dress of, for example, a Big Bertha, also means a superior product that will "add yards to your game." The boutique manufacturers have poured millions into research and development, patents, market surveys, advertisements, and the other various forms of marketing in the effort to produce a superior, marketable, and recognizable golf club. It is pure conspicuous consumption; these clubs are the Cadillacs of the 1950s or the Porsches of the Millennium. It is somewhat ironic that intellectual property's stepchild, the lowly trade dress, is the only option available to protect the look, the feel, and the "ambiance" of a boutique golf club.

The lead case of *Callaway Golf Co. v. Golf Clean, Inc,.* makes it clear what must be done to gain protection. As with Callaway's Big Bertha, the manufacturer must arbitrarily combine its features in such a manner that the clubs are inherently distinctive. The clubs, in fact, have acquired secondary meaning. The features claimed by Callaway as its trade dress are primarily nonfunctional. Golf Clean made the court's job easier by being greedy and copying detail by detail so that confusion was likely, intended, expected, anticipated, and hoped for.

CHAPTER 9

Trade Secrets

Walter T. Champion, Kirk D. Willis,
Patrick K. Thornton, and Joey Barajas

Some would say that trade secrets are the stepchildren of intellectual property. But perhaps it's better said that trade secrets are the precursors of intellectual rights, and that trade secrets possess their own rights, value, and meaning. A wise-talking dog once said that everything could be a trade secret if it's not illegal. Another truism is that once the cow gets out of the barn, then that cow is gone; with trade secrets, when the cat's out of the bag, you probably have lost your indigenous trade secret rights.

Trade secrets and the misappropriation of trade secrets are closely related to the other intellectual property causes of action. Trade secret law affords developers of useful commercial information a civil remedy against anyone who wrongfully obtains and uses that business secret. Unlike patent and copyright law, there is no comprehensive federal statute that controls trade secret law. Trade secret law acknowledges that companies seek to control their valuable information in secret so they can maintain a competitive advantage.

Trade secrets are very much a part of the sports and entertainment industries. The information contained in a football play book is a trade secret. For example, in November 2010, a Connecticut high school football coach was suspended for using an opposing quarterback's missing armband during the first half of the game. The armband, of course, contained numerous "trade secrets" in the guise of plays, audibles, signals, etc. The high school principal suspended the coach after he admitted using the list of coded plays.

"A trade secret may consist of any formula pattern, device, or compilation of information which is used in one business, and which gives him an opportunity to obtain an advantage over competitors who do not know or use it" (RESTATEMENT OF TORTS §757 comment b [1937]). Factors considered in determining whether trade secrets exist include:

1. The extent to which information is known outside business;
2. The extent to which information is known to those inside the business;
3. The precautions taken by holder of trade secrets to guard the secrecy of information;
4. The savings earned and the value to the information holder as against the competitor;
5. The amount of information or money expended in obtaining and developing information; and
6. The amount of time and expense it would take for others to acquire and duplicate information[1]

In *Harvey Barnett, Inc. v. Shidler,* 338 F.3d 1125 (10th Cir. 2003), an operator of a program for infant swimming instruction sued former employees for misappropriation of trade secrets. The questions were whether library books and information downloaded from the Internet could qualify as trade secrets—and whether the infant swimming instruction program could qualify as a protectable trade secret even though individual elements of it were in the public domain. However, a novelty candy company president who sought to license "Pit Crew Chew" gum or candy sued a candy marketer, alleging misappropriation of trade secrets associated with marketer's launch of similar "Champion Chew" product, lost on the grounds that his trade secrets were not entitled to protection.

Businesses develop trade secrets and make every effort to protect those secrets from their competitors. Trade secrets are a valuable piece of intellectual property to any business. If a competitor attempts to misappropriate a trade secret, they can be sued. The Uniform Trade Secrets Act defines a trade secret as "information... that (i) derives independent economic value... from not being generally known to, and not being readily ascertainable by, proper means by other persons who can obtain economic value from its disclosure or use, and (ii) is the subject of efforts that are reasonable under the circumstances to maintain its secrecy." Of course, there is the infamous "spygate," where Coach Bill Belichick was accused of surreptitiously videotaping the signals and visual coaching instructions of the New York Jets. These signals and instructions were clearly trade secrets that were illegally misappropriated.

"A trade secret is protected against disclosure or use if knowledge of that trade secret was acquired by improper means, breach of confidence, via a third party who acquired the secret through improper means or breach of confidence (with notice to that effect) or acquired through mistaken disclosure (with notice of that mistake)."[2]

> Trade secrets law can protect information about how to design, manufacture, market and sell products, how to attract and service customers, and how to grow market share. It can protect information ranging from quantitative trading strategies and algorithms to future dress designs to sales strategies to bid proposals to material sourcing, manufacturing and quality control protocols, much of which cannot be protected at all by other intellectual property regimes. It can protect against incursions by trusted insiders, including employees, consultants, and business partners, as well as by external thieves and hackers. And it can afford those protections for so long as the information remains a trade secret which in some cases can be decades.[3]

The key is that the holder of the trade secret, for example, the Baltimore Colts as holder of their play book, must vigilantly pursue and protect their trade secrets.

> Protecting trade secrets is hard work. While the trade secrets owner escapes the initial rigors of the patent registration process, it must practice constant vigilance in adopting, following, and refining reasonable measures to protect its secrets. It must then bring considerable finesse to the process of seeking effective judicial relief when its trade secrets are at risk. Virtually every important new trade secret decision emphasizes the importance of protection in identifying trade secrets and the need for presenting evidence, not simply boilerplate conclusions or unwarranted presumptions, in asserting or defending trade secret claims. Developing a nuanced factual record and helping the court draft appropriate remedies is key to both sides in evaluating, preventing, and resolving trade secrets claims.[4]

Trade secret litigation is all the rage. "Newswires are abuzz with accounts of the 'turnaround verdict' in the epochal 'Bratz' litigation, where the jury rejected claims that Mattel's rival, MGA Entertainment, had stolen Mattel's secret ideas for Bratz dolls and instead found *Mattel* liable for $88.4 million for acquiring MGA's trade secrets through un-lawful marketing activities."[5] Remember, the subject matter of a trade secret must be secret.

Confidential Business Information

In the *Triple Tee Golf* litigation, wrongful misappropriation of the seven alleged trade secrets was defined as follows:

a. The first trade secret of the Plaintiff was for an adjustable weighting system in a "hollow back" club, so the distribution of weight in the golf club head could be changed to obtain a de-sired flight path and distance of a golf ball. The Plaintiff con-templated this could be accomplished through one of three methods: (1) use of an existing sole plate, with a distance weight distribution, and fixed by Allen screws or other means could be removed or replaced by a new sole plate with a different weight distribution, (2) insertion of additional weight into the hollow of the club, or the sole, to obtain a different weight distribution, and (3) use of weighted metal bands, with a distinct weight dis-tribution, spanning across the hollow, but inside the outside boundary of the club head, fixed by Allen screws or other means that could be removed or replaced by a metal band with a dif-ferent weight distribution.

b. The second "trade secret" is that a peripheral band could be placed around the perimeter of the hollow to secure in place either inserted weights . . . or the metal bands. . . .

c. The third "trade secret" is a twenty-seven point weighting sys-tem on a three dimensional x, y, and z coordinate system within the space of the "hollow back" golf club head and secured with one of the methods set forth above. There would be three weight boxes along the front of the face, from left to right along the y axis, three weight boxes from the bottom of the club head to the top of the club head along the z axis, and three weight boxes from the front of the club head to the rear of the club head along an x axis, to create one or more of twenty-seven weighted coordinates in the three-dimensional space of the "hollow back" club. The adjustable weights, as set forth above, would be changed in the twenty-seven point weighing system to obtain different weight distributions in the club head, to alter the flight of the golf ball when struck to accommodate the desires and needs of the golfer. At all times the weights and weighting system would stay within the perimeter of the club, as delineated by the peripheral bands, to comply with all rules and regulations of golfing.

d. The fourth "trade secret" is a system to analyze the swing of a golfer to determine any defect thereof, and whether the optimal striking point ("sweet spot") on the face of the golf club should be adjusted by utilizing the twenty-seven point weighting system to produce the distance and flight path of the golf ball desired by the golfer. The golfer's swing would be captured by video, and then processed through a computer program, to be written and developed by qualified programmers, to analyze the golf swing, and determine the placement of the twenty-seven point weighting system to correct the swing, or to produce a desired flight path or distance of the golf ball, by positioning of the optimal striking point ("sweet spot") on the face of the golf club.

e. The fifth "trade secret" is a naming or designation system for golf clubs. Instead of a "1 Wood" or a "4 Iron" or a "Pitching Wedge" or a "Putter," the golf clubs would be named or designated through lofts and description of the purpose for the club. . . .

f. The sixth "trade secret" builds upon the concept described in the fifth "trade secret." The sixth "trade secret" is to move away from a standardized set of golf clubs with a set number of woods/drivers, a set number of irons, a set number of wedges, and a putter, with a uniform weight distribution throughout the set of clubs. The new set of golf clubs would be assembled using non-uniform/different weight distributions, as set forth above, to achieve different flight paths, distances, and purposes. The twenty-seven point weighting system would be combined with different lofts to enable the golfer to choose specific clubs for specific needs and desires for his game. The golfer could choose as many, or as little a number, clubs as he wanted to complete a set of golf clubs. All of the golf clubs would be branded the same, and designated or named using the naming system set forth above. The lofts that are available to the golfer would be in two increments. This will, by its very nature, create golf clubs with non-standard loft. One example of this type of club that was envisioned by the Plaintiff was a 22 Driver.

g. The seventh "trade secret" is the way in which all of the foregoing ideas would be marketed toward the general public as one coherent system. The first target consumer would be children and junior golfers, because there were no major golf club manufacturers who directed sets of clubs toward junior golfers. The junior golfer would be provided a set of clubs with just the basic "hollow back" golf club head. Instead of a set of golf clubs with a large number of clubs to understand, the basic junior set would contain only a few clubs, for designated purposes, with different lofts . . .[6]

In the *Fox Sports Net Worth* litigation, a sports television network sued a major league baseball team and its C.O.O. for misappropriation of trade secrets. The Minnesota Uniform Trade Secrets Act prohibits the improper acquisition, use, or disclosure of trade secrets. Fox cannot meet its burden of establishing that the C.O.O. or the Twins were privy to any of its confidential information. Fox argues that the C.O.O. had access to trade secrets by his knowledge of its financial information and business contacts. The court disagrees. First, the court notes that the C.O.O. was general manager at Midwest Sports Channel (MSC) but had left by the time MSC was purchased by Fox. Therefore, any information the C.O.O. may have had related only to MSC. Fox concedes that it entered into other telecast agreements after the C.O.O. left, rendering his knowledge of its financial information outdated. Obsolete information cannot form the basis for a trade secret claim because the information has no economic value.[7]

In *Hoffman v. Impact Confections, Inc.,* plaintiff alleges that Impact misappropriated its trade secrets, consisting of the designs, plans, ideas concepts, and other proprietary materials regarding "Pit Crew Chew." Even if the concepts and plans concerning "Pit Crew Chew" satisfy the first prong of this definition, Impact has presented evidence that Ollie Pop did not make reasonable efforts to maintain the secrecy of the information. Under its non-disclosure agreement, the parties were required to take certain steps to designate information as confidential. Because Ollie Pop never designated the information at issue as "confidential," the information was not protected by the agreement. Plaintiff also has not presented evidence that Ollie Pop took other reasonable steps to maintain the secrecy of the information. Therefore, plaintiff's trade secret claim will fail and Impact is entitled to summary judgment.[8]

In *Welsh v. Big Ten Conference, Inc.,* the defendant, the Big Ten Conference, Inc., is a group of academic institutions that sponsors athletic programs and championships. The plaintiff, Robert W. Welsh, is a longtime supporter of Big Ten athletics. Beginning in 1997, Welsh began working on a business plan for Big Ten that included ideas for television programming such as talk shows, live auctions of Big Ten merchandise and memorabilia, and the re-broadcast of memorable past games. One of Welsh's ideas was for the "Big Ten Networks," a satellite cable television station providing in-depth coverage of sports and the culture of Big Ten. Welsh intended that he, through his company Big Ten Development, would implement the business plan for Big Ten.

After some initial discussions with Big Ten and the receipt of correspondence indicating Big Ten's initial interest in working with Big Ten Development, Welsh set up a meeting to present his plan. On May 18, 1998, Welsh presented his plan to Big Ten in a written business plan dated May 1998 and annotated "Confidential." Shortly after the meeting, Big Ten told Welsh that it had decided not to pursue the business relationship. However, it retained Welsh's materials, despite the fact that it had acknowledged the confidential nature of the business plan. Several years later, Big Ten introduced the Big Ten Network, which included several programming ideas that resembled those proposed by Welsh in 1998. Welsh filed suit for violations of the Illinois Trade Secrets Act.[9]

The Uniform Trade Secret Act

In 1979, the Uniform Trade Secrets Act was approved by the National Conference of Commissioners of Uniform State Laws. Since that date, the Act has been adopted by 20 states: California, Colorado, Connecticut, Delaware, Illinois, Indiana, Kansas, Louisiana, Maine, Minnesota, Nevada, North Dakota, Oklahoma, Oregon, Rhode Island, Virginia, Washington, West Virginia, and Wisconsin.

A trade secret is defined under the Act as information, including a formula, pattern, compilation, program, device, method, technique, or process, that:

1. Derives independent economic value, actual or potential, from not being generally known to, and not being readily ascertainable by proper means by, other persons who can obtain economic value from its disclosure or use, and
2. Is the subject of efforts that are reasonable under the circumstances to maintain its secrecy. U.T.S.A. § 1(4).

This broad definition contains several significant departures from the common law. First, the Act eliminates the Restatement's requirement that the trade secret be "used in one's business." The Act extends protection to a plaintiff who has not yet had the means or the opportunity to put the trade secret to use. As a result, trade secret protection for discoveries made during research may be easier to prove in jurisdictions that have enacted the Uniform Act than in jurisdictions following the Restatement definition. This definition also includes information that has a negative commercial value; that is, the results of lengthy and expensive research that proved that a particular process will not work.

The Act also requires the plaintiff to demonstrate a "reasonable effort" to maintain the secrecy of the information. The effort required is that which is reasonable under the circumstances; courts do not expect extreme and unduly expensive procedures. Thus, in jurisdictions in which the Act has been adopted, companies should ensure the confidentiality of business information by adopting and enforcing formal trade secret protection plans.[10]

Covenants Not to Compete

In most states, incomplete covenants will be enforced if the covenant is designed to protect against unfair and illegal conduct on behalf of the former employee. This is done to insulate the employer from competition. The current standards are to stand by covenants that are reasonable while restricting negative conduct. There is no uniform standard for creating and producing enforceable restrictive covenants, particularly because litigation typically arises only *after* the covenants have been breached, and, therefore, the reasonableness of the covenants is often evaluated with the benefit of hindsight not available at the time of drafting. Regularly, courts view non-compete agreements more harshly when the employer attempts to stand by the agreement.

Because covenants not to compete are viewed as restraints of trade, they are evaluated against a standard of reasonableness as opposed to a strict contract construction standard. When analyzing the enforceability of these covenants, courts balance the concerns of the employer in guarding its property in regard to public policy and trade restrictions. A court will have to balance an employer's tangible interests and the hardship of an employee due to restricted job opportunities. Courts differ in their treatment of overly broad covenants. Some courts hold non-compete agreements totally unenforceable if they are overly broad and unreasonable in scope or duration.[11]

In a widely-reported trade secrets case, which I call *"Bimbo,"* the court found that the plaintiff had made a compelling factual showing of likely risk and granted an injunction to prevent a top executive who knew all three secrets (the recipe, the engineering, and the process) for placing the nooks and crannies in Thomas's English muffins, as well as the profitability and cost savings plans for his former employer, from commencing competing employment with competitor Hostess (*Bimbo Bakeries USA, Inc. v. Botticella,* No. CIV.A. 10–0194, 2010 WL 571774 [E.D. Pa. Feb. 9 2010]). Botticella was subject to a confidentiality agreement but was not bound by a non-compete agreement.

Another decision finding the plaintiff had shown evidence that disclosure would be inevitable is *Samsung Telecommunications America, LLC v. Ogle,* No. 09–09210 (Dallas Co. Dist. Ct. July 23, 2009), which granted a temporary restraining order to prevent the former chief marketing officer of Samsung Telecommunications from assuming similar responsibilities for competitor Motorola despite the lack of a non-compete agreement. The former employer presented evidence that the two companies were head-to-head employers at a critical time period during which equipment suppliers would be negotiating concessions with the telecommunications carriers. Finding that the plaintiff had taken reasonable precautions to maintain trade secrets, that Ogle had agreed to protect them, that the trade secrets would necessarily be placed at immediate risk in the new position, and that "once confidential and proprietary information and/or a trade secret is disclosed it is forever lost." The court granted a temporary restraining order prohibiting Ogle from, among other things, working in a capacity involving the negotiations or holding of "arrive periods" with or marketing to telecommunications carriers. Subsequent proceedings have not been reported. The case is a good example of the importance of defining the secrets at issue, showing the need for narrowly tailored restraints, and explaining the unique time sensitivity of the specific proposed competitive activities.[12]

In 1966, Dr. Harvey Barnett, the founder and president of Infant Swimming Research (ISR), began to develop the Infant Swimming Research program, which plaintiffs describe as a scientific, behavioral approach to pediatric drowning prevention. This program utilizes a method known as "swim, float, swim" and contains nearly two thousand "prompts and procedures" for teaching infants as young as six months old how to survive in the water. Additionally, the ISR program maintains safety protocols to keep children safe during instruction and provides a "BUDS" Record Sheet allowing parents to monitor children's bodily functions, diet, and sleep in order to evaluate physical responses to the ISR program.

Judy Heumann, Ann Shidler, and Alison Geerdes, defendants in the case, are former ISR instructors who left the company in early 2000.

While employed by ISR, Heumann, Shidler, and Geerdes each signed a "Non-disclosure and Confidentiality Agreement" and a license agreement containing a further "confidentiality of Information" provision as well as a "Covenant Not to Compete." As quoted in *Harvey Barnett, Inc. v. Shidler*:

> Notwithstanding these agreements on leaving ISR in 2000, the three former employees started Infant Aquatic Survival, a new company devoted to teaching infant and child swimming in Colorado. It is this conduct that is the subject of the litigation. Defendants' program is allegedly similar to the ISR program in that it utilizes the same "swim, float, swim" method, implements some of the same safety protocols, uses a Daily Health Data Sheet similar to the BUDS sheet, uses a comparable registration form, and distributes a comparable parent resource book to parents of children enrolled in the IAS program. It is also uncontested that defendant Shidler's husband sought to reserve the names Harvey Barnett, Inc., and Infant Swimming Research, Inc., with the Colorado Secretary of State. On more than one occasion, defendants falsely advertised that their program, IAS, had been in business since 1990.
>
> ISR filed in district court a complaint against the defendants, alleging state-law claims of misappropriation of trade secrets, breach of contract, and unjust enrichment as well as unfair competition and deceptive trade practices under the CCA, along with federal claims of trademark infringement and misleading trade practices under the Lanham Act. ISR then sought a preliminary injunction to prevent the defendants from teaching the ISR program to other instructors. Following an evidentiary hearing, the district denied ISR's request for a preliminary injunction as to Heumann and Shidler. Subsequently, the defendants moved for summary judgment, which was granted. In its ruling, the district court concluded that the ISR program was not a trade secret as a matter of law and dismissed ISR's misappropriation-of-trade-secrets claim. The district court further concluded that both the covenant not to compete and the confidentiality provision in the license agreement were not enforceable, and dismissed ISR's breach-of-contract claim. As to ISR's remaining claims—trademark infringement and misleading trade practices under the Lanham Act, and violations of the CCPA— the court concluded that because ISR failed to advance sufficient evidence on each element those claims must be dismissed as well. ISR appeals the grant of summary judgment to defendants.[13]

International Agreements for the Protection of Trade Secrets

The first international agreement containing any explicit provisions for the protection of trade secrets was the North American Free Trade Agreement (NAFTA), signed by the U.S. on December 8, 1993. The following year, the legislation implementing the TRIPS Agreement, which contains similar provisions on the protection of "undisclosed information," was passed by Congress. There is also a regional agreement within the United States and Central America called the Central American Free Trade Agreement, with protections similar to NAFTA.[14]

Economic Espionage Act

The Economic Espionage Act, 18 U.S.C. §§ 1831–1839, creates prosecutions, most of which involve offers by defendants to sell secrets belonging to others. Several have involved sting operations, photographs, and even videotapes. Companies that believe their secrets have been stolen now may have a potent tool, offering the possibility of fines up to $10,000,000 and jail terms of up to 15 years, depending upon who orchestrated the theft. To avail themselves of this tool, however, trade secrets owners must first be sure to take reasonable measures to protect their secrets. They then must interest the U.S. Attorney and, ultimately, the Justice Department, in prosecuting. And they must be careful to cooperate with, but not dominate, the prosecutors to avoid a determination that they have so controlled the investigation as to compromise the prosecutor's impartiality.

The Act also presents serious risks to companies that do not have well-documented, thoughtful procedures in place to discourage theft or receipt of others' secrets. Wrongful acts by even one employee can subject a corporation to potential liability under the Act. The company that has not designed, supplemented, and enforced "an effective program to prevent and detect violation of law" may be subject to particularly severe penalties. Such a program may afford an added benefit by emphasizing respect for trade secrets; a trade secrets compliance program designed to protect against receipt of others' secrets may lead to greater care being used to protect the company's own secrets. As regards the elements of an effective program, policies will differ, in part based on the industry and corporate culture.[15]

Sports Playbooks as Trade Secrets

"Businesses constantly create, plan, produce, reproduce, and formulate strategies in order to gain a competitive advantage over others in the marketplace. . . . Companies seek the protection of intellectual property laws to secure proprietary rights in their innovations. The benefits of that protection stem from the rights of exclusion afforded by intellectual property law. The right to prevent others from gaining or using information can foster economic success and advancement." Nowhere is this truer than in the world of professional sports.[16]

"In the NFL, playbooks are treated like trade secrets." However, whether and how a court might actually apply trade secret law to playbooks remains a matter of speculation.[17]

The National Football League is "full of grown men playing a boy's game for a tycoon's fortune."[18] Professional football is a business. Franchises buy stadiums, sell tickets, pay salaries to players, coaches, and assistants, sell broadcasting rights to television stations, sell advertising rights to marketers, design logos, create uniforms, and license rights to clothing designers and vending suppliers. Like all other businesses, NFL teams compete in a market to outperform each other in hopes of achieving public notoriety and earning substantial profits. When the team wins, the franchise as a whole wins. Players and coaches may get new contracts with higher salaries, and owners profit from increased marketing exposure through television, radio, advertising, and other associated sales. If a team continuously succeeds against its opponents the team may even enjoy a profitable trip to the Super Bowl.

Successful coaching is one key to winning games in the NFL. Successful coaching means, in part, having an experienced coach and talented players. More importantly, though, a team needs a game plan for approaching upcoming games. The game plan revolves around the creation, design, and scripting of specific plays to be run in a certain game against a particular opponent. These players are formally memorialized in playbooks and practiced in advance by the players who execute them during the games. The coaching staff decides when to utilize certain plays at different points in the game. The compilation of these pre-designed plays is known as a playbook of scripted sports plays.[19]

An individually scripted play is the combined movement of the eleven participants on the field for one team at one point in time. This entails the total pattern of each player's actions in relation to the movements of others on the team. Scripted plays are pre-designed, orchestrated events that are created in preparation for an upcoming game. In general, an individual play is secretly developed in collaboration with other assistants within the team organization, introduced in practice sessions to those players who will then carry out the play, and ultimately included in a formal playbook.[20]

An individual play is a method of advancing the ball downfield or a process for obtaining a score. A play includes the formation of players on the field before the series of movements before that play begins and contains the combined movements of all eleven players for the duration of the play. It concludes when each player's assignment has ended. Thus, it is this series of actions as a whole that is the key to a particular play's success. The ingenuity of the coach and players is what makes the next scripted play better than the last. No single play will necessarily succeed against any one defense at any one time against any one team. A play is neither one formation nor just an individual player's athletic move. It's like a game of chess. A play does not account for incidental uncertainties that may occur during execution such as opposing players falling down or missing tackles. Furthermore, a specific, magic number of plays that are to be created for a particular game down does not exist. Most importantly, plays depend on timing. The design includes information pertaining to when particular plays will be utilized. The plays are scripted to include a combination of movements from the time of the break of the huddle before the snap to the audible calls made by the quarterback at the line of scrimmage and then to the specific patterns of runs, blocks, cuts, and turns made until the play is whistled dead by an official. Determining when each particular element of this sequence of events should occur is part of the creative process. The element of surprise is often the key to the success of a particular play. The secret nature of the playbook thus creates the competitive advantage for the team.[21]

Trade Secrets Acts in E-commerce

To qualify for trade secret protection, a plaintiff need only show that it took reasonable precautions. The threshold is not high. As a general rule, the courts do not require that extreme and unduly expensive procedures be taken to protect trade secrets against flagrant industrial espionage. In *Religious Technology Center v. Netcom On-Line Communication Services, Inc.*, 923 F. Supp. 1231 (9th Cir. 1995), the court held that reasonable efforts to maintain secrecy "can include advising employees of the existence of a trade secret and limiting access to the information on a need to know basis, as well as requiring employees to sign confidentiality agreements." The plaintiff "had made more than an adequate showing" on the issue of whether there were reasonable efforts to maintain the secrecy of its documents: using locked cabinets and safes; logging and identifying the materials; making the materials available to only a handful of sites worldwide; attaching electronic sensors to the documents; using locked briefcases for transporting works; using alarms, photo identifications, and security personnel; and requiring confidentiality agreements for all those given access to the materials.

At a minimum, owners of confidential trade secrets information should require their employees to sign confidentiality agreements with respect to such information. Steps should also be taken to mark the information so that it is easily identified as confidential and to ensure that employees know how to recognize and handle such information. Companies should also make access available on a "need to know basis." Companies may also want to limit access to confidential trade secret information through locked facilities, identification requirements, and acceptable surveillance measures. In the case of computer information, access may be controlled by use of electronic labeling, electronic locks, passwords, warning screens and encryption or coding. "Shrink-wrap licenses" are also used, usually in connection with computer software, to limit disclosure by purchasers by stating directly on the product package that the use of the product by anyone other than the licensee constitutes an agreement to certain nondisclosure terms.[22]

The Internet has enabled individuals to widely disseminate protected trade secret information. However, trade secrets law still protects the holder of a trade secret against disclosure or use when the knowledge is gained, not by the owner's volition, but by some improper means.

The United States District Court for the Northern District of California addressed the issue of the effect of posting trade secrets on the Internet in the *Religious Technology Center* case. The Court held that where an anonymous person posted trade secret information on the Internet, the defendant who downloaded the information could not be held liable for misappropriation of trade secrets because the posting of the trade secret information over the Internet destroyed the trade secret protection, even if the trade secret information was obtained by wrongful means (923 F. Supp. at 1255–1257). Although the defendant could not rely on his own improper posting as a defense to the plaintiff's misappropriation claims, "Evidence that another individual has put the alleged trade secrets into the public domain prevents plaintiff from further enforcing its trade secret rights in those materials." The Court held that although the "Internet has not reached the status where a temporary posting on a news group is akin to publication in a major newspaper or on a television network, those with an interest in using the Church's trade secrets to compete with the Church are likely to look to the news group. Thus, posting works to the Internet makes them generally known to the relevant people—the potential competitors of the Church." The Court acknowledged that it was "troubled by the notion that an Internet user, including those using 'anonymous remailers' can destroy valuable intellectual property rights by posting them over the Internet, especially given the fact that there is little opportunity to screen postings before they are made . . . Thus, the anonymous (or judgment proof) defendant can permanently destroy valuable trade secrets, leaving no one to hold liable for the misappropriation."[23]

CHAPTER 10

The Right of Publicity

The right of publicity is the right to control the commercial use of one's identity. The right of publicity becomes even more significant in the fast-paced information technology age, where images are processed at amazing speeds through and by a variety of mechanisms and sources. It actually emanates from tort law and the right of privacy, although some may consider the right of publicity a member of the intellectual property family. The right of publicity is the: "inherent right of every human being to control the commercial use of his or her identity."[1]

Professor William Prosser wrote in a 1960 California Law Review article that the right of privacy gave rights to four different torts commonly referred to as "Prosser's Four Torts of Privacy." These four torts were eventually included in the Restatement of Torts. The four categories are:

1. The use of a person's name, picture, or other likeness for commercial purposes without permission;
2. Intrusion on an individual's affairs or seclusion;
3. Publication of information that places a person in a false light;
4. Public disclosure of private facts about an individual that an ordinary person would find objectionable.[2]

The majority of states now recognize "the use of a person's name, picture or other likeness for commercial purposes without permission" as a viable cause of action for infringement of the right of publicity. Many states have passed statutes dealing with the right of publicity. The right of publicity grants a person the exclusive right to control the commercial value and exploitation of his or her name, likeness, or personality.[3] It protects the commercial interests of athletes and entertainers in their identities.[4] Other privacy torts protect primarily personal interests, whereas the right of publicity primarily protects the property interest in the publicity of one's name.[5]

The United States Supreme Court has decided only one right of publicity case, *Zacchini v. Scripps-Howard Broadcasting,* 433 U.S. 562 (1977). In *Zacchini,* an individual performed a "human cannonball" act that was subsequently shown on the local news. The court dismissed the broadcast company's First Amendment defense, recognizing a right of publicity for Zacchini's entire act (all ten seconds).

In a right of publicity case, a plaintiff who alleges that a right of publicity has been appropriated must prove that a name or identity was appropriated for some advantage, usually one of a commercial nature.[6] This presents no issue where a plaintiff's name or pictures are used in the advertisement for defendants' products.[7] Under common law and the Restatement (Second) of Torts, a plaintiff's right of publicity is protected even without the showing of a commercial use.[8] For example, a court recognized a cause of action in favor of the plaintiff where the defendant forged the plaintiff's name on a tax return.[9]

The Right of Publicity in Sports

In today's media-driven sports and entertainment industries, athletes have become celebrities both on and off the field. Sports fans can now watch their favorite sports stars through a variety of forms of media 24 hours a day, 7 days a week. Sports and the reporting of sporting events has become international news. David Beckham, Tiger Woods, Peyton Manning, and Serena Williams are not only great athletes but have now become celebrities in their own rights with large followings of fans. Fans cannot seem to get enough news about their sports, and this also includes off the field news, sometimes involving the most excruciating details about the private lives of athletes and entertainers. Many high-profile athletes have retained public relations firms to control and monitor their public images because of the value of those images. Both sports and entertainment agents understand their clients have "star power," which can translate into endorsement value. Many corporations will pay athletes large sums to endorse their products. In 2010, PGA golfer Tiger Woods made $90.5 million in earnings; $70 million came from endorsements. NBA player LeBron James was second in endorsements for professional athletes at approximately $30 million.[10] Athletes, entertainers, and their agents understand their value and take appropriate measures to protect and enhance the name and image of their clients. Entertainers, much like athletes, have substantial commercial value. Movie stars, actors, celebrities, and others who have grabbed the spotlight and headlines, some without even really achieving anything whatsoever, such as Paris Hilton, have developed a commercial value in their names.

Not only must athletes protect their commercial value, they also must protect their public image as well. An athlete's or an entertainer's public image can affect his or her endorsement value. No athlete wants bad press or to create a poor public image; therefore, many sue to protect their right of publicity and to prevent others from profiting from using the name, likeness, image, and goodwill that the athlete has created and earned.

Many areas of the law come into play when the commercial value of an athlete's name or likeness is at stake: the common law right of privacy, the statutory right of publicity, federal and state trademark laws, unfair competition laws, and defamation law. U.S. courts have been willing to extend the right of publicity to names, nicknames, caricatures, and even voices.[11]

There have been numerous lawsuits which have explored and defined the right of publicity in a variety of contexts.[12] In *Muhammad Ali v. Playgirl*, 447 F. Supp. 723 (S.D.N.Y. 1978), Ali sued the women's magazine, alleging that it was using his likeness when it published a drawing of an African American boxer sitting in a corner of a boxing ring who had Ali's facial features. The deciding factor was the addition of the phrase "the Greatest," which is undoubtedly the nom de guerre of Muhammad Ali. The court found in favor of Ali, indicating that the right of publicity is not limited to an actual photograph but could be based merely on the use of the physical characteristics of the individual.

In a case involving football great Elroy "Crazylegs" Hirsch, Hirsch sued a manufacturer of shaving lotion, alleging that the company's use of his nickname "Crazylegs" to describe its shaving lotion was in violation of his right of publicity. He alleged that because he had used that nickname for many years as both a collegiate and amateur football player, his right of publicity had been infringed. The court remanded the case to the trial court, stating that the disputed identification issue would not prevent his claim.[13]

Kareem Abdul-Jabbar was an outstanding collegiate basketball player. Abdul-Jabbar sued General Motors Corporation (GMC) for its use of his former name, Lewis Alcindor, over a television advertisement that appeared years after Abdul-Jabbar completed his college playing days.[14] A television commercial played during the 1993 NCAA men's basketball tournament stated, "How about some trivia?" Immediately thereafter, the words "You're talking to the champ" appeared on the screen. Then a voice asked, "Who holds the record for being voted the most outstanding player of this tournament?" The following words appeared on the screen: "Lewis Alcindor, UCLA, '67, '68, '69." A voice then asked, "Has any car made the *Consumer Digest's* Best Buy List more than once? The Oldsmobile Eighty-Eight has." The commercial then showed the car for several seconds, stated that the 88 had made the list three years in a row, and gave the price. The commercial ended by showing the on-screen message, "A Definite First Round Pick," with a voice adding, "It's your money" and a final printed message, "Demand Better, 88 by Oldsmobile." GMC had never obtained consent from Abdul-Jabbar to use his name. After Abdul-Jabbar complained to GMC, the ad was withdrawn. Abdul-Jabbar sued, saying the use of his name was likely to confuse consumers as to his endorsement of the automobile. GMC asserted that Abdul-Jabbar had lost the rights to his birth name because he had "abandoned" his former name through nonuse. The court found in favor of Abdul-Jabbar, stating:

> While the Lanham Act has been applied to cases alleging appropriation of a celebrity's identity, the abandonment defense has never to our knowledge been applied to a person's name or identity. We decline to stretch the federal law of trademark to encompass such a defense. One's birth name is an integral part of one's identity; it is not bestowed for commercial purposes, nor is it "kept alive" through commercial use. A proper name thus cannot be deemed "abandoned" throughout its possessor's life, despite his failure to use it, or continue to use it, commercially.
>
> In other words, an individual's given name, unlike a trademark, has a life and a significance quite apart from the commercial realm. Use or nonuse of the name for commercial purposes does not dispel that significance. An individual's decision to use a name other than the birth name—whether the decision rests on religious, marital, or other personal considerations—does not therefore imply intent to set aside the birth name, or the identity associated with that name.
>
> While the issue of whether GMC's use of the name Lew Alcindor constituted an endorsement of its product is far from clear, we hold that GMC cannot rely on abandonment as a defense to Abdul-Jabbar's Lanham Act claim.[15]

Even though they can receive no compensation for playing football, American college football players can become major stars in their own right. Some can produce substantial revenue for their universities. However, under National Collegiate Athletic Association (NCAA) rules, student athletes are considered amateurs who are not able to earn money while playing college football. In *Keller v. Electronic Arts, Inc.,* 2010 WL 530108 (N.D. Cal.), a former collegiate football player sued, claiming his right of publicity was infringed upon by the makers of a video game which had placed his picture on the front cover of the game. Sam Keller, a former college quarterback, argued that NCAA and Electronic Arts, Inc. (EA) infringed upon his right of publicity. He argues that the NCAA failed to honor its own rules dealing with amateur student-athletes and that the NCAA should be held liable for an infringement of his right of publicity because they knowingly approved of EA's use of Keller's likeness in the videogame.

Sam Keller is a former starting quarterback for the Arizona State University and the University of Nebraska football teams. EA develops interactive entertainment software. It produces, among other things, the "NCAA Football" series of video games. In the games, consumers can simulate football matches between college and university teams. To make the games realistic, EA designs the virtual football players to resemble real-life college football athletes. Keller claims that these virtual players are nearly identical to their real-life counterparts: they share the same jersey numbers, have similar physical characteristics, and come from the same home state. To enhance the accuracy of the player depictions, Keller alleged, EA sends questionnaires to team equipment managers of college football teams. Although EA omits the real-life athletes' names from "NCAA Football," Keller asserted that consumers may access online services to download team rosters and the athletes' names and upload them into the games.

Sam Keller also alleged that the NCAA violated his Indiana right of publicity. The NCAA argued that his claim failed as a matter of law because he did not allege that it used his image or likeness. Keller responded that the NCAA used his likeness because it "expressly reviewed and knowingly approved each version of each NCAA-brand videogame. . . ." Under Indiana law, personalities have a property interest in, among other things, their images and likenesses. A personality is a living or deceased person whose image and likeness have commercial value.

To determine whether a work is transformative, a court must inquire into whether the celebrity likeness is one of the "raw materials" from which an original work is synthesized, or whether the depiction or imitation of the celebrity is the very sum and substance of the work in question. The question is whether a product containing a celebrity's likeness is so transformed that it has become primarily the defendant's own expression rather than the celebrity's likeness. The word "expression" means something other than the likeness of the celebrity.

Here, EA's depiction of the plaintiff in "NCAA Football" is not sufficiently transformative to bar his California right of publicity claims as a matter of law. In the game, the quarterback for Arizona State University shares many of plaintiff's characteristics. For example, the virtual player wears the same jersey number, is the same height and weight, and hails from the same state. EA does not depict Keller in a different form; he is represented as what he was: the starting quarterback for Arizona State University.

Although "NCAA Football" is based on Keller's "public affairs," EA is not entitled to the statutory defense because its use of plaintiff's image and likeness extends beyond reporting information about him. Accordingly, plaintiff's California statutory and common law right of publicity claims are not barred as a matter of law.

One of the first cases to recognize an athlete's right to his own image is *O'Brien v. Pabst Sales Co.*, 124 F.2d 167 (5th Cir. 1941), *cert. denied* 315 U.S. 823 (1942). Quarterback Davey O'Brien sued a beer producer that used his picture as a football player without his permission. O'Brien had been actively involved in organizations that spoke out against the use of alcohol. He sued Pabst for invasion of privacy. Although O'Brien lost his case, Justice Holmes in a dissenting opinion stated that although there was no controlling authority on the issue, O'Brien still clearly had a property right in his endorsement.

> . . . I think, under the Texas common law, the appellant is entitled to recover the reasonable value of the use in trade and commerce of his picture for advertisement purposes, to the extent that such use was appropriated by appellee.
>
> The right of privacy is distinct from the right to use one's name or picture for purposes of commercial advertisement. The latter is a property right that belongs to every one; it may have much or little, or only a nominal value; but it is a personal right, which may not be violated with impunity.

Don Newcombe was an outstanding major league baseball player. He is also a recovering alcoholic. The 1956 National League's Most Valuable Player sued Coors over its use of a picture of a baseball player who was shown in a picturesque baseball stadium in a wind-up position that Newcombe claimed was him (*Newcombe v. Adolf Coors Co.*, 157 F.3d 686 [9th Cir. 1998]). Newcombe argued that the figure in the advertising was him and was used without his consent, asserting appropriation of his right of publicity. Unbeknownst to the artist, the photograph he had used for his model was actually a photo of Newcombe pitching in the 1949 World Series at Ebbets Field in Brooklyn. The situation was further complicated because Newcombe was a recovering alcoholic and because of Newcombe's position as the spokesperson for the National Institute for Drug and Alcohol Abuse.

In *Montana v. San Jose Mercury News,* 40 Cal. Rptr. 2d 639 (Cal. Ct. App. 1995), former NFL quarterback Joe Montana sued a newspaper over its reproduction of an artist's rendition of him in the Super Bowl. He alleged that the newspaper misappropriated his name and likeness for commercial purposes by reproducing in poster form newspaper pages containing his photograph, thereby violating his right of privacy. The court found against the famous quarterback based on First Amendment grounds. The court stated in part that

> [i]n the instant case, there can be no question that the full page newspaper accounts of Super Bowls XXIII and XXIV, and the 49'ers' [sic] four championships in a single decade, constituted publication of matters in the public interest entitled to First Amendment protection. Montana, indeed, concedes as much. The question he raises in this appeal is whether the relatively contemporaneous reproduction of these pages, in poster form, for resale, is similarly entitled to First Amendment protection. We conclude that it is. This is because Montana's name and likeness appeared in the posters for *precisely* the same reason they appeared on the original newspaper front pages: because Montana was a major player in the contemporaneous, newsworthy sports events. Under these circumstances, Montana's claim that SJMM used his face and name solely to extract commercial value from them fails.[16]

In *Facenda v. NFL Films, Inc., et al.,* 2007 WL 1314632 (E.D. Pa. 2007), the estate of the legendary sportscaster John Facenda (commonly referred to as "the voice of God") sued over the use of his voice in the video game *Madden NFL '06.* The estate asserted claims for invasion of privacy, as well as unauthorized use of name or likeness under the Pennsylvania Right of Publicity Statute and under the Lanham Act. The court dismissed the right of privacy claim but found that the estate was entitled to recover under the Lanham Act as well as the state's right of publicity statute. The court found that although Facenda's voice was used only briefly, it added commercial value to the video game and therefore was actionable.

In *Pooley v. National Hole-In-One Ass'n*, 89 F. Supp. 2d 1108 (D. Ariz. 2000), the defendant used plaintiff Don Pooley's picture for a mere six seconds in its advertisement. Does that limited use appropriate and violate an individual's right of publicity? According to the court, it did. The court stated: "It capitalized on Plaintiff's name, reputation, and prestige in the context of an advertisement. The promotional videotape went one step further and implied a false connection between the Plaintiff and its business. The Court finds that the use of Plaintiff's identity was strictly commercial and not protected by the First Amendment. . . ."[17]

Kareem Abdul-Jabbar was, by all accounts, a great NBA player and an amusing co-pilot in *Airplane*. His "sky hook" dominated the league for many years. Should he capitalize on his "sky hook" and use the term in marketing? In fact, that is exactly what he did.[18]

In January 2010, Shaquille O'Neal sued a Las Vegas company over the word "Shaqtus." When O'Neal played for the Phoenix Suns, he was known as "the Big Cactus" and "the Big Shaqtus."[19]

Right of Publicity for Entertainers

Entertainers also have commercial value in their name and likeness. They must take every measure to ensure parties are not appropriating their rights of privacy in some manner (voice, characters, likeness, photographs, initials, nicknames, etc.). It is primarily an element of a right of publicity case that the plaintiff be reasonably recognizable or identifiable or in other words that the plaintiff be capable of identification "from the objectionable material itself." It is not essential that the plaintiff's name be used. What is important is whether appropriation of the plaintiff's identity has occurred.

Midler v. Ford Motor Co., 849 F.2d 460 (9th Cir. 1988), "centers on the protectability of the voice of celebrated chanteuse from commercial exploitation without her consent." Even though the district court described the defendants' conduct as that "of the average thief," that court nonetheless believed that there was no legal principle preventing the imitation of Midler's voice.

The Appeals Court, however, looked at it differently. The Ford Company, in their "Yuppie Campaign," acquired the services of a sound-alike (in fact, one of the Hurlettes, the Divine Miss M's backup singers) and instructed her to imitate Midler's voice in a rendition of "Do You Want to Dance." The value of her voice is what the market would have paid for Midler to have sung the commercial in person. A voice is as distinctive and personal as a face. The human voice is one of the most palpable ways identity is manifested. The singer manifests herself in the song. To impersonate her voice is to pirate her identity. The *Midler* court held only that when a distinctive voice of a professional singer is widely known and is deliberately imitated in order to sell a product, the sellers have appropriated what is not theirs and have committed a tort in California. Midler had made a showing sufficient to defeat summary judgment, that the defendants exploited Midler's identity for their own profit in selling their product.

Similarly, in *White v. Samsung Electronics America, Inc.*, 971 F.2d 1395 (9th Cir. 1992), a well-known television star, Vanna White, sued, arguing that her image had been recreated by a robot in a corporate advertisement that infringed upon her right of publicity. The court was called upon to determine whether her right of publicity was infringed and whether her name and likeness had been appropriated through the use of the robot ad.

In running a particular advertisement without Vanna White's permission, defendants attempted to capitalize on White's fame to enhance their fortune, so to speak. Plaintiff Vanna White is the hostess of "Wheel of Fortune," one of the most popular game shows in television history. An estimated 40 million people watch the program daily. Capitalizing on the fame which her participation in the show has bestowed on her, White markets her identity to various advertisers.

The Vanna White ad depicted a robot, dressed in a wig, gown, and jewelry that was consciously selected to resemble White's hair and dress. The robot was posed next to a game board instantly recognizable as the Wheel of Fortune game show set, in a stance for which White is famous. The caption of the ad read: "Longest-running game show. 2012 A.D." Defendants referred to the ad as the "Vanna White" ad. Unlike the other celebrities used in the campaign, White neither consented to the ads, nor was she paid.

White argued that the district court erred in granting summary judgment to defendants on White's common law right of publicity claim. In *Eastwood v. Superior Court*, 149 Cal. App. 3d 409, 417, 198 Cal. Rptr. 342 (1983), the California court of appeals stated that the common law right of publicity cause of action "may be pleaded by alleging (1) the defendant's use of the plaintiff's identity; (2) the appropriation of plaintiff's name or likeness to defendant's advantage, commercially or otherwise; (3) lack of consent; and (4) resulting injury." The *Eastwood* court did not hold that the right of publicity cause of action could be pleaded only by alleging an appropriation of name or likeness. *Eastwood* involved an unauthorized use of photographs of Clint Eastwood and of his name. Accordingly, the *Eastwood* court had no occasion to consider the extent beyond the use of name or likeness to which the right of publicity reaches. That court held only that the right of publicity cause of action "may be" pleaded by alleging, *inter alia,* appropriation of name or likeness, not that the action may be pleaded *only* in those terms.

Television and other media create marketable celebrity identity value. Considerable energy and ingenuity are expended by those who have achieved celebrity value to exploit it for profit. The law protects the celebrity's sole right to exploit this value, whether the celebrity has achieved her fame out of rare ability, dumb luck, or a combination thereof. The *White* court declined to eviscerate the common law right of publicity. White has alleged facts showing that defendants had appropriated her identity.

In the case of *Elvis Presley International Memorial Foundation v. Crowell,* 733 S.W.2d 89 (Tenn. Ct. App. 1987), the question of whether a right of publicity survives an individual's death was at issue. Many entertainers remain popular even in death. The estates of entertainers can earn millions of dollars even after the death of the entertainer. James Dean and Marilyn Monroe[20] have both grown in stature in death, but Elvis Presley still remains "the king," even in death (that is, if he is dead). The overwhelming majority of cases hold that the right of privacy is personal and non-assignable and dies with the holder of the right of publicity.[21]

The court emphasizes that "[i]t would be difficult for any court today, especially one sitting in Music City U.S.A., practically in the shadow of the Grand Ole Opry, to be unaware of the manner in which celebrities exploit the public's recognition of their name and image. The stores selling Elvis Presley tee shirts, Hank Williams, Jr.'s bandannas or Barbara Mandrell satin jackets are not selling clothing as much as they are selling the celebrities themselves."

There are few everyday activities that have not been touched by celebrity merchandising. This, of course, should come as no surprise. Celebrity endorsements are extremely valuable in the promotion of goods and services. They increase audience appeal and thus make the commodity or service more sellable. These endorsements are of great economic value to celebrities and are now economic reality.

The court concludes, "[u]nquestionably [that] a celebrity's right of publicity has value. It can be possessed and used. It can be assigned, and it can be the subject of a contract. Thus, there is ample basis for this Court to conclude that it is a species of intangible personal property."

In *Topheavy Studios, Inc. v. Doe,* 2005 WL 1940159 (Tex. App.), the court dealt with the issue of a release in the context of a right of publicity claim. Jane Doe and two of her friends were enjoying spring break in

South Padre Island, Texas. Topheavy Studios was on the island to shoot film footage of young women to use in their video game titled "The Guy Game." The advertisement on the box of the game stated:

> The Guy Game puts you in the world's wildest party spot for the steamiest Spring Break action ever! Shot live at South Padre Island, this Red-Hot Trivia Challenge lets you play with over 60 smokin' co-eds during Spring Break Insanity, as they proudly show off their "assets" for your personal enjoyment. You bring the party and we'll supply the game—YOU'LL SCORE EVERY TIME!

Doe agreed to be a contestant in the game. She signed a release given to her by Topheavy with a fake name that appeared on a fake identification and which also said she was 21, which was false. She was actually only 17. She received twenty dollars as "prize money" for her participation in the contest. After the game was released, Doe's brother informed her that he saw her on the game exposing her breasts. Doe sued Topheavy on multiple theories, including invasion of privacy and misappropriation of her likeness. Topheavy said Doe consented to the use of her likeness. Doe said the release she signed was voidable because she was a minor at the time she signed the release. The Texas Court of Appeals found that a question of facts existed as to whether the release was voidable and as to Doe's claim for invasion of privacy. The Court of Appeals upheld the district court's ruling, which had issued an injunction against Topheavy preventing their further distribution of the game.

In *Henley v. Dillard Department Stores,*[22] the famous musician Don Henley of the Eagles, sued after the department store chain ran a newspaper advertisement for a shirt they named a "Henley." The ad showed a photograph of a man wearing a "Henley" with the inscription "This is Don" in large print. Within the ad, the words "This is Don's Henley" also appeared with an arrow pointing to the shirt. It also included: "Sometimes Don tucks it in; other times he wears it loose—it looks great either way. Don loves his Henley, you will too." The district court found that Henley's right of publicity was infringed upon by Dillards, stating: "By appropriating Plaintiff's name or likeness, Defendant received the benefit of celebrity endorsement without asking permission or paying a fee."

Generally, it is not unlawful for a person to adopt a name that is similar to the plaintiff as long as he or she does not pass themselves off as the plaintiff.[23] In *T.J. Hooker v. Columbia Pictures Industries,*[24] the plaintiff, a professional wood carver, who was well known for his carvings of ducks and other fowl, sued Columbia, arguing that the police drama,

T.J. Hooker, was, among other theories, a misappropriation of his name and likeness for the "defendants' advantage and benefit." The court in ruling for the defendant stated:

> it is apparent that plaintiff has failed to allege a tortious appropriation of his name. Plaintiff does allege that [d]efendants' . . . use of plaintiff's name appropriates the right of publicity in plaintiff's celebrated name. But this broad, conclusory allegation cannot substitute for allegations of fact showing that the defendants used the name T.J. Hooker as a means of pirating plaintiff's identity. By his own admission, the commercial value of plaintiff's name is in the field of wildlife art. Hunters, sportsmen, and collectors identify plaintiff's name with fine carvings of ducks and other fowl. There is nothing in the complaint which can be construed as an allegation that the defendants adopted the name T.J. Hooker in order to avail themselves of plaintiff's reputation as an extraordinary woodcarver.
>
> Plaintiff admits that the fictional television series at issue here is a police drama. It is difficult to imagine a subject further removed from the life of T.J. Hooker the artisan. The facts and circumstances alleged by plaintiff provide no basis upon which it can be found that the name T.J. Hooker, as used in the defendants' fictional television series, in any way refers to the real T.J. Hooker.

Famous people come from all areas of society. In *Rosa Parks v. LaFace Records*,[25] a case argued on behalf of Ms. Parks by Johnnie L. Cochran Jr., the civil rights icon, sued a rap artist over a song entitled "Rosa Parks." The lyrics of the song stated in part: "Ah ha, hush that fuss. Everybody move to the back of the bus. Do you wanna bump and slump with us? We the type of people make the club get crunk."

Ms. Parks sued on several legal theories, including right of publicity. The court cited relevant Michigan law, stating: "A right of publicity claim is similar to a false advertising claim in that it grants a celebrity the right to protect an economic interest in his or her name." The defendants claimed their use was protected under the First Amendment to the U.S. Constitution.[26] The United States Court of Appeals reversed the lower's court's decision to grant summary judgment to defendant stating that ". . . we believe that Parks' right of publicity claim presents a genuine issue of material fact regarding the question of whether the title to the song is or is not wholly unrelated to the content of the song. A reasonable finder of fact could find the title to be a disguised commercial advertisement or adopted solely to attract attention to the work."

Johnny Carson was forever linked with Ed McMahon's catch phrase, "Here's Johnny." Remember Jack Nicholson in *The Shining*? This was sufficient to prove his identification in a right of publicity action. In *Carson v. Here's Johnny Portable Toilets, Inc.,* 498 F. Supp. 71 (E.D. Mich. 1980), the plaintiff, Johnny Carson, was the star of *The Tonight Show.* At the opening of the show, he was introduced with a buoyant "Here's Johnny." The phrase also referred to him in other entertainment appearances, in news articles and cartoons, for a chain of restaurants called Here's Johnny, and in the marketing of men's clothing by Johnny Carson Apparel, Inc. The phrase "Here's Johnny" was "generally associated with Johnny Carson by a substantial segment of the television viewing public. Carson sued the defendant, Here's Johnny Portable Toilets, Inc., which was engaged in the business of renting, selling, and servicing portable toilet cabanas. Carson sued for an injunction, alleging, among other claims, a violation of his right of publicity. Of course, a portable toilet cabana is a "john" by any other name. But you can see why Johnny Carson was not too keen about this type of brand dilution.

The Court held that Carson was entitled to relief for the violation of his right of publicity, not because the defendant has used his name, but because the catch phrase "Here's Johnny" had come to identify Carson. The court reasoned that "a celebrity's legal right of publicity is invaded whenever his identity is intentionally appropriated for commercial purposes. . . . Here there was an appropriation of Carson's identity without using his 'name.'"

CHAPTER 11

Unjust Enrichment

Walter T. Champion, Kirk D. Willis,
Patrick K. Thornton, and Joey Barajas

Unjust enrichment is a judicially developed area of law that expresses corrective justice. The term "unjust enrichment" is founded upon the equitable principle that a person should not be allowed to enrich himself unjustly at the expense of another. The Second Circuit has stated that unjust enrichment applies in situations where no legal contract exists, "but where the person sought to be charged is in possession of money or property which in good conscience and justice he should not retain, but should deliver to another."[1]

Unjust enrichment in intellectual property in the simplest form is the concept that it is unjust for an entity to reap where it has not sown. Unjust enrichment is a prerequisite for enforcement of the doctrine of restitution. In its substantive sense, unjust enrichment refers primarily to situations in which the defendant has received something that of right belongs to the plaintiff, for example, if it was received by mistake or theft. In intellectual property, unjust enrichment promotes creative and intellectual ideas and provides the first creator with a remedy in the event that someone has profited from the work of the original creator. However, it is clear that not every loss B suffers at A's hands is a wrongful one; and not every gain A secures at B's expense is an unjust one. For instance, the manufacturer who first marketed a diminutive bottle in the shape of a desk telephone cannot prevent the production of other novel bottles in the shape of miniature trunks, handbags, automobiles, violins, and opera-glasses. In intellectual property cases, the idea may be used by all so long as the risk of confusion is avoided. No particular kind of nastiness must be proven to support a restitution recovery. Unjust enrichment is not wrongful so long as it is: (1) unearned and unrecompensed; (2) results from the labor or other resources of plaintiff; (3) not transferred to defendant to satisfy one's legal duty or with donative intent; and (4) occurs in contexts where reasons that deny restitution are absent.[2]

The Supreme Court and the Human Cannonball

In *Zacchini v. Scripps-Howard Broadcasting Company*, the U.S. Supreme Court discusses both incentives for creators and unjust enrichment in upholding against a First Amendment challenge of a state right of publicity in performances. In this case, the Court spoke approvingly of state restrictions on the copying of intangibles on grounds of preventing unjust enrichment and of providing economic incentive to creators. The plaintiff does not complain about the fact of exposure to the public but rather about its timing and manner. Zacchini welcomes some publicity but seeks to retain control over the means and manner as a way to maximize the monetary benefits that flow from such publication.[3]

Zacchini's fifteen-second "human cannonball" act, in which he is shot from a cannon into a net some 200 feet away, was, without his consent, videotaped in its entirety and broadcast at a county fair in Ohio by a reporter for the Scripps-Howard Broadcasting Company. Zacchini brought a damages action in state court against the broadcasting company, alleging an "unlawful appropriation" of his "professional property." The broadcasting company responded that it is constitutionally privileged to include in its newscasts matters of public interest that would otherwise be protected by the right of publicity, absent the intent to injure or to appropriate for some nonprivileged purpose. The Court sided with Zacchini in concluding that:

> Wherever the line in particular situations is to be drawn between media reports that are protected and those that are not, we are quite sure that the First and Fourteenth Amendments do not immunize the media when they broadcast a performer's entire act without consent. The Constitution no more prevents a State from requiring respondent to compensate petitioner for broadcasting his act on television than it would privilege respondent to film a broadcast a copyrighted dramatic work without liability to the copyright owner, or to film and broadcast a prize fight, or a baseball game, where the promoters or the participants had other plans for publicizing the event.

In summary, the Court in *Zacchini* found that the broadcasting company would be unjustly enriched if it did not compensate Zacchini for broadcasting his act on television. Zacchini was deprived of compensation when the broadcasting company showed Zacchini's entire act without consent and the broadcasting company "reaped benefits where it had not sown" because the broadcasting company reaped a benefit by gaining an audience without paying compensation to Zacchini for his act.

Sports Radio Broadcasts and Unjust Enrichment

Another case that highlights unjust enrichment is the case of *Pittsburgh Athletic Co. v. KQV Broadcasting Co.*[4] The defendant in this case is a Pittsburgh radio station, KQV, which had broadcast play-by-play news of the Pittsburgh Pirates games through information obtained from paid observers whom the radio station had stationed at vantage points outside Forbes Field who can see over the enclosure of that field and observe the plays as they are made. This practice was done without the consent of the Pittsburgh Pirates, who are owned by the plaintiff, Pittsburgh Athletic Company. The Pirates licensed the exclusive right to broadcast play-by-play descriptions or accounts of the games played by the Pirates to General Mills, Inc. The National Broadcasting Company also has a licensing agreement with General Mills, Inc., to broadcast by radio over stations KDKA and WWSW play-by-play descriptions of these games. Pittsburgh Athletics Co. sued to enjoin the unauthorized KQV broadcasts of the Pirates' games. The court enjoined KQV's activities, concluding that the ball club, by reason of its creation of the game, its control of the park, and its restriction of the dissemination of news therefrom, has a property right in such news and the right to control its use for a reasonable time following the games. The court held that KQV had misappropriated the property rights of the Pirates in the "news, reports, descriptions or accounts" of the Pirates' games; that such misappropriation resulted in KQV's "unjust enrichment" to the detriment of the Pirates; and that KQV's actions constituted "unfair competition," "fraud on the public," and a violation of unspecified provisions of the Communications Act.

There are also many instances where courts focus on free riding leads to an assumption on the part of the courts that all enrichment derived from use of an intellectual property right is necessarily unjust. This gives a glimpse of the complications that come with unjust enrichment in intellectual property cases. Some examples of the court assuming all enrichment derived from the use of intellectual property is unjust involve extension of intellectual property rights to cover uses that do not cause harm *per se* to the owner of the intellectual property interest. Some courts see any use of a trademark by a competitor or third party as problematic, for example, not because it deprives the trademark owner of sales, confuses consumers, or increases search costs, but because it reflects "trading on the goodwill" of the trademark owner and, therefore, appropriates value that properly belongs to the trademark owner.

Recording Artists and Unjust Enrichment

In *Oliveira v. Frito-Lay, Inc.,*[5] a recording artist brought an action against the potato chip seller and others involved in promotion of the seller's products, claiming Lanham Act violations and state law claims on grounds the defendants allegedly infringed the artist's trademark rights by using a recording of the artist singing her signature song in a television commercial for potato chips. The United States District Court for the Southern District of New York dismissed, and the artist appealed. The Court of Appeals held that: (1) the artist did not have trademark rights in recording, but (2) the artist's complaint failed to admit that she had no contract rights pertaining to public the release of her recorded performance.

Astrud Oliveira, known professionally as Astrud Gilberto, appeals from the dismissal of her suit by the United States District Court for the Southern District of New York. The defendants are Frito-Lay, Inc., a well-known seller of potato chips, and other entities engaged in the promotion of Frito-Lay products. Among numerous claims, the complaint alleged that the defendants infringed her trademark rights under § 43(a) of the Lanham Act, 15 U.S.C. § 1125(a), by using a famous 1964 recording of Gilberto singing "The Girl from Ipanema" in a television commercial for Frito-Lay's baked potato chips. The complaint also alleged claims under New York State law, including violation of the plaintiff's right of publicity under New York Civil Rights Law § 51, unjust enrichment and unfair competition. With respect to the federal claim under the Lanham Act, the district court dismissed based on its conclusion that no reasonable jury could find that defendants' use of plaintiff's performance in their commercial implied an endorsement by plaintiff of Frito-Lay's potato chips. With respect to the state law claims, the court ruled that, upon the publication of her recorded performance in 1964, plaintiff lost her common law rights in the recording.

The court affirms the dismissal of the Lanham Act claim for somewhat different reasons. As for the dismissal of the state law claims, the court improperly assumed facts adverse to plaintiff. The court vacates the grant of judgment in favor of the defendants on those claims; the court remands for the dismissal of the state law claims without prejudice to their being refiled in state court.

In 1964, Gilberto recorded "Ipanema" accompanied by Stan Getz on saxophone and her then-husband, Joao Gilberto, on the guitar. The 1964 recording became world famous.

In 1996, defendant Frito-Lay began to market "Baked Lays" Potato Crisps, a low-fat baked potato chip. It introduced the product with a thirty-second television advertisement created by its advertising agency, defendant BBDO Worldwide, Inc. The ad shows several famous models reclining by a swimming pool. The 1964 recording of Ipanema plays in the background. As the camera pans from one model to the next, each looks crestfallen that the bag of Baked Lays in her hands is empty. The camera moves on to Miss Piggy, also reclining by the pool, who has been eating the chips and passing the empty bags to the models, while singing along with plaintiff's recording. A voice-over identifies Baked Lays and adds, "With one and a half grams of fat per one-ounce serving, you may be tempted to eat like a. . . ." "Don't even think about it!" interrupts Miss Piggy.

"Ipanema" was written by Vinicius de Moraes and Antonio Carlos Jobim. Jobim registered the composition with the U.S. Copyright Office in 1963 and renewed the registration in 1991. Norman Gimbel composed the English lyrics for the song and registered a U.S. copyright for them in 1963, renewing in 1991. The 1964 recording at issue in this case was made for the recording company Verve, which is now a subsidiary of PolyGram Records, Inc. PolyGram Records claims to own the master of the recording. It distributes the recording, along with Gilberto's rendition of several other popular songs, on various albums and CDs under the Verve Records label.

In order to use the recording in the Baked Lays commercial, BBDO purchased the synchronization rights from Duchess Music Corporation on behalf of Jobim and Gimbel Music Group on behalf of Gimbel. BBDO also purchased a license to use the master recording from Poly-Gram Records. It paid more than $200,000 for the licenses. Apparently believing that Gilberto had retained no rights in the recording, BBDO did not seek her authorization to use it in the ad.

Gilberto was not involved in the production of the 1964 recording other than as lead singer. She did not compose the music, write the lyrics, or produce the recording. According to her complaint, when recording the song, she did not sign any contract or release with the recording company or the producers, and she was not employed by them.

Gilberto received a Grammy award for the recording, which immediately became a smash hit and launched her now thirty-five year career in singing. She claims that as the result of the huge success of the 1964 recording and her frequent subsequent performances of "Ipanema," she has become known as The Girl from Ipanema and is identified by the public with the 1964 recording. She claims as a result to have earned trademark rights in the 1964 recording, which she contends the public recognizes as a mark designating her as a singer. She contends, therefore, that Frito-Lay could not lawfully use the 1964 recording in an advertisement for its chips without her permission.

Gilberto's complaint at first asserted "false implied endorsement" under Section 43(a) of the Lanham Act, 15 U.S.C. § 1125(a), as well as five pendent claims under New York law, including unfair competition through violation of a common law copyright and interference with her right of publicity in violation of N.Y. Civ. Rights Law § 51. The defendants moved to dismiss for failure to state a claim under Fed.R.Civ.P. 12(b)(6); the district court granted the motion as to the five state-law claims but denied the motion as to the Lanham Act claim.

The court ruled against dismissing the Lanham Act claim because it was "not entirely implausible" that the plaintiff could prove that the audience might interpret the inclusion of the 1964 recording in the ad as implying Gilberto's endorsement of Baked Lays. The claim for unfair competition was dismissed because the court found Gilberto failed to allege a property right in the 1964 recording. In 1964, the federal copyright law gave no protection to recorded performances; as for any common law rights Gilberto had possessed in the recording, the court concluded that she had relinquished them upon publication of the work. Noting, however, that by pleading exceptional circumstances, she might be able to overcome the presumption of relinquishment upon publication, the court granted her leave to replead the unfair competition claim. As to the claim for interference with her right to publicity under N.Y. Civ. Rights Law § 51, the court dismissed on the ground that the statute applied only to the use of a "name, portrait or picture," and Gilberto did not allege such a use.

Gilberto then moved for reconsideration of the portions of the June 13, 1997, order dismissing her unfair competition claim and her claim under N.Y. Civil Rights Law § 51. The district court denied the motion as to the unfair competition claim without leave to replead. As to the right of publicity claim, however, the court noted that in 1995, the year before the defendants aired the commercial, N.Y. Civil Rights Law § 51 was amended to include not only unauthorized use of a name, portrait and picture, but also the unauthorized use of a person's voice. The court therefore granted Gilberto leave to replead the claim under § 51 to allege wrongful use of her voice.

Gilberto then filed a second amended complaint. The complaint again raised a claim under Section 43(a) of the Lanham Act. This time, however, the claim was framed in significantly broader terms not merely for "false implied endorsement," but more generally, for "capitalizing on plaintiff's valuable reputation and goodwill in a way that is likely to cause confusion or deceive as to the affiliation, connection, or association of defendants with plaintiff, or as to the sponsorship or approval of defendants' goods by plaintiff." In addition, the complaint raised a claim of trademark dilution under § 43(c), 15 U.S.C. § 1125(c) and five state-law claims, two of which were for unfair competition and violation of N.Y. Civ. Rights Law § 51. The complaint also raised a new state-law claim for unjust enrichment. The defendants moved pursuant to Fed.R.Civ.P. 12(b)(6) to dismiss all the claims, except the one under § 43(a) of the Lanham Act.

The district court granted the motion. It dismissed the dilution claim because, in the court's view, there is no Federal trademark protection for a musical work. As to the right of publicity claim under § 51, now pleaded to allege unauthorized use of Gilberto's voice, the court ruled that no valid claim was pleaded because an exception to liability arises under § 51 when the plaintiff has sold or disposed of the voice embodied in the production. By recording "Ipanema" without a contract, the plaintiff placed her recorded voice in the public domain and thus "disposed of" her rights in her recorded voice. The court dismissed the claims for unfair competition and unjust enrichment on the theory that both claims required Gilberto to plead a common law property right in the recording, which she failed to do.

Defendants then moved for summary judgment on the remaining claim under § 43(a) of the Lanham Act. The district court granted the defendants' motion and dismissed the case for two reasons: first, Gilberto lacked standing to raise a Lanham Act claim, and second, that no reasonable jury could find for the plaintiff on her claim of implied endorsement." Gilberto challenged the dismissal of her claims for trademark infringement under the Lanham Act and violation of N.Y. Civil Rights Law § 51, unfair competition, and unjust enrichment.

To the extent Gilberto's claim depended on the theory of implied endorsement, the court agreed with the district court that a fact finder could not reasonably find an implied endorsement and affirm its judgment. Had Gilberto not amended the Lanham Act claim in her first amended complaint, which was captioned "False Implied Endorsement in Violation of 15 U.S.C. § 1125(a)," and which seemed to rely solely on the implied endorsement theory, this reasoning might dispose of the Lanham

Act claim. The second amended complaint, however, broadened the Lanham Act claim. It expressly asserted that the performance of her signature song constituted an unregistered trademark and that the defendants' use of the recording of the plaintiff's performance in its advertisement capitalized on the plaintiff's valuable reputation and goodwill and was likely to cause confusion or to deceive as to the affiliation, connection, or association of the defendants with the plaintiff.

Gilberto argued that the song is her signature piece and the centerpiece of all her concert appearances, that the public associates her performance of "Ipanema" with her, and that she bills herself as "The Girl from Ipanema" and operates an informational website under that name.

The district court's ruling did not expressly address this branch of the plaintiff's Lanham Act claim. The court did say in explaining its dismissal of the trademark dilution claim, under 15 U.S.C. § 1125(c)(1), that there is no federal trademark protection for a musical work, which may explain why the court found it unnecessary to address further her trademark infringement claim on the basis that the protection of a musical work falls under the rubric of copyright, not trademark law.

The fact that musical compositions are protected by the copyright laws is not incompatible with the notion that they also qualify for protection as trademarks. Graphic designs may be protected by copyright, but that does not make them ineligible for protection as trademarks. The Act defines a trademark as including any word, name, symbol, or device, or any combination thereof, used by a person to identify and distinguish his or her goods from those manufactured or sold by others and to indicate the source of the goods (15 U.S.C. § 1127). The Court sees no reason why a musical composition should be ineligible to serve as a symbol or device to identify a person's goods or services. In *Qualitex Co. v. Jacobson Products Co., Inc.,* 514 U.S. 159 (1995), the U.S. Supreme Court considered whether a color could serve as a mark. In deciding that it could, the Court reviewed the broadly inclusive language of the statutory definition and observed that the courts and the Patent and Trademark Office have authorized trademark protection for a particular shape—a Coca-Cola bottle; a particular sound—NBC's three chimes; and even a particular scent: plumeria blossoms on sewing thread. NBC's three chimes is "a particular sound" consisting of three sounds, in a specified order, with a specified tempo, on specified instruments, which essentially constitutes a brief musical composition. For many decades it has been commonplace for merchandising companies to adopt songs, tunes, and ditties as marks for their goods or services, played in commercials on the radio or television.

An *Oliveira* panel considered whether a musical composition could serve as a trademark *for itself* and concluded it could not. *See EMI Catalogue Partnership v. Hill, Holliday, Connors, Cosmopulos Inc.*, 228 F.3d 56, 64 (2d Cir. 2000). The court reasoned that granting to a song the status of trademark *for itself* would stretch the definition of trademark too far and would cause disruptions as to reasonable commercial understandings. Compare to *Sinatra v. Goodyear Tire & Rubber Co.*, 435 F.2d 711, 712 (9th Cir.1970), which rejected the claim by singer Nancy Sinatra that her song "These Boots Are Made for Walking" is so identified with it that it has acquired a secondary meaning such that another person could not sing it in a commercial.

For similar reasons, the *Oliveira* court concludes that, at least upon the showing made by Gilberto, the law does not accord her trademark rights in the recording of her signature performance. Plaintiff has not cited a single precedent throughout the history of trademark supporting the notion that a performing artist acquires a trademark or service mark signifying herself in a recording of her own famous performance. The "signature performance" that a widespread audience associates with the performing artist is not unique to Gilberto. Many famous artists have recorded such signature performances that their audiences identify with the performer. Yet in no instance was such a performer held to own a protected mark in that recording (*Oliveira*, at 62).

It is true that there are instances in which courts have protected the "persona" of an artist against false implication of endorsement generally resulting from the use of look-alikes or sound-alikes. In *Waits v. Frito-Lay, Inc.*, 978 F.2d 1093, 1107 (9th Cir.1992), the court affirms judgment for plaintiff, Tom Waits, the famous throaty-voiced singer, on false implied endorsement claim for use in a snack-food commercial of a singer who imitated a gravelly singing style while praising defendant's product; similarly, in *White v. Samsung Elecs. Am., Inc.*, 971 F.2d 1395, 1400–01 (9th Cir.1992), the court held that there was genuine issues of material fact precluding summary judgment as to false implied endorsement claim brought by Vanna White, the hostess of the "Wheel of Fortune" game show, for use in an advertisement for VCRs of a look-alike caricature robot endorsing defendant's product. In *Allen v. National Video, Inc.*, 610 F. Supp. 612, 627–28 (S.D.N.Y.1985) the court upheld actor Woody Allen's claim of false implied endorsement for use in an advertisement for video-rental stores of a look-alike renting videos from defendant. But these authorities do not help Gilberto. The use of her recorded song has not taken her persona, and the district court concluded that she could not sustain a claim of implied endorsement.

The court could not say it would be unthinkable for the trademark law to accord to a performing artist a trademark or service mark in her signature performance. And if Congress were to consider whether to extend trademark protection to artists for their signature performances, reasons might be found both for and against such an expansion. The *Oliveira* court recognized the previously unknown existence of such a right might be profoundly disruptive to commerce. Numerous artists who could assert claims similar to Gilberto's would bring suit against entities that had paid bona fide license fees to all known holders of rights. Indeed, artists who had licensed users under their copyrights and had received fees for the copyright license could bring suits claiming additional compensation for infringement of trademark rights. The *Oliveira* court saw no justification for altering the commercial world's understanding of the scope of trademark rights.

The court perceived no need in the interests of fairness to expand the scope of trademark, since the law affords performing artists a number of other protections even for performances made before the federal copyright statute was expanded in 1972 to cover sound recordings, including significant protections that may be secured by contract.

The dismissal of Gilberto's Lanham Act claim was affirmed. The grant of judgment to the defendants on the New York law claims under Civil Rights Law § 51, unfair competition, and unjust enrichment, was vacated. These state law claims were remanded with instruction to dismiss them without prejudice so that they could be repleaded in the courts of New York. The court in *Oliveira v. Frito-Lay, Inc.* remanded the case for further proceedings because the state law claims on unfair competition and unjust enrichment needed to be clearly decided by the New York courts.

Motion Pictures and Unjust Enrichment

In *Orion Pictures Co., Inc. v. Dell Pub. Co., Inc.*,[6] a producer and distributor of a motion picture derived from a book sued the publisher of the paperback version of the book and moved for preliminary injunction. The District Court held that: (1) even though the defendant marketed the novel under the title "A Little Romance" before the plaintiff's film was released under same title, the title had attained a secondary meaning and was protectable under doctrine of unfair competition, where the plaintiff had engaged in extensive prerelease campaign to advertise the film and its title and it was clear from the defendant's own promotional literature and advertising, and particularly from its cover page inscription, that the defendant was counting on the plaintiff's publicity as primary means by which to promote sale of the book, and (2) likelihood of confusion of consumers as to the source of the novel and film was sufficient for recovery under Lanham Act and under standards for common law unfair competition, where the buyer of the book would be likely to assume that it bore very close resemblance to film.

The plaintiff's motion for a preliminary injunction presents an interesting question concerning the plaintiff's motion picture, derived from a book, and the defendant's paperback version of the book, published to exploit the publicity and interest generated by the movie. A French author, Patrick Cauvin, published a book in French entitled $E = MC^2$, *Mon Amour* (edition Jean Claude Lattes, 1977), which was quite popular in Europe. As a result of the book's success, it came to the attention of an American group headed by the plaintiff, Orion Pictures Company, a New York company, which decided to produce and distribute a film based upon the book. Orion obtained the services of Pan Arts Associates, Inc., whose principal stockholder is director George Roy Hill, to film the story. Pan Arts obtained the motion picture rights to the book and prepared a screenplay from it.

The production of the motion picture, retitled "A Little Romance," generated extensive publicity in the news media and the trade journals. This publicity noted that the picture would be directed by Hill and would star the preeminent British actor Sir Laurence Olivier. Orion stated that it had spent, or was committed to spend, over $4 million to advertise and promote the film. Defendant, Dell Publishing Co., Inc., a New York corporation, learned in late 1977 of the plan to make the movie based on $E = MC^2$, *Mon Amour,* and contracted with the French author and his publisher to obtain the English translation and paperback publication rights to the book. Dell bought the right to market the book under any title it desired but, according to its editorial director, intended from the start to use the same title for the book as would be used by the movie.

Commencing in the spring and continuing through the summer of 1978, officials of Dell negotiated with Orion and attempted to arrange a mutually beneficial tie-in between the release of the book and the movie. In August of 1978, Orion informed Dell of its intention to release the film under the title "A Little Romance." Dell immediately decided to publish its book under the same title, and so instructed its employees.

In early 1979, Orion decided that it would not be in its best interest to go forward with the proposed tie-in agreement. This decision was allegedly based on director Hill's conclusion that, as a result of substantial rewriting and alterations in the story line, the screenplay for the movie had departed from the original book to such a degree that there was no longer much similarity between the two. As an alternative proposal, Orion offered to allow Dell to publish a novel based upon the screenplay. This offer was found unacceptable by Dell since, besides having already spent $25,000 to obtain the French author's rights to the original work, it also had a royalty arrangement with Cauvin which might have been breached by the sale of a new literary work derived from the screenplay. When the negotiations failed, Orion notified Dell that it would not enter into any tie-in agreement. Orion at no time consented to the use of its title for the paperback book.

Despite the lack of any agreement, Dell, apparently in the belief that Orion had no protectable interest in the title or in the publicity that the movie would generate, went forward with the publication of its paperback under the title "A Little Romance." The defendant also chose to include on the front cover of the book the pronouncement that it was "NOW A MAJOR MOTION PICTURE," along with a drawing of three people who bore noticeable resemblances to Laurence Olivier and the two child stars of the picture with the Eiffel Tower and Paris in the background. Dell's publicity releases sent to potential wholesalers and retailers of the book rested heavily upon the movie tie-in, commenting that the movie, considering its director and stars, would be sure to receive intense promotion and publicity that was formulated to help pitch the Dell book, since the release of a major film will boost sales of its translation as a greatly acclaimed French novel.

Dell published and distributed 125,000 copies of the book throughout the United States and Canada, with wholesale distribution completed on April 26, 1979. The wholesalers in turn have distributed their volumes to retailers, and, undoubtedly, many of the books have already been sold to the public.

The plaintiff moved for a preliminary injunction restraining defendant from using the title "A Little Romance" and from unfairly competing with it in any manner. The complaint alleges that the defendant has violated § 43(a) of the Lanham Act, 15 U.S.C. § 1125(a), § 368-d of the New York State General Business Law (McKinney's 1968), and the common law standard for unfair competition. Plaintiff also seeks an order directing the defendant to reacquire and to destroy all copies of the book previously published and delivered.

The relative rights of the parties, of course, cannot be assessed in a vacuum. The defendant contends that the movie is a relatively faithful transposition of the book to a different medium, and the plaintiff contends that the movie is, at best, only loosely based on the French work. To resolve these differences, the Court has read the book and seen the movie.

The basic plot of both works is the same. Two very precocious children, an American girl and a French boy, meet in Paris and have an innocent romance. The romance, however, does not find favor with the girl's family. The children, with the help of an elderly rogue, run away to Italy, are apprehended in Venice, returned to their families in France, and, finally, are permanently and poignantly separated, with the girl's family returning to the United States. In transforming a written work into a film, there are, of necessity, certain changes that have to be made. The average book has several times as much material as the average-length movie can absorb. In rare instances, when dealing with a short, simple work, for example Hemingway's *Old Man and the Sea,* it is possible to reproduce all of the essential action of the book. In other instances, movies have retained no more of the original book than its title. Occasionally, a film will contain only a portion of the story found in the book.

This movie makes a number of changes in locations, characters, and details. The additions and deletions, however, are no more than are ordinarily encountered in the transformation of a written work into a film. For instance, the part of the elderly man, played by Olivier, grows from a quantitative presence of 20 percent in the book to one of 40 percent in the motion picture. This proportional change is achieved primarily by deletions of material from the book, rather than by additions to the film. Another change in the film, which could have been of some importance— that of advancing the age of the children from eleven to thirteen, preadolescent to adolescent—in fact had little impact on the story line, as the degree of sexual maturity attributed to the characters in the movie did not increase, a result which perhaps indicates a difference in view between France and the United States as to the age of sexual maturity.

Nonetheless, the movie is substantially different from, and better than, the book. The book has a series of alternating chapters with each chapter narrated in the first person by one child or the other, setting forth an introspective appraisal of their lives and their relationship to each other. Because the children are not only unusually precocious, but also surprisingly self-aware and mature, these appraisals contain lengthy reflections on society in general which, after awhile, tend to become somewhat tedious. There are extensive passages dealing with the main characters' self-consciousnesses and their fantasies of things to come. A major theme of the book is that the brilliant child is, as a result of his superior intelligence, separated from his peers and alienated from the world at large. In contrast, the movie avoids much of all this by taking a purely objective view of the children and their relationship. As a consequence, it moves along at a fast and enjoyable pace and never loses its charm. The court concluded that if one were to read the book first, the entertaining achievement of the film would not be anticipated.

The proper legal result, however, is not self-evident from this critical analysis. The plaintiff charges that the defendant deliberately sought a "free-ride" on the millions of dollars plaintiff is spending on advertising and that the publication and distribution of the paperback will diminish the popularity of the movie.

For a film's title to be protectable under the doctrine of unfair competition, it is necessary that the title have attained some secondary meaning. Thus, a title which, through publicity and use, has come to be associated in the minds of a substantial number of people with a certain type of film produced by a particular individual, may be protected from use by others.

The defendant claims initially that since it marketed its book before the picture opened, no secondary meaning in the title could have developed, and thus no unfair competition could have occurred. The Court did not agree. Even if the work has not been released, a sufficient amount of prerelease publicity of the title may cause the title to acquire recognition sufficient for protection. Thus, in *Metro-Goldwyn-Mayer, Inc. v. Lee,* 212 Cal.App.2d 23, 27 Cal. Rptr. 833 (1963), a California court found that as a result of an extensive advertising campaign, the film title "The Wonderful World of the Brothers Grimm" had been publicized sufficiently to achieve a secondary meaning, even though the film itself was at that time uncompleted. With "A Little Romance," the plaintiff similarly engaged in an extensive pre-release advertising campaign to advertise the film and its title. Moreover, it is clear from the defendant's own promotional literature and advertising, and particularly from its cover page inscription, that the defendant was counting on the plaintiff's publicity as the primary means by which to promote the sale of the book. Such an attempt to "pass off" by the defendant is, it has been held, "not only evidence of likelihood of confusion, but of secondary meaning as well" (*See The National Lampoon, Inc. v. American Broadcasting Co.,* 376 F. Supp. 733, 747 (S.D.N.Y.), aff'd, 497 F.2d 1343 [2d Cir. 1974]).

Even if no secondary meaning in the title "A Little Romance" had as yet been firmly established, this would not preclude relief. In *W. E. Bassett Co. v. Revlon, Inc.,* 435 F.2d 656, 661 (2d Cir. 1970), the Court held that when dealing with a descriptive term, which would include a film title, there is an inference of a secondary meaning (*See Blake Publishing Corp. v. O'Quinn Studios, Inc.,* no. 79 Civ. 783 [S.D.N.Y. May 1, 1979]). At a minimum, an inference of secondary meaning was established. There also appears to be growing support for the proposition that a secondary meaning in the making should be protected, at least to the extent of preventing intentional attempts, as by the defendant here, to capitalize on the efforts and good-will of others. (See 3 R. Callmann, Unfair Competition Trademarks and Monopolies §§ 77.3, at 356 [3d ed. 1971]).

Relief may also be afforded to the plaintiff under § 368-d of the New York State General Business Law, and New York's common law of unfair competition, claims over which this Court has pendent jurisdiction. Under New York law, relief is not limited to situations where the plaintiff has proven a secondary meaning in the mark or title. Rather, the controlling question in determining whether there has been a state law violation is whether the acts are fair or unfair, according to principles of equity. (See, *Santa's Workshop, Inc. v. Sterling*, 282 App. Div. 329, 330, 122 N.Y.S.2d 489 [1956]). Utilizing this standard, the court held that the defendant acted unfairly in using the title "A Little Romance," and in explicitly advertising it to be the same work as the film.

Having determined that the title "A Little Romance" is sufficiently identifiable with the plaintiff's film to be entitled to protection from unfair competition, the court then determined whether there is any likelihood that an "ordinarily prudent purchaser" would be misled or simply confused as to the source of the goods in question. It is clear that no consumer could confuse, literally, the book with the movie. Consumers are, however, interested in the transmedium relationship of such works. While a person buying the book after seeing the movie would, if he studied the credits carefully, realize that he was purchasing the original literary work and not a novel based on the screenplay, he would be likely to assume that the book bore a very close resemblance to the film, especially in light of the inscription, "NOW A MAJOR MOTION PICTURE." Conversely, a person attending the movie, after reading the book, would be quite surprised at the different impact achieved by the film. The defendant's book, by virtue of its title and inscription, gives the impression that it is the "official" novel version of the film and, therefore, highly similar in content to it. In promoting such an impression, the defendant has misled the public.

In determining the relief to be afforded, the bad faith of the defendant in adopting the plaintiff's title and art work and in overstating the relationship between the film and the book are substantial factors to be considered. In view of the likelihood of consumer confusion, plus the possible injurious effect the book might have upon the public's desire to see the movie, injunctive relief was deemed to be appropriate. The effect of the infringement and unfair competition in this instance, as is usually the case with claims of this nature, is neither determinable nor compensable by money damages.

The practical problem in framing the appropriate relief, however, is that the books are already in the hands of retailers and the reading public. It would be difficult, if not impossible, to recapture them.

In trade secret law, unjust enrichment encompasses a wide array of remedies. As the prime example, according with the Uniform Trade Secrets Act § 3(a), trade secret law allows plaintiffs to recover a share in profits the trade secret thief makes from the secret.[7]

In *Kewanee Oil Co. v. Bicron Corp.*,[8] the court rejected patent preemption, noting that trade secret law goes beyond patent law by protecting values beyond incentives to create, such as commercial morality and privacy. The court in *Kewanee* states that trade secret law protects a fundamental right of human privacy.

In *Sun Media Systems, Inc. v. KDSM, LLC,*[9] an advertising company, Sun Media Systems, Inc., sued television broadcasters, KDSM LLC., for trade secret misappropriation, among other claims, after defendants discontinued use of plaintiff's services, yet allegedly continued using plaintiff's advertising methods. The relationship between the two companies was that KDSM engaged Sun Media to conduct advertising campaigns through direct mail for the broadcasting station. The Iowa Uniform Trade Secrets Act provides that an owner of a trade secret is entitled to recover damages for the misappropriation of that trade secret, for the defendant would be unjustly enriched if it were allowed to profit off the trade secrets of the plaintiff. The court found that Sun Media provided little more than vague and unparticularized responses to the question of what constituted a trade secret and concluded that Sun Media Systems did not have a trade secret.

CHAPTER 12

Unfair Competition

Walter T. Champion, Kirk D. Willis,
Patrick K. Thornton, and Joey Barajas

A branch of intellectual property law, "unfair competition" is a term applied to all dishonest or fraudulent rivalry in trade and commerce but is particularly applied to the practice of endeavoring to substitute one's own goods or products in the markets for those of another for the purpose of deceiving the public. This deception is commonly accomplished by imitating or counterfeiting the name, title, size, color scheme, patterns, shape, or distinctive peculiarities of the article, or by imitating the shape color, label, wrapper, or general appearance of the package, or other such simulations. The imitation is used as a way to mislead the general public or deceive an unwary purchaser while not quite amounting to an absolute counterfeit or to the infringement of a trademark or trade name. Generally, acts of deception, bad faith, fraud, or oppression, or acts against public policy because of their tendency to unduly hinder completion, are considered unfair competition. Unfair competition laws have been established to protect consumers and businesses and help prevent illegal merchandizing. An example of unfair competition in the context of intellectual property would be infringement of trade dress. This may involve such things as imitating a competitor's distinct style of golf clubs or establishing a company with the similar name of another company already established in the particular field.[1]

Unfair Competition by Trade Dress Infringement

Trade dress protection is available for nonfunctional features if they distinguish the goods' origins. The Lanham Act provides protection against the creation of confusion by the simulation of a product's packaging, but now it also includes the product's configuration and ornamentation.

In *Callaway Golf Co. v. Golf Clean*, 915 F. Supp. 1206 (M.D. Fla. 1995), the manufacturer of "Big Bertha" woods and irons, claimed that the defendants' golf clubs, "Canterbury Big Bursar Irons" and "Professional Big Brother Tour" irons, infringe upon Callaway's trademarks and trade dress in violation of the Lanham Act. Golf Clean, Inc. is a small corporation which manufactures and markets a golf club and a ball cleaning device called "Golf Clean." It also assembles, sells, and distributes golf clubs through its retail outlets. One of the products sold by Golf Clean is the Canterbury Big Bursar irons, which look almost identical to Callaway's Big Bertha irons.

Callaway Golf Company manufactures and markets high-quality golf clubs. Callaway introduced its original Big Bertha golf club, the Big Bertha driver, in January 1991, and the Big Bertha fairway metal woods in 1992. The Big Bertha clubs have been extremely successful for Callaway; in fact, plaintiffs claim they are the best-selling premium priced metal woods in the world. As a complement to its highly successful Big Bertha metal woods, Callaway developed a line of Big Bertha irons. These irons, which Callaway introduced into the market in early 1994, have been phenomenally successful and have generated more than $147 million in sales.

Callaway's marketing strategy is to design clubs that are "Demonstrably Superior and Pleasingly Different." Accordingly, the company emphasizes in its Big Bertha advertisements the shape and design of the irons, a design which Callaway promotes as in keeping with its successful Big Bertha woods. Callaway's Big Bertha irons possess the following features:

1. A wide top line with a peened finish similar to that on the striking face of the club;
2. A semicircular relief facet on the sole of the club;
3. A large, straight cut rear cavity;
4. The lowermost score lines on the striking face painted white with the bottom score line being shorter than the others and centered under them;
5. Set in the rear cavity of the club head, the Big Bertha Irons medallion, which itself features:
   a. a unique and distinctive shape and layout;
   b. the federally-registered Callaway logo appearing in an arched script;
   c. the federally-registered Big Bertha logo appearing in a flared rectangular box;

   d. the "IRONS" designation in block writing on a colored back-
     ground immediately below the Big Bertha logo; and,
   e. a red, black, and silver color scheme.

The success of Callaway's clubs, both woods and irons, has resulted
in a cottage industry of "knock off" clubs, and the company has vigorously attempted to protect their interests. Prior to this lawsuit, Callaway
successfully obtained permanent injunctions in California and South
Carolina against retailers and distributors of the Canterbury Big
Bursar.

Just like Callaway's Big Bertha irons, defendants' Canterbury Big
Bursar irons exhibit nearly identical features:

1. A wide top line with a smooth finish in contrast to the peened finish
   on the striking face of the club;
2. A semi-circular relief facet on the sole of the club;
3. A large, straight cut rear cavity; and,
4. The lowermost score lines on the striking face painted white with the
   bottom score line being shorter than the others and centered under
   them.

The court notes that this similarity is not happenstance. Prior to filing
its papers in this case, Callaway telephonically ordered a set of "Canterbury Big Bursar" irons from Golf Depot in Clearwater, Florida. After
inspecting these clubs, Callaway dispatched an investigator to visit one
of Golf Depot's stores and masquerade as a customer for the Canterbury
Big Bursar irons. A Golf Depot salesperson told this investigator that the
Big Bursar irons were made "from the same molds used by Callaway."
Defendant's effort to copy Callaway's club includes matching the shape,
script, color, and size of Callaway's Big Bertha medallion.

Before the district court can issue a preliminary injunction, Callaway
must show: (1) a substantial likelihood of success on the merits (i.e.,
that defendants have infringed on Callaway's trade dress and trademarks); (2) an irreparable injury if the injunction is not granted; (3) that
Callaway's threatened injury outweighs the threatened harm the injunction may cause defendants; and (4) the granting of the injunction will
not disserve the public interest. Of these four factors, the final three are
demonstrably in favor of Callaway for reasons that are set forth below.
Therefore, the focus of the court's analysis is on the first factor, which
is the likelihood of success on the merits of Callaway's claim of trade
dress infringement.

Trade dress infringement is an implied federal cause of action based upon a portion of the Lanham Act §43, 15 U.S.C. §1125. The term "trade dress" refers to the total image of a product and may include features such as size, shape, color combinations, texture, graphics, or even particular sales techniques. To succeed on the merits of a trade dress infringement claim, Callaway must prove: (1) that its trade dress has a quality of inherent distinctiveness or has otherwise acquired secondary meaning in the marketplace; (2) that the features of the trade dress are primarily non-functional; and (3) that the trade dress of the products is confusingly similar.

The court found that Callaway's Big Bertha irons are inherently distinctive and have acquired secondary meaning. In evaluating the inherent distinctiveness of Callaway's trade dress, a court must consider: (1) whether it is a common, basic shape or design; (2) whether it is unique or unusual in a particular field; and (3) whether it is a mere refinement of a commonly adapted and well known form of ornamentation for a particular class of goods viewed by the public as a dress or ornamentation for the goods. If a product is inherently distinctive, secondary meaning need not be demonstrated.

The Callaway Big Bertha Iron's trade dress undeniably incorporates the common, basic shape and design of a golf club. As defendant correctly points out, the cavity back design, a wide sole, and scoring on the club's face, are common features in golf clubs. However, trade dresses often use common lettering styles, geometric shapes, or colors. While each of these elements alone would not be inherently distinctive, their combination and the total impression that the dress gives to the observer makes the item distinctive.

The various ornamental and colorful designs of the Callaway Big Bertha Irons were deliberately chosen so as to produce a unique total image for the clubs—an image Callaway touts as "demonstrably superior and pleasingly different." Callaway adopted a "chunky" and "aggressive" wide top line for their club that is almost unique in the field (the Ping Zing club has a similar wide top line). The semicircular relief facet on the sole of the club is a distinctive design of this manufacturer. Added to these peculiar characteristics are the club's other features: namely, the large, straight cut rear cavity, the distinguishing white lowermost score lines, and the unique Callaway medallion in the cavity's inset. All these components produce a distinctive club. Indeed, when Callaway introduced their Big Bertha irons in 1994, they looked noticeably different than any other club on the market. Callaway's arbitrary combination of features makes their Big Bertha Irons inherently distinctive.

Because Callaway's irons are inherently distinctive, secondary meaning need not be demonstrated. A court should consider the following factors in assessing secondary meaning: (1) the length of time and manner of its use; (2) the nature and extent of its use; and (3) the efforts made in the direction of promoting a conscious connection, in the public's mind, between the mark and a particular source of origin.

Callaway has bombarded the golfing consumer with the image of its Big Bertha Clubs by spending over $5 million in advertising. Significantly, Callaway's ads and other promotional materials prominently feature the club head, thus emphasizing its unique and distinctive appearance. Callaway has sold over $147 million worth of the clubs, thereby establishing that the clubs are extremely popular amongst golfers. Numerous articles have been written profiling the development and success of the Callaway Big Bertha Irons. These facts, coupled with defendant's nearly exact duplication of the Big Bertha and its representations that the Canterbury Big Bursar was made from the same molds as the Callaway Big Bertha, establish that the Big Bertha has acquired secondary meaning.

Trade dress is protectable only if it is primarily nonfunctional. Notwithstanding this requirement, individual elements of the trade dress can be functional and the entire package still protected under the Lanham Act. Factors to consider are whether a particular design is superior, whether there are alternative trade dress configurations available, and whether a particular design is comparatively simple or cheap.

There are numerous clubs on the market that incorporate individual features of Callaway's trade dress. Hence, alternative trade dress configurations that serve the same function are available to competitors. Further, there is no evidence that Callaway's design is superior to that of other clubs, or that it is comparatively simple or cheap. Granting Callaway an exclusive right to use the Big Bertha trade dress will not hinder effective competition by others. Based upon this test, Callaway's trade dress is deemed to be primarily nonfunctional.

The primary factor in determining trade dress infringement under the Lanham Act is the likelihood of confusion resulting from the defendant's adoption of a trade dress similar to the plaintiff's. The elements that must be considered to determine likelihood of confusion are: the strength of the trade dress, the similarity of design, the similarity of the product, the similarity of retail outlets and purchasers, the similarity of advertising media used, the defendant's intent, and actual confusion. The issue does not turn upon one party's position supporting a majority of these factors; instead, the court must evaluate the weight each factor deserves and then make its ultimate decision. The appropriate weight each factor should be given varies with each case.

a. *Strength of Trade Dress.* Callaway's trade dress is strong; it has spent millions on advertising and placing the image in the golfing public's eye. Accordingly, the Court determined that the trade dress is inherently distinctive and has acquired secondary meaning, and that Callaway Big Bertha golf clubs have a strong trade dress.

b. *The Similarity of Design.* The similarity of design test is nothing more than a subjective eyeball test. After eyeballing the clubs, even after a lengthy gaze, the Callaway Big Bertha and the Canterbury Big Bursar look almost exactly alike. The Professional Big Brother's design copies Callaway's club, even with defendants' change in logo. Hence, this factor weighs heavily in Callaway's favor.

c. *Similarity of Retail Outlets and Purchasers.* The possibility of confusion is greater when products have similar trade channels and predominant consumers. Callaway clubs are sold at off-course retail golf shops. Defendants sell their clubs at their own retail stores as well as to other off-course golf shops. Defendants' employee admits to having sold customers Big Bertha clubs at defendant's store. Thus, the trade channels must necessarily be similar if both clubs are being sold at defendant's store.

d. *Similarity of Advertising Media.* Callaway advertises its clubs in various golf related print media and general circulation publications, as well as on television and through professional golfer endorsements. There is no evidence that defendants use any of these media to advertise their product. Because Callaway bears the burden of proof for its motion, this factor must be weighed in favor of defendants.

e. *Defendants' Intent.* If a plaintiff can show that a defendant adopted a mark with the intent of deriving benefit from the reputation of the plaintiff, that fact alone may be sufficient to justify an inference that there is confusing similarity.

f. *Actual Confusion.* However, since the court found that defendant's proposed Professional Big Brother is substantially the same as the Canterbury Big Bursar, therefore, defendant's argument is without merit. Callaway's survey, although not dispositive on the issue of actual confusion, suggests that discovery in this case may well reveal more evidence of actual confusion.

g. *Callaway has Demonstrated Likelihood of Confusion.* In summary, Callaway has adequately demonstrated the factors necessary for a finding of likelihood of confusion. Callaway's trade dress is fairly strong, defendants' clubs are nearly identical to the Callaway Big Bertha, the products are sold in similar retail outlets, defendants' affirmatively intended to misrepresent its product as materially the same as Callaway's, and there is at least some indication of actual confusion. These factors weigh heavily in favor of a conclusion that Callaway has established a likelihood of confusion.

The Callaway Big Bertha arbitrarily combines its features in such a manner that the clubs are inherently distinctive; further, the clubs have acquired secondary meaning. The features claimed by Callaway as its trade dress are primarily nonfunctional. Finally, defendants' product is confusingly similar to the Callaway Big Bertha and is likely to be confused by the end user as having some connection to Callaway.

Accordingly, the court recommended that a preliminary injunction be issued prohibiting defendants from:

a. Manufacturing, producing, distributing, circulating, selling, offering for sale, importing, exporting, advertising, promoting, displaying, shipping, marketing, or otherwise disposing of "Canterbury Big Bursar Irons," "Professional Big Brother Tour" irons, Big Bursar Iron heads, or Big Bursar Iron medallions;
b. Manufacturing, producing, distributing, circulating, selling, offering for sale, importing, exporting, advertising, promoting, displaying, shipping, marketing, or otherwise disposing of any golf club iron head or club that:
   1. Has a polished sole plate with a semi-circular relief facet; a heavy or wide top line with a peened or pebbled finish; a striking face with a peened finish, having horizontal score lines with the bottommost score line shortened and centered in the middle of the striking face, and the two bottom score lines painted a contrasting color; and a large, straight cut rear cavity with a finish similar to that on the top line of the club head; substantially similar to the head on Callaway Golf's Big Bertha Irons; or
   2. Has a medallion substantially similar to Callaway Golf's Big Bertha Irons medallion.
c. Using a trade dress confusingly similar to that of Callaway Golf's in the overall appearance of its Big Bertha Irons and/or in the appearance and shape of its Big Bertha Iron medallion in connection with the advertising, promotion, offering, marketing, manufacture, sale or other disposal of iron heads or irons;

d. Using, manufacturing, producing, distributing, circulating, selling, offering for sale, importing, exporting, advertising, promoting, displaying, shipping, marketing, or otherwise disposing of any iron heads, irons or other products or things, not manufactured by Callaway Golf, that bear any simulation, reproduction, counterfeit, copy or colorable imitation of Callaway Golf's Registered Trademarks, including the Callaway and Design Trademark;
e. Removing from any premises under their possession, custody or control, any goods or things bearing any simulation or colorable imitation of Callaway Golf's trade dress or Registered Trademarks;
f. Disposing in any manner of any merchandise or thing in their possession, custody or control bearing any colorable imitation of Callaway Golf's trade dress or Registered Trademarks; and
g. Disposing in any manner of any documents or other records evidencing the source or wholesale purchasers of the pertinent clubs, club heads, or medallions.

In *Callaway Golf Co. v. Golf Clean, Inc.*, the trade dress of the golf club was inherently distinctive; therefore, it is unfair competition to allow defendant to copy plaintiff's design detail by detail so that confusion is likely, intended, expected, anticipated, and hoped for.

Movie Merchandising

In *Dreamwerks Prod. Group, Inc. v. SKG Studio,*[2] a promoter of science fiction merchandise, Dreamwerks, sued defendant, a movie production company, for trademark infringement under the Lanham Act and state law. Dreamwerks argued that consumers were likely to be confused by the two marks. DreamWorks SKG argued that science fiction merchandise promotion and movie making were not related, and that plaintiff targeted a specific segment of consumers, while defendant targeted everyone. Applying a multi-factor test, the court found that "DreamWorks SKG" sounded exactly like "Dreamwerks" and that the minor spelling differences were not enough to distinguish the two marks. Noting that many movie production companies sell and promote merchandise with their movies, the court found that the two businesses were related enough to create the likelihood of confusion necessary to state a trademark infringement claim.

Dreamwerks, a company hardly anyone has heard of, sues entertainment colossus DreamWorks SKG, claiming trademark infringement. This is the reverse of the normal trademark infringement case, where the

well-known mark goes after a look-alike, sound-alike, feel-alike unknown that is trying to cash in on the famous mark's goodwill. The twist
here is that Dreamwerks, the unknown, was doing business under that
name long before DreamWorks was a twinkle in Hollywood's eye.
Dreamwerks is, therefore, the senior mark, and it argues that its customers will mistakenly think they are dealing with DreamWorks, the junior
mark. Is that wishful thinking?

EVERYONE has heard of DreamWorks SKG, established in 1994
by the three hottest names in Hollywood: Steven Spielberg, Jeffrey
Katzenberg, and David Geffen, each of whom graciously contributed
an initial to form the SKG part of the trademark. DreamWorks is a film
studio, having produced such well-advertised movies as *The Peace-
maker*, *Amistad*, and *Mouse Hunt*. Like other movie studios, Dream-
Works participates more generally in the entertainment business, having created DreamWorks Interactive, a joint venture with software
giant Microsoft; GameWorks, which is a micropub and virtual reality
video arcade for the 90s; and DreamWorks Toys, a joint venture with
toy maker Hasbro.

Less well known is Dreamwerks Production Group, Inc., a small
Florida company that since 1984 has been in the business of organizing
conventions in the Northeast and Midwest, mostly with a Star Trek
theme. At a typical Star Trek convention, Dreamwerks draws customers with a star like the late DeForest Kelley (Bones), Leonard Nimoy
(Spock), or Michael Dorn (Worf from *Star Trek: The Next Generation*). For an admission fee of $25 or so, customers get autographs,
meet fellow Trekkies, compete in costume contests, listen to pitches for
upcoming movies, and browse the products of vendors who have
rented space at the convention. Dreamwerks sometimes presents previews of science fiction and adventure/fantasy movies produced by the
major studios, such as *Batman Returns*, *Dracula*, *Aladdin*, and *Jurassic
Park*. Dreamwerks clearly caters to the pocket-protector niche (a.k.a.,
nerds or geeks), and its convention business has never really taken off.
But the longevity of the enterprise illustrates its remarkable resilience,
not unlike the starship Enterprise itself.

Because Dreamwerks registered its mark with the United States Patent and Trademark Office in 1992, it holds the senior mark and is the
plaintiff here. It claims that DreamWorks SKG is causing confusion in
the marketplace by using a mark too similar to its own and is doing so
with respect to goods and services that are similar to those that Dreamwerks offers. What could be better for Dreamwerks than to have people
confuse it with a mega movie studio? Many an infringer has tried to

manufacture precisely such confusion and thereby siphon off the good-will of a popular mark. Not so, answers Dreamwerks, apparently in earnest. It is not interested in fooling consumers, and it claims to suffer ill will when people buy tickets under the misimpression that they are dealing with DreamWorks rather than Dreamwerks. Dreamwerks also frets that its own goodwill will be washed away by the rising tide of publicity associated with the junior mark. Dreamwerks points out some-what wistfully that it hopes to expand its business into related fields and that these avenues will be foreclosed if DreamWorks gets there first. Fi-nally, Dreamwerks notes that whatever goodwill it has built now rests in the hands of DreamWorks; if the latter should take a major misstep and tarnish its reputation with the public, Dreamwerks too would be pulled down.

These are not fanciful or unreasonable concerns, though they may be somewhat exaggerated by the hope of winning an award or settlement against a very solvent DreamWorks. The court cannot guess to what extent these harms are likely nor whether they are offset by any extra goodwill plaintiff may inadvertently reap as a result of mark confusion. The narrow question presented whether Dreamwerks has stated a claim for trademark infringement sufficient to survive summary judgment. The district court held that Dreamwerks had not, because the core func-tions of the two businesses are so distinct that there is no likelihood of confusion as a matter of law.

The test for likelihood of confusion is whether a "reasonably pru-dent consumer" in the marketplace is likely to be confused as to the ori-gin of the goods or service bearing one of the marks. In *AMF, Inc. v. Sleekcraft Boats*, 599 F.2d 341, 348–49 (9th Cir. 1979), the court listed eight factors to facilitate the inquiry: (1) strength of the mark; (2) prox-imity or relatedness of the goods; (3) similarity of sight, sound and meaning; (4) evidence of actual confusion; (5) marketing channels; (6) type of goods and purchaser care; (7) intent; and (8) likelihood of ex-pansion. The factors should not be rigidly weighed. Rather, the factors are intended to guide the court in assessing the basic question of likeli-hood of confusion.

In the usual infringement case, these factors are applied to determine whether the junior user is palming off its products as those of the senior user. Would a consumer who finds a running shoe marked "Miké" be bamboozled into thinking that it was manufactured by Nike? Especially if Miké had a "swish" instead of the Nike's famous swoosh? In a reverse infringement case, there is no question of palming off, since neither jun-ior nor senior user wishes to siphon off the other's goodwill. The question in such cases is whether consumers doing business with the senior user might mistakenly believe that they are dealing with the junior user. More specifically, the question here is whether a reasonable consumer attending a Dreamwerks-sponsored convention might do so believing that it is a convention sponsored by DreamWorks.

Before performing a Vulcan mind meld on the "reasonably prudent consumer," the court notes that if this were an ordinary trademark case rather than a reverse infringement case—in other words, if DreamWorks had been there first and Dreamwerks later opened up a business running entertainment-related conventions—there would be little doubt that DreamWorks would have stated a case for infringement sufficient to survive summary judgment. The reason for this, of course, is that a famous mark like DreamWorks SKG casts a long shadow. Does the result change in a reverse infringement case because the long shadow is cast by the junior mark? The court thinks it does not.

Three of the *Sleekcraft* factors are pivotal here: (1) arbitrariness of the mark; (2) similarity of sight, sound, and meaning; and (3) relatedness of the goods. "Dreamwerks" is an arbitrary and fictitious mark deserving of strong protection. Had Dreamwerks chosen a descriptive mark like Sci-Fi Conventions, Inc., or a suggestive mark like Sci-Fi World, some confusion with the marks of legitimate competitors might be expected. DreamWorks argues that the word "Dream" makes the Dreamwerks mark suggestive of a company which brings sci-fi dreams to life. But "Dream" is used in too many different ways to suggest any particular meaning to the reasonable consumer. At best, "Dreamwerks" conjures images related to fantasy, hope, or reverie. It's too great a mental leap from hopes to Star Trek conventions to treat the mark as suggestive. The Dreamwerks mark deserves broad protection.

Sight, sound, and meaning are easy. There is perfect similarity of sound, since "Dreamwerks" and "DreamWorks" are pronounced the same way. There is also similarity of meaning: Neither literally means anything, and to the extent the words suggest a fantasy world, they do so equally. Similarity of sight presents a slightly closer question. The man-in-the-moon DreamWorks logo, when presented in the full regalia of a movie trailer, is quite distinctive. But "DreamWorks" often appears in the general press and in industry magazines without the logo, leaving only the slight difference in spelling. Spelling is a lost art; many moviegoers might think that Miramax and Columbia Pictures are movie studios. Moreover, a perceptive consumer who does notice the "e" and lower-case "w" in Dreamwerks might shrug off the difference as an intentional modification identifying an ancillary division of the same company. While the court recognizes that spelling matters, the court is not sure substituting one vowel for another and capitalizing a middle consonant dispels the similarity between the marks.

The clincher is the relatedness of the goods. Twenty years ago, DreamWorks may have had an argument that making movies and promoting sci-fi merchandise are different businesses promoting different products. But movies and sci-fi merchandise are now as complementary as baseball and hot dogs. The main products sold at Dreamwerks conventions are movie and TV collectibles and memorabilia; the lectures, previews, and appearances by actors which attract customers to Dreamwerks conventions are all dependent, in one way or another, on the output of entertainment giants like DreamWorks.

The district court emphasized that Dreamwerks has carved out a narrow niche in the entertainment marketplace, while DreamWorks controls a much broader segment. Dreamwerks targets Trekkies; DreamWorks targets everyone. But the relatedness of each company's prime directive is irrelevant. Rather, the court must focus on Dreamwerks's customers and ask whether they are likely to associate the conventions with the DreamWorks studio. Entertainment studios control all sorts of related industries: publishing, clothing, amusement parks, computer games and an endless list of toys and kids' products. In this environment it's easy for customers to suspect DreamWorks of sponsoring conventions at which movie merchandise is sold. Other studios are rapidly expanding their merchandising outlets: Universal Studios has theme parks in California, Florida, and Japan with dozens of stores selling movie-related products, and Disney is helping transform New York's Times Square into a G-rated shopping center. Dreamwerks convention-goers might well assume that DreamWorks decided to ride the coattails of Spielberg's unparalleled reputation for sci-fi/ adventure films (*Jaws, E.T., Close Encounters, Raiders, Jurassic Park*) into the sci-fi merchandising business.

The court does not decide the ultimate question presented in this case, whether DreamWorks SKG infringes the trademark held by Dreamwerks Production Group, Inc. The court only remands for trial. While it is somewhat unusual for a famous mark to defend its very existence against a much lesser known mark, DreamWorks is in no different a position than any other new company which must ensure that its proposed mark will not infringe on the rights of existing trademark holders. Counsel for DreamWorks conducted a diligent search and discovered the Dreamwerks mark, yet failed to make accommodations or select a different mark. Counsel complains that a ruling in favor of Dreamwerks will leave little room for new marks to develop, since almost every combination of words has been taken by someone doing business somewhere in what may be a loosely related field. But this is not true of fanciful marks—marks that have no connection to the product or service offered. Fanciful marks not only give the trademark holder a pristine legal landscape, they also add to the splendor of our language by giving us new ways to express ourselves. If you received junk e-mail, you were spammed. The childish antics of politicians are Mickey Mouse. Lousy, mindless work is a McJob. A quick fix is a Band-Aid. Glitz and ditz make for a Barbie World. Calling something the Rolls Royce of its class is shorthand for referring to a refined product targeted at those with expensive tastes. And maudlin family gatherings make for Kodak moments. None of these phrases had any meaning before the trademark was absorbed into the language; each is evidence of how commerce and culture transform each other. A clever new trademark diversifies both the marketplace and the marketplace of ideas; a takeoff or copy of a mark, even if accidental, adds nothing but confusion. This dispute could have been avoided had DreamWorks been more careful, or a tad more creative, in choosing its name.

The court in *Dreamwerks Prod. Group, Inc. v. SKG Studio* reversed and remanded the case for further proceedings because the minor spelling differences in "DreamWorks" and "Dreamwerks" were not enough to distinguish the two marks and would likely create confusion necessary to state a trademark infringement claim. This would lead to unfair competition between the two companies because movie production companies sell and promote merchandise with their movies, therefore merging into the field in which Dreamwerks primarily does business.

In *TGC Corp. v. HTM Sports, B.V.*,[3] TGC Corporation, a manufacturer of seamless-palm gloves sued its marketer, Head Sports, Inc. and HTM Sports B.V. for, *inter alia*, unfair competition by misappropriation of trade secrets, alleging that the marketer wrongfully continued to produce the gloves using manufacturer's know-how after manufacturer became economically defunct. The "unfair competition" claim was understood to be essentially a claim for trade dress infringement under § 43(a) of the Lanham Act, 15 U.S.C. § 1125(a). The court entered judgment on a jury verdict for manufacturer and then granted marketer's motion for judgment as a matter of law. It held that the golf glove characteristics manufacturer claimed were protectable—certain sizing specifications, the thinness of the leather used, and the thumb stretch—were physical features that were all readily observed and easily ascertained or duplicated and, therefore, were not trade dress. Specifically, the seamless palm that purportedly wicks away moisture from the palm is functional and readily observable to the eye. Other manufacturers such as Nike make such gloves, and there is no secondary meaning that can be shown; therefore, it is not protectable as a trade secret or trade dress.

CHAPTER 13

Deceptive Trade Practices

Deceptive trade practices are a type of intellectual property—basically, false advertising and/or false designation of established trademarks. A form of deceptive trade practices is so-called ambush marketing, where a deceptive trademark and/or packaging (usually alleging trade dress violations) is issued without authority. It is the misdirection of the consumer by false or deceptive information. For example, in *State v. Granite Gate Resorts, Inc.,* 1998 WL 240133 (Minn. 1998), *aff'd* 568 N.W.2d 715 (Ct. App. Minn. 1997), the State of Minnesota sued an out-of-state Internet gambling operator, alleging false advertising deceptive trade practices, for advertising on the Internet that defendant's sports betting site, WagerNet, licensed in Belize, was legal. Defendant knew that it was violating the Wire Act (18 U.S.C. § 1084) by allowing Minnesota residents to transmit bets by the use of a wire in foreign commerce. Since these services were illegal, Granite Gate engaged in false advertising deceptive trade practices and consumer fraud by knowingly misrepresenting that their sports handicapping service and proposed sports bookmaking services were lawful.[1]

In *Buckeye Assocs., Ltd. v. Fila Sports, Inc.,* 1985 WL 1108513 (D. Mass.), plaintiff Buckeye Associates sued defendants Fila USA and Fila Italy, seeking damages for alleged violations of the federal antitrust laws, breach of contract, misrepresentation, interference with advantageous relations, unfair and deceptive trade practices in violation of the Massachusetts Consumer Protection Act, violation of the Massachusetts Antitrust Act, and violations of the California Unfair Trade Act. Buckeye fails to establish personal jurisdiction over the defendants.

In *Central Manufacturing, Inc. v. Brett,* 2009 WL 3624679 (7th Cir.), the court discussed the trademark rights in the word "stealth" owned by a Chicago-based corporation and whether they could not pursue a trademark infringement suit against a sporting goods company that sold "stealth" baseball bats. This trade infringement suit was based on alleged misinformation and lies. Plaintiff could not prove the existence of "stealth brand products" or that any were sold except as they "existed" on their "sales quote sheets," which failed to rise above mere advertising and could not establish continuous use. The following text comes from the court transcript:

> In 2001, Brett joined Tridiamond sports, Inc., a manufacturer of baseballs, baseball bats, gloves, and other related accessories, to form Brett Brothers Sports International, Inc. Tridiamond was incorporated in 1997 by Joe Sample, a former airline executive who had served as vice president and president of International Ambassador, a company specializing in the organization of travel programs. International Ambassador was purchased in 1996 by former Major League Baseball Commissioner Peter Ueberroth, and informal conversations with Ueberroth soon gave Sample an idea. Ueberroth mentioned the difficulty some players had in adjusting from the use of metal baseball bats at the high school and collegiate levels to the wood bats of professional baseball. Initially introduced in the early 1970s as a cost-saving alternative for leagues operating under a smaller budget due to the breakability of wood bats, metal bats were eventually believed to generally outperform wood ones. . . . Because the use of metal bats may inflate hitting statistics, a player's professional prospects may be misevaluated, and the shift to wood bats may reveal a great player to be merely very good one—the difference, potentially, between a highly compensated major league career and a decade spent on buses shuttling from Appleton to the Quad Cities.

The stealth bats are constructed of laminates from hand-selected and graded hardwoods. The patented Boa reinforcement on the handle significantly enhances durability. The choice of wood for the barrel has proven to greatly reduce the chipping and flaking characteristic in one-piece ash bats.

The plaintiffs in this action, Central Manufacturing, Inc., and Stealth Industries, are both controlled by Leo Stoller, who serves as president and sole shareholder. Stoller also operates a number of other companies. Stoller alleges that his companies have been using the "Stealth" trade name and mark for a wide range of products since at least 1982. Indeed,

Stoller registered the Stealth mark for boats, motorcycles, bicycles, microwave-absorbing automobile paint, billiard and dart equipment, auto locks, window locks, comic books, lawn sprinklers, metal alloys, pest elimination devices, among other products (*S Industries, Inc. v. Ecolab, Inc.*, 1999 WL 162785, at *1 [N.D. Ill.]). In 1984, Stoller filed a trademark registration with the United States Patent and Trademark Office (through one of his other companies, Sentra Manufacturing), claiming ownership of the Stealth mark for goods such as tennis rackets and balls, golf clubs and balls, basketballs, baseballs, soccer balls, cross bows, tennis racket strings and shuttle cocks. The mark was awarded to Sentra in 1985 and was transferred to Central in 1997. In 2001, Central filed a mark application with the PTO for use of the Stealth word mark on baseball bats, softball bats and t-ball bats. Later that year, Central entered into an agreement with Blackwrap, Inc., for use of the Stealth word mark on its bats, and a similar agreement with Easton Sports, Inc., in 2003, and in 2004, the U.S. PTO extended use of the mark to baseball bats. Thereafter, having become aware of Brett Brothers' use of the Stealth word mark Central believed that, because it had registered the "Stealth" mark for "baseballs and other sporting goods" in 1985, Brett Brothers was guilty of infringement and unfair competition.

Leo Stoller is no stranger to trademark litigation. Indeed, one might say it is the essential part of his business strategy. Upon learning of the Stealth bat, Stoller sent Brett Brothers a cease-and-desist letter claiming ownership of the stealth mark for use on baseball bats, alleging infringement, and demanding a $100,000 licensing fee. Brett Brothers refused, and Stoller filed suit. Such an action can succeed, however, only if, among other things, the plaintiff owns the mark. Registration is prima facie evidence of ownership, but established use by a nonregistrant is a valid defense to a registrant's infringement claim. For this reason, the district court concluded that Brett Brothers' established use of the Stealth mark on baseball bats since 1999 precluded any infringement on the basis of Central's 2004 registration.

Although Stoller produced documents related to the development, commercial use and sales volume of goods bearing the Stealth mark, it offered nothing about any specific transaction—nothing about quantity, particular products, names of buyers, or dates of sale.

The case lacked merit on all counts. Central had filed its infringement lawsuit without evidence of any sales of baseballs or baseball bats to support its claim to rights in the "stealth" mark for such products. It ignored requests to produce documents to support its claim, forcing the defendant's lawyers to go to court to compel action. Stoller offered confused, misleading deposition testimony with unfulfilled promises of cooperation. And the documents that were eventually produced effectively made a mockery of the entire proceeding. The court had no trouble upholding the award of fees and costs.

False Advertising under the Lanham Act

Lanham Act (trademarks) false advertising consists of literally false claims and misleading claims. A claim that was literally false, and thus an action under the Lanham Act, was initiated by a boast by a billiard table seller that he was "Ohio's largest" distributor of Brunswick products.

The Lanham Act, also known as the Trademark Act of 1946, is codified at 15 U.S.C.S. § 1051 *et seq.*; § 43(a) (15 U.S.C.S. § 1125(a), which protects against false advertisement and trademark infringement and provides as follows:

a. Civil Action. (1) any person who, on or in connection with any goods or services, or any container for goods, uses in commerce any word term, name, symbol, or device, or any combination thereof, or any false designation of origin, false or misleading description of fact, or false or misleading representation of fact, which
   A. is likely to cause confusion, or to cause mistake, or to deceive as to the affiliation, connection, or association of such person with another person, or as to the origin, sponsorship, or approval of his or her goods, services, or commercial activities by another person, or
   B. in commercial advertising or promotion, misrepresents the nature, characteristics, qualities, or geographic origin of his or her or another person's goods, services, or commercial activities shall be liable in a civil action by any person who believes that he or she is or is likely to be damaged by such act.

Defendant BHA Billiards claims that it was family-owned since 1949, but plaintiff correctly contends that this falsely implies that BHA has been in the billiards business since 1949 and owned by one family. However, BHA has been owned by two different families and has been in the billiards business for only a few years. This can be reasonably construed to mean that BHA has been in the billiards business since 1949, and that there has been a continuity of family ownership since that time. Therefore, these two statements might be misleading. However, the statement

that Brunswick is "The World's Leader in Billiards" is a general assertion or exaggerated claim of superiority, which constitutes "puffery,"
which is not actionable under the Lanham Act.

In *Aviva Sports, Inc. v. Fingerhut Direct Marketing, Inc.*, 2011 WL
6257317 (D. Minn.), plaintiffs sought relief of defendant's inflated advertising (pun intended).

Aviva manufactures and sells, among other things, inflatable water
slides and pools. In 2001, Aviva Sports, L.L.C. began selling inflatable
slides for children to use in swimming pools. It expanded its product
line so that by 2006, it had twelve fixed-air inflatable slides and pools,
generating sales of $1.69 million. Manley began selling inflatable wa-
ter slides and pools in or around 2003. Manley sells both fixed-air and
constant-air products. Both Manley's and Aviva's products were available in retail stores, such as Menard, Fingerhut, and K-Mart, as well
as through the Internet. In 2006, the giant retailer Target began carrying Manley's products along with Aviva's products. . . .

In 2007, Aviva created a prototype of a constant-air slide, which
it presented at Target's competitive line review. According to Aviva,
it was told not to pursue this product because Manley already
'owns' the market for constant-air slides. Sometime thereafter,
Aviva ceased its efforts to market its constant-air slide—Aviva currently sells no constant-air products. Also in 2007, Target stopped
selling Aviva's inflatable pools and slides in its stores. That same
year, Shoremaster, Inc. acquired Aviva Sports, L.L.C. and created
Aviva Sports, Inc. (the plaintiff in this action). This resulted in significant internal changes at Aviva, including the loss of a number of
employees. Between 2007 and 2010, Aviva's sales of its inflatable
pools and slides declined. By 2010, Aviva's inflatable products generated sales of only approximately $544,290 . . .

In May 2009, Aviva sued Manley and four retailers for alleged
patent infringement and violations of the Lanham Act and Minnesota UDTPA. According to Aviva, advertisement and/or packaging for ninety-five of Manley's products contain false or fraudulent
representations. Specifically, Aviva argues that Manley superim-
posed scaled-down images of children onto images of its products
to make the products appear larger than they actually are. Further,
Manley supposedly uses larger, custom-made products for its photo
shoots, rather than the actual products being advertised. As a result
of this alleged manipulation, Aviva claims that Manley's advertisements violate the statutes' false advertising provisions. Aviva argues

that Manley's false advertising has injured and will continue to injure Aviva through a diversion of sales and loss of goodwill.

The court agrees with Aviva; however, it did not present evidence of actual losses, and, therefore, could not seek actual damages.

Football concussions are at the center of a heated national debate on the long-term safety of our national sport (with apologies to baseball). There are billion-dollar lawsuits against the National Football League that seek to collect damages for the disproportionate negative mental disabilities that plague former football players. This appears to be especially true for multiple-concussion injuries. So, anything that could possibly stop the occurrence of multiple concussive events would be extremely marketable and profitable. Enter the case of *Riddell, Inc. v. Schutt Sports, Inc.,* 2010 WL 3729676 (D. Wisc. 2010), where plaintiff's claims that wearers of "Riddell Revolution Youth helmets" were 31 percent less likely to suffer a concussion was literally false, but competitor's Lanham claim was rejected since they failed to identify pecuniary losses and because the Lanham Act was not designed to protect manufacturers from their competitor's deceptive trade practices.

False Designation under the Lanham Act

Bluestar Management, LLC v. The Annex Club, 2010 WL 4666077 (N.D. Ill.), discusses false designation Lanham Act lawsuits in the context of competing baseball fan clubs. Defendant began to spread false rumors to city inspectors.

> The complaint further alleges that the Wrigley Rooftop Club is currently paying for a 'sponsored result' advertisement on the website <www.purelocal.com> that features a photograph of the Wrigley Done Right roof top building adjacent to a link to the website for the Wrigley Rooftop Club. Aside from being a direct competitor of the Wrigley Rooftop Club, Wrigley Done Right is situated in a well-known building that is twice as wide and better located than the Wrigley Rooftop Club.
>
>   Additionally the complaint alleges that defendants have intentionally used their collective power and influence to preclude Wrigley Done Right from joining the Wrigley Rooftop Association . . . , an association of most of the Special Club License holders and operators of Wrigley rooftop venues. Without membership in the Rooftop Association, Wrigley Done Right is prevented from participating in organized meetings with the local community and

alderman to discuss issues related to operation of the rooftops, including new ordinances and license requirements, and to advocate on behalf of its business interests.

Defendants have also allegedly interfered with Wrigley Done Right's sales by interfering with its inclusion on the <ballparkroof tops.com> website. From approximately January 7, 2008, until May 5, 2008 . . . defendants repeatedly refused to list Wrigley Done Right on the <ballparkrooftops.com> website and instead fraudulently linked it to his own rooftop's website <wrigleyfieldrooftopclub .com>. This allegedly resulted in lost sales for Wrigley Done Right.

Section 43(a) of the Lanham Act, 15 U.S.C. § 1125(a)), which provides, in relevant part, that:

(1) any person who, on or in connection with any goods or services, or any container for goods, uses in commerce any word, term, name, symbol, or device, or any combination thereof, or any false designation of origin, false or misleading description of fact, or false or misleading representation of fact, which (A) is likely to cause confusion, or to cause mistake, or to deceive as to the affiliation, connection, or association of such person with another person, or as to the origin, sponsorship, or approval of his or her goods, services, or commercial activities by another person, or (B) in commercial advertising or promotion, misrepresents the nature, characteristics, qualities, or geographic origin of his or her or another person's goods, services, or commercial activities, shall be liable in a civil action by any person who believes that he or she is or is likely to be damaged by such act. To state a claim under § 1125(a)(1)(B) for false designation plaintiff must allege: (1) that the defendant used a false designation of origin or false description or representation or in connection with goods or services; (2) that such goods or services entered interstate commerce; and (3) that the plaintiff is a person who believes he is likely to be damaged as a result of the misrepresentation.

False designation claims are generally "passing-off" or "reverse passing-off" that involve a misuse of a name or trademark. Here, in short, "Wrigley Done Right has stated a claim of false designation under the Lanham Act against the promoter of a competing Wrigley Field fan group based on an Internet advertisement photograph."

Duplications of Identifying Marks

In determining the lawfulness under a state deceptive trade practice statute of particular practices which were claimed to constitute unfair competition, the courts have held that under particular circumstances, findings of violations of particular state deceptive trade practice or consumer protection statutes are established by evidence or allegations of the use of trade names, corporate names, or other identifying names that are similar to other names already in use; the use of marks that were similar to other marks already in use; and the sale of goods that were physically similar to other goods being sold.

Cease-and-desist letters asserting British news agency's copyright in upcoming broadcast coverage of Princess Diana's funeral did not have sufficient nexus with consumer protection concerns to support video distributor's claim under Illinois Consumer Fraud and Deceptive Business Practices Act; statements were not directed to the market generally, did not have a direct bearing on the market for home video tapes of the funeral, and had no direct effect on consumers (*American Broadcasting Co. v. Maljack Productions, Inc.,* 34 F. Supp. 2d 665 [N.D. Ill. 1998]).

In action by restaurant chain franchisor against owner of restaurant for violations of state's unfair and deceptive trade practices act, and other violations, after defendant began to use term "Longhorn Steakhouse," which allegedly infringed on plaintiff's service mark "Long Horn Steaks," trial court found that plaintiff was entitled to relief, where defendant had engaged in "palming off," which consisted of defendant's attempt to market its restaurant as if it were a part of plaintiff's restaurant chain (*Contemporary Restaurant Concepts, Ltd. v. Las Tapas-Jacksonville, Inc.,* 753 F. Supp. 1560 [M.D. Fla. 1991]).

In *Kazmaier v. Wooten,* 761 F.2d 46 (1st Cir. 1985), plaintiff claimed exclusive right to "World's Strongest Man" and unsuccessfully sued for unfair or deceptive trade practices on the basis that there was no confusion with defendant who acted in television commercials as the "World's Strongest Man" since defendants were in their rights to use the contested title.

In *Rolls Royce Motors, Ltd. v. A & A Fiberglas, Inc.,* 428 F. Supp. 689 (C.D. Ga. 1977), the court held that a violation of the Georgia Deceptive Trade Practices was established by evidence that defendant, a seller of plastic and fiberglass products, manufactured and sold automobile customizing kits that included a simulated grill and hood ornament bearing a striking resemblance to the front grill and hood ornament on Rolls-Royce automobiles, which grill and hood ornament were registered trademarks of the plaintiff, the manufacturer of Rolls-Royce. Pointing out that the Act authorized injunctive relief where the defendant passed off goods or services as those of another or caused a likelihood of confusion or misunderstanding, the court explained that the crux of a complaint based on the Act was the likelihood of confusion between their striking similarities. And further explaining that the secondary meaning of the plaintiff's trademarks was conclusively established by the marks' registered status, the court concluded that the likelihood of confusion was reasonably apparent. The court therefore ordered that the defendant be permanently enjoined from copying or initiating the plaintiff's trademarks in connection with the manufacture, advertising, and sale of its customizing kits.

Upon evidence that a manufacturer and marketer of embroidered cloth emblems made and sold emblems which were duplications of identifying marks used by the member clubs of the National Football League without authorization from the League's exclusive licensing agent, the member clubs, or the League itself (*National Football League Properties, Inc. v. Consumer Enterprises, Inc.,* 26 Ill. App. 3d 814, 327 N.E.2d 242 [1975]), the court upheld the issuance of a preliminary injunction prohibiting the manufacturer from, *inter alia,* manufacturing and selling such emblems, which injunction was based on an allegation, that the manufacturer had engaged in deceptive trade practices in violation of the Illinois Deceptive Trade Practices Act. The court explained that the identifying marks, when affixed to merchandise manufactured by the league's licenses, were entitled to trademark protection, and pointed out that relief can be granted where there is a likelihood of confusion as to the source of goods, even though the goods involved are not in direct competition, and "palming off" of goods is not shown. The court concluded that a likelihood of confusion existed concerning the source of the manufacturer's emblems.

Using its reasoning set forth in *National Football League Properties, Inc. v. Consumer Enterprises, Inc.,* the court held in *National Football League Properties, Inc. v. Dallas Cap & Emblem Mfg., Inc.,* 26 Ill. App. 3d 820, 327 N.E. 2d 247 (1975), that the plaintiff, the exclusive licensing agent of the member clubs of the National Football League, demonstrated a probability of success on its claim that the defendant, a manufacturer and marketer of embroidered cloth emblems, engaged in deceptive trade practices in violation of the Illinois statutory law by making and selling, without authorization, embroidered cloth emblems that were duplications of the marks used by the member clubs of the National Football League. The court thus upheld the issuance of an injunction which, as modified, prohibited the defendant from, *inter alia,* manufacturing and selling such emblems. Evidence of a consumer survey showed that a random sample of persons who were shown emblems manufactured by the defendant identified the emblems with football teams, and that a majority of the persons making such identification believed that the emblems, or the clothing to which the emblems were affixed, were authorized by the teams.

Plaintiff holder of copyrights and trademarks pertaining to "Superman" and "Wonder Woman" was entitled to summary judgment against defendant "singing telegram" franchisors and franchisee under statutes prohibiting unfair or deceptive trade practices where defendants caused likelihood of confusion as to source, sponsorship, and approval of their services and as to affiliation, connection, and association between defendants and plaintiff through use of balloons, costumes, and names of plaintiff's characters (*DC Comics, Inc. v. Unlimited Monkey Business, Inc.,* 598 F. Supp. 110 [N.D. Ga. 1984]).

Defendant's use of trade name "Star Mart" and "Star-1" logo for its convenience stores attached to service stations supported unfair competition claim by supermarket operator that was already using similar name and mark (*Star Markets, Ltd. v. Texaco, Inc.,* 945 F. Supp. 1344 [D. Haw. 1996]).

Action for trademark infringement was stated by champagne distributor against marketer of popcorn and its president, where defendants distributed and sold popcorn as *"Champop"* (*Schieffelin & Co. v. Jack Co. of Boca, Inc.,* 725 F. Supp. 1314 [S.D. N.Y. 1989]).

Where there was no likelihood of confusion between plaintiff's use of registered word "Sunspots" in connection with stationery and greeting-card designs and defendant's use of words "Sun Spots" for line sports apparel, actions based on alleged trademark violation and deceptive trade practice would not lie (*Carrington v. Sears, Roebuck & Co.,* 683 P.2d 1220 [Hawaii App. 1984]).

Where the essence of an action by plaintiff distributor of "troll dolls" against competitor was alleged infringement of trade dress rights and false designation of origin, plaintiff had no cause of action under New York Consumer Protection Act since the purpose of each act was to remedy deceptive trade practices, not to redress claims such as trade dress infringement, which involves no issue of public interest (*EFS Mktg. v. Russ Berrie & Co.,* 836 F. Supp. 128 [S.D. N.Y. 1993]).[2]

CHAPTER 14

Domain Names

Related aspects of trademarks are the relatively recent phenomena of domain names and cybersquatting. In order to locate a business web page on the Internet, there is a need to know its Internet address. The addresses are the key to effective communication. By typing in a certain series of letters, numbers, and symbols, which are referred to as the Internet domain name, the user gains access to the intended website. Domain names are usually the company's nickname, trade name, abbreviation, ticker name, or catch phrase. Many problems exist because domain names are classified as trademarks.[1] In sports, fans are now able to receive the latest news of their favorite teams and players, and in the entertainment world, fans can catch the latest gossip of their favorite celebrity ("Oh, no she didn't"). But what happens when a famous trademark is being used as a domain name by another party? If an individual fraudulently steals a domain name and tries to sell it, is that the same as stealing intellectual property? This sounds like cybersquatting, which is defined as the registration of domain names of well-known trademarks by non-trademark holders who then try to sell the name back to the legitimate mark holder. The purchaser of the domain name holds another party, many times a famous athlete or well-known entertainer, as a commercial hostage. However, the Anticybersquatting Consumer Protection Act of 1999 (ACPA) deals with cybersquatters who attempt to register an athlete's or entertainer's domain name, or a similar-sounding name, and then use it as an alleged fan website. These cybersquatters purchase famous domain names in the hope of making money by selling the name back to those famous individuals. However, the First Amendment can sometimes protect these cybersquatters.[2]

The interesting case of the young Tiger baby, Charlie Axel Woods, explains the vagaries of cybersquatting in a situation where the "famous" person is in actuality only the son of a famous person. Of course, young Charlie Axel's father is Eldrick "Tiger" Woods; TIGER WOODS itself is the subject of U.S. Trademark Registration. Charlie Axel Woods is the second child of Tiger and his former wife, Elin Nordgren; he was born on February 8, 2009, and of course this was a major media moment. The domain name <charlieaxelwoods.com> was registered on February 9, 2009, by a complete unknown, one Josh Whitford. Tiger quite naturally complained that Whitford was not using the domain name in connection with any bona fide use or making any legitimate noncommercial or fair use of the domain name. Whitford argued, however, that the disputed domain name was not confusingly similar to any registered or common law trademark associated with Tiger Woods. The panel concluded that the personal name "Charlie Axel Woods" is not protectable as a common law trademark or service mark. Tiger was able to present no evidence that "Charlie Axel Woods" was ever used in connection with the sale of commercial goods or services or that his name never acquired any secondary meaning.[3] A key question in maintaining a domain name is to prove that the famous person has built up "commercial value" in his or her name. Famous ballplayer Barry Zito was able to use that argument in wrestling away his domain name, <barryzito.com>, from the registrant, and having WIPO return his domain name to him.[4]

The famous gladiator/actor and ultimate fighting championship superstar, Chuck Liddell, fought again in a battle for his domain name, <http://www.chuckliddell.com>, which was registered by Comdot Internet Services in 2004. This domain name provided links to other Liddell-associated sites; however, CHUCK LIDDELL was an unregistered mark; therefore, Liddell had to prove prior to filing that the public associated goods or services related to CHUCK LIDDELL, the domain name, with the person Chuck Liddell. CHUCK LIDDELL has acquired a secondary meaning so that he had common law rights to the CHUCK LIDDELL trademark. Since the domain name was identical to the CHUCK LIDDELL mark, and since the domain name was used to attract users only for commercial gain the domain name was registered in bad faith and the WIPO panel rightfully transferred it back to Liddell.[5]

A certain Vernard Bonner registered a domain name referring to "official superbowl parties." The NFL objected to <http://www.officialsuperbowlparties.com> on the grounds that it owned the mark "Super Bowl." Bonner's domain name was identical or confusingly similar to the mark SUPERBBOWL. The NFL proved that Bonner had no legitimate interests in the name and that he registered it in bad faith, and thus it was transferred to the NFL. The same analysis works with <superbowlcon cierge.com> with the same result.[6] Similarly, the registered domain name of <http://www.kareemabduljubbar.com> was confusingly similar to the trademark "Kareem Abdul-Jabbar," which was, of course, owned by the famous NBA superstar. But defendant had no legitimate interest in the name and thus registered in bad faith.[7]

Allen Stanford is a well-known former cricket player who is still very famous (in cricket circles) as both a cricket sponsor and innovator. One Krishna Mohunlal registered the disputed domain name <http://www .allenstanfordcricket.com> that collects information about worldwide cricket with a number of click-through links leading to cricket websites. Stanford did not register his common law rights to his name, and that use of his name by Mohunlal was unauthorized. It was held that his name was used in bad faith, since it was used solely to attract cricket lovers and fans of the great Allen Stanford for commercial gain.[8] (Allen Stanford is to cricket what Pele is to soccer or Michael Jordan is to basketball.)

Ohio State University (and its famous Buckeyes motif) sued a website that featured the trademark "Buckeye" accompanied by its name and distinctive use of school colors in its website and its football publication. Ohio State demonstrated a strong likelihood of success on the merits of its claim for trademark infringement and unfair competition.[9]

The domain name <browns.com> is intrinsically similar to the registered trademarks of the Cleveland Browns: "Cleveland Browns" and "Browns." The Browns allege that the domain name <browns.com> was identical to their trademark, "Browns," and confusingly similar to "Cleveland Browns" and that the holder registered and used the domain name in bad faith.[10]

Domain name dispute settlements usually begin with complaints filed with the World Intellectual Property Organization (WIPO) Arbitration and Mediation Center. The Center then verifies that the complaint satisfies the formal requirements of the Uniform Domain Name Dispute Resolution Policy, the Rules for Uniform Domain Name Dispute Resolution Policy, and the WIPO Supplemental Rules for Uniform Domain Name Dispute Resolution Policy.

In *Russell Brands, LLC v. Cognata,* the disputed domain name was <spalding.net>. Complainant owns numerous trademark registrations evidencing exclusive rights to the trademark SPALDING in connection with sporting and fashion goods. Complainant is also the owner of the domain name <spalding.com> and <spaldingequipment.com>. A.G.

Spalding & Brothers opened their first sporting goods store in 1876. It is undisputed that the SPALDING trademark is well-known, particularly in connection with sporting goods of all kinds. Defendant has no rights or legitimate interests in respect of the disputed domain name. Complainant has never granted, assigned, licensed, sold, or transferred any rights in its trademarks to defendant, who has no links with the complainant and has no authorization to use the name SPALDING. Defendant did not build his reputation with the disputed domain name and does not have any rights over a trademark, company name, or business name equivalent or including SPALDING, nor does defendant associate the disputed domain name with a good faith offering of goods and services. These circumstances indicate that the disputed domain name was registered or acquired primarily for the purpose of disrupting the business of the complainant and preventing the complainant from reflecting its trademark in a corresponding domain name, which would be of interest for him.[11]

However, a WIPO panel in *Rugby World Ltd. v. Gyrre,* found against the complainant, Rugby World Cup, in the interpretation of the disputed domain name <worldcup2011.com>. Complainant is beneficially owned by the International Rugby Board (IRB), which was founded in 1886 and is the world governing and lawmaking body for the game of rugby union. Rugby union is played in more than 100 countries. In 1989, the IRB established complainant and assigned to it all rights in the Rugby World Cup tournament. Since 1987, the Rugby World Cup tournament has been held every four years. The 2011 Rugby World Cup was won by the "All-Blacks" of New Zealand. It is beyond dispute that the 2011 Rugby World Cup has received a great deal of publicity and is a well-known event. However, there are numerous other sports and competitive pursuits which hold "world cup" events. For instance, the FIFA Football World Cup is the best known "world cup" in the sporting world. In the year 2011, there were numerous "world cup" events, including Cricket World Cup 2011, FIFA Women's World Cup 2011, Dubai Racing World Cup 2011, FIFA U-20 World Cup 2011, Dance World Cup 2011, FIFA U-17 World Cup 2011, FIFA World Cup 2011 in Japan, Snowboarding World Cup 2011, and FIFA Beach Soccer World Cup 2011.

The domain name was registered on August 7, 2009. Defendant Andreas Gyrre has some relationship with Euroteam AS, a Norwegian company that operates the website to which the domain name resolves. Defendant Gyrre is listed as "Chairman of the Board" on the website. Euroteam's business includes the legal resale of tickets to sporting events. Gyrre and Euroteam do not conceal the fact that they intend to take advantage from the descriptive nature of the words "world cup 2010." Complainant clearly holds rights in the registered marks RUGBY WORLD CUP and RUGBY WORLD CUP 2011. But the question remaining is whether the disputed domain name is confusingly similar to these marks. The panel concludes that the domain name may be somewhat similar to these marks but not confusingly so. Without the word "rugby" attached to "world cup," there is nothing to set apart this "world cup" from the many other "world cups."[12]

E-Commerce

E-commerce includes domain names, but it also covers all other Internet issues. A domain name is the threshold to recognizing commercial enterprises. It is the porthole, especially when the domain name contains a recognized trademark. The Internet Corporation for Assigned Names and Numbers (ICANN) manages the generic top-level domain (gTLD) system. In 1999, ICANN adopted a Uniform Domain-Name Dispute Resolution Policy (UDRP). The Anticybersquatting Consumer Protection Act amends § 43 of the Trademark Act and assures that a person who registers, traffics, or uses a domain name in bad faith for profit will be civilly liable if the name is identical or confusingly similar to a registered trademark; or if the domain name dilutes a famous work or if the name is a protected trademark, word, or name. Metatags are embedded in the hypertext markup language (HTML) used to create websites. The tags, which are not visible to web page viewers, contain data such as keywords, which are then used by search engines to locate websites. Courts have ruled that someone who uses another individual's trademark in a metatag or in some other unauthorized way in conjunction with e-commerce may be guilty of trademark infringement.[13]

In *Roger Cleveland Golf v. Price,* plaintiff, a manufacturer and distributer of golf clubs, golf equipment, and apparel, alleges that defendants operate and are the registrants of the domain names copycat-clubs.com, worldtimegolf.com, and legacygolfclubs.com. Each of these domain names resolves to an online store advertised as a "wholesaler" that carries a wide selection of the newest clubs from brands such as Callaway golf, Ping golf, Nike golf, Taylor Made golf, Titleist golf, Cobra golf, Mizuno golf, Cleveland golf, Yes, and Odyssey putters. The store bills itself as "your one stop shop for the best *COPIED* and *ORIGINAL* golf equipment on the Internet."

In 2009, a mystery shopper working for plaintiff made a purchase of several CLEVELAND® brand golf clubs. The plaintiff has since determined that the golf clubs the mystery shopper received were counterfeit. Another defendant, Bright Builders, was found to have a role in the creation and support of the business model and websites through which plaintiff's trademarks were allegedly infringed.[14]

In *Bugoni v. Kappas,* plaintiff, a resident of Boca Raton, Florida, sues the PTO, the NFL, and four individuals "believed to be located in Germany." The plaintiff alleges that "sometime in 2008," he "conceived" an invention while watching football at a local sports bar and "likely drinking beer." The invention appears to be a camera capable of video and audio transmission that may be installed in an NFL Regulation Football. The plaintiff alleges that he produced the "earliest design documents" in 2009, paid for and was "granted" a trademark number on May 22, 2011, and applied for a patent on August 15, 2001, but he could not pay the fee; nor could he pay it before the application was abandoned.

On July 25, 2011, the plaintiff allegedly purchased the Internet domain name BallCam.com, where he then published the prototype of his invention. On October 14, 2011, an article was published on the Internet, allegedly naming the individual defendants as inventors of a device that is of the same nature as described by the plaintiff's patent application. The plaintiff sought, among other relief, to enjoin non-governmental defendants from using intellectual property or claiming intellectual property rights to his invention and to compel the PTO to waive the patent application fee. Because the plaintiff's claims against the non-governmental defendants necessarily depended upon a patent that did not exist, he could not establish his legal standing to sue, and the case therefore was dismissed.[15]

Cybersquatting

"Cybersquatters" is a name given to individuals who attempt to profit from the Internet by reserving and later reselling or licensing domain names back to the companies that invested time and money in developing the goodwill of the trademark.[16] The intent behind the Anticybersquatting Consumer Protection Act was to promote the growth of online commerce and to protect trademark holders from cybersquatting or the bad faith and abusive registration of distinctive marks as Internet domain names with the intent to profit from the mark's goodwill.[17] Cybersquatters "warehouse" a great many domain names that are similar to other famous or known trademarks. At one time, cybersquatters could evade punishment by not selling domain names; however, now, courts use multiple registrations of domain names as one factor in determining bad faith intent.[18]

In *Sporty's Farm L.O.C. v. Sportsman's Market, Inc.,*[19] a Court of Appeals decided a case under the Anticybersquatting Consumer Protection Act (ACPA) for the first time. The plaintiff, Sportsman's Market, Inc., was an aviation catalog company that had used the logo "Sporty's" since the 1960s and registered the nickname in 1985 with the PTO. In 1995, the defendant, Omega, a "scientific process measurement and control instruments" mail order catalog company, entered the aviation catalog business and registered "sportys.com" as its domain name. In 1996, Omega transferred the domain name to Sporty's Farm a subsidiary of Omega. Sporty's Farm advertised its Christmas tree business on the Internet site. Soon after the domain name transfer to Sporty's Farm, Sportsman's found out that the domain name had been registered and requested it back.[20] The court held that Sportsman's trademark in "Sporty's" was an inherently distinctive trademark.[21] The court concluded that Sporty's Farm infringed on sportsman's legal rights by using the domain name sportys.com.[22]

In *Shields v. Zuccarini,*[23] the U.S. District Court for the Eastern District of Pennsylvania dealt with the ACPA as regards a graphic artist and creator of "Joe Cartoon," a collection of cartoons. In 1997, the artist Joseph Shields registered the domain name www.joecartoon.com. After the Joe Cartoon site became popular, defendant John Zuccarini registered five different domain names varying slightly from "www.joecartoon .com," such as joescartoon.com, joecarton.com, joescartoons.com, joe-cartons.com, and cartoonjoe.com. Plaintiff filed suit, but then the defendant changed the site's content displaying only a message stating it was an apolitical protest because of Joe Cartoon's allegedly anti-animal bias. The key question to decide is whether "Joe Cartoon" was a "distinctive or famous mark entitled to protection" under the ACPA. The court determined that Joe Cartoon was distinctive and/or famous, and then the court had to decide whether Zuccarini's domain names were identical or confusingly similar to Shields's mark, which they found to be so.

The next question was whether Zuccarini acted with bad faith. Although Zuccarini agreed that he was protesting Joe Cartoons' use of depictions of brutality to animals, the court found that his real purpose was to make money. This was a clear violation of the ACPA based on the fact that defendant had neither legal right to register the domain names nor any business use of variations on Joe Cartoon.[24]

It is an absolute truth that marketing fuels fan fanaticism in sports and entertainment (e.g., Lady Gaga!). An off-shoot of this phenomenon is the official team website that both markets the team and extends the trademarked brand. But with their popularity comes initiation of the domain name, so as to siphon off some of the franchise's potential. Forty years ago, no one would have imagined that sports franchises could earn so much "extra" money from sources as diverse as luxury suites, marketing including baseball caps, jerseys, etc., PSL's (permanent seat licenses, which are not actually permanent), and stadium naming rights. So, how do we stop cybersquatting of right-sounding, allegedly fan-oriented domain names? Also "[t]he explosion of the Internet has opened the doors for sports fans to receive the latest news on their favorite teams and players. Websites such as http://www.espn.com and http://www.cbssportsline.com are standard vocabulary in the average sports fan's vernacular."[25]

In *Con Way, Inc. v. Conwayracing.com,* Plaintiff initiated an action for cybersquatting against the domain name CONWAYRACING.COM. Plaintiff provides supply chain and logistical services to a wide range of businesses worldwide. It also sponsors the Con Way Racing team in the NASCAR Craftsman Truck Series and is the owner of the CONWAY.COM domain name. Plaintiff owns numerous trademark registrations that include or are derived from "CON WAY," including the service mark of "CON WAY," for use in "supply chain, logistics, and reverse logistics services."

Plaintiff alleges that the domain CONWAYRACING.COM is a website that serves as a search directory that provides links to companies that provide goods and services associated with racing, including NASCAR racing. Plaintiff further contends that the domain name infringes upon its trademark and violates the ACPA and that it has the effect and intent of confusing the public and plaintiff's customers and diluting plaintiff's mark.

The court concludes that the domain name, "CONWAYRACING.COM," is confusingly similar to plaintiff's mark, "CON WAY," and that "CON WAY" is a strong and famous mark that is associated with the sponsorship of racing activities, and the name "CONWAYRACING.COM" is similar to, and apparently derived from, plaintiff's mark.[26]

Shaquille O'Neal, of course, is the famous now-retired basketball superstar, sometime actor, part-time deputy sheriff, and respected literacy advocate. He began his career in the NBA in 1992. He was famously nicknamed "Shaq"; he is also president, secretary, and treasurer of Mine O' Mine, Inc. ("MOM"), and he has granted MOM the exclusive right to sublicense his name, image, and likeness and to register, exploit, and protect the word "Shaq" and Shaq formative marks, including, among others, "Shaq," "Shaqtacular," "Shaq Attaq," and "Shaq's All Star Comedy Jam." MOM's federal registration of the Shaq mark for T-shirts and other goods was issued in 1998 based on the first use of the mark in 1995.

On February 6, 2008, O'Neal was traded to the Phoenix Suns. Around that same time, sportswriters and others dubbed him "The Big Cactus" and "The Big Shaqtus." While playing for the Phoenix Suns, O'Neal wore an orange jersey with the number 32. On or about March 30, 2008, "True Logo Fan, Inc." registered <Shaqtus.net> as a domain name with GoDaddy. Girmar Anwar is listed as the administrative contact for <Shaqtus.net> and the owner and registrant.

On or about March 31, 2008, Calmese registered "Shaqtus" as an Arizona trade name with the Arizona Secretary of State for "clothing/advertising." Calmese hired Michael Herzog of Vision Animation Studios to create the image of the Shaqtus. The Shaqtus took the form of a cactus with the facial expression of a man wearing an orange basketball jersey bearing the name "Phoenix Shaqtus" and the number 32 and bouncing a basketball.

In 2008 and 2009, ESPN aired commercials featuring O'Neal encountering a cactus bearing O'Neal's face in the Arizona desert. On or about December 4, 2009, Calmese sent a letter to ESPN which stated that he is the co-owner of the "Shaqtus" trademark and trade name and has been selling clothing articles and advertisements with the same "Shaqtus" trademark since 2008 at Shaqtus.NET and Shaqtus.COM. ESPN responded that MOM is the owner of the federal registration for the mark Shaq and that any claim of property would stem from that registration and that their use of "Shaqtus" was done with O'Neal's consent. MOM then demanded that Calmese et al. cease and desist from all use of the Shaqtus mark, transfer <Shaqtus.net> to MOM, and cancel his Arizona trade name registration for Shaqtus.

MOM asserted that there is a high likelihood of confusion because, among other similarities, the marks start with the same four letters, which are uniquely known to refer to O'Neal, and Calmese clearly intended to refer to the name given to O'Neal by sportswriters when O'Neal was traded to the Phoenix Suns, which was "Shaqtus," a combination of "Shaq" and "cactus."

MOM sells T-shirts with the Shaq mark, and Calmese sold T-shirts with the Shaqtus mark. The shirts are complementary because they are both shirts that reference the same NBA player. There are no different classes of T-shirt consumers, and T-shirts with the Shaq mark are identical in use and function as T-shirts with the Shaqtus mark.

Both Shaqtus and the Shaq mark begin with the same four letters and, therefore, when consumers read and hear the two terms, Shaqtus and Shaq, they see and hear words that are similar in sight and sound. Further, since Shaq and Shaqtus have both been used to refer to O'Neal, the marks are similar in meaning. MOM owns a family of marks containing the surname Shaq, including Shaq, ShaqTACULAR, and Shaq ATTAQ. The Shaqtus mark also contains the Shaq scope of MOM's family marks. In short, there are no genuine issues of material fact, and MOM is entitled to judgment as a matter of law on its trademark infringement claims; anything related to the Amazing Shaq is unique, especially if defendant's sole goal is to piggyback on his trademarked famous nicknames solely for the acquisition of filthy lucre.[27]

CHAPTER 15

Intellectual Property in Cyberspace

Cyberspace is the universe of information that is available from computer networks and is the connective tissue of society-at-large. The question is how authors, inventors, artists, composers, athletes, advertisers, marketers, and creative folks in general are going to get paid for the use of their intellectual property. Intellectual property is of course old school, horse and buggy, and the printed book (whatever that is), but the information superhighway changes everything. Those changes are what we must mark, appreciate, understand, and learn how to use those changes so as to deter infringement and effectively pursue Internet copyright violators.

Domain names and cybersquatting are the indicators and signs that mark, symbolize, and police the intellectual property of artists and athletes. These domain names are a part of the Internet, which is also home to the World Wide Web. There are many aspects of intellectual property in cyberspace that affects sports and entertainment. For example, e-commerce allows moviegoers the opportunities to purchase movie or concert tickets and sports fans the chance to purchase game tickets, Dallas Cowboys shirts, and autographed Mickey Mantle baseballs. There is also sports broadcasting as visualized through the Internet and boxing matches. "Between iTunes, Vcast, TiVoPSP, Windows Media, cellular phones, public WiFi, and available broadband Internet access, the consumer is already well on the way towards multiplatform, on-demand access to worldwide content" (Patrick Turner, "Digital Video Copyright Protection with File-Based Content," 16 Media L. & Pol. 165 [Summ. 2007]). And let's not forget mobile entertainment and ringtones. The music business was significantly changed through the advent of digital technology. In the 1980s, there was digital sampling to illegal Internet downloads accompanied by home copying, which was first done via blank cassettes and then by CD "rippers" and "burners" and file sharing over peer-to-peer exchange technologies.

> . . . [T]wo forces of technological change have recently vested in ordinary people the ability to produce complex forms of media. First is the democratization of the means of media production—the explosion of inexpensive high-quality cameras, microphones, musical instruments, sound-recording equipment, and personal-computer-based editing systems. Second is the democratization of the means of distribution—the Internet, broadband access, computer-based burning and printing of CDs and DVDs, on-demand book publishing, and user-driven web applications such as YouTube, Flickr, and RSS, all of which permit the distribution of video and other content to potentially huge audiences. (Erik Johnson, "Rethinking Sharing Licenses for the Entertainment Media," 26 Cardozo Arts & Ent. L.J. 391, 393 [2008])

The Internet[1]

The Internet is an international network of interconnected computers. An integral part of this information superhighway is the World Wide Web (www), which is an Internet hypertext-based global multimedia information network. Professor Paul Goldstein of Stanford Law School believes that "[i]f the defining attribute of intellectual assets is that they can be used by countless numbers of consumers across national borders and never be exhausted, then the Internet may be the first distribution technology to fully capture this unique quality. By detaching inventions, entertainment, and advertising from the physical products that embody them, the Internet, even more than television and radio before it, enables the transmission of content at virtually no cost" (Paul Goldstein, "Intellectual Property: The Tough New Realities that Could Make or Break Your Business," 152 [NY: Portfolio, 2007]).

In *Reno v. ACLU*, 117 S.Ct. 2329 (U.S. 1997), the U.S. Supreme Court looked at whether two statutory provisions that were enacted to protect minors from "indecent" and "patently offensive" communications on the Internet abridged First Amendment Freedom of Speech. The Court held the Communications Decency Act of 1996 did not prevail over the government's interest in encouraging freedom of expression in a democratic society, which outweighs any theoretical but unproven benefit of censorship.

Copyright problems probably began with Johannes Gutenberg and the moveable press: mass-produced books ultimately segued into the information superhighway (Tomlinson at 62). "One of the main distinctions between professional copyright pirates and consumer copyright pirates is that professional infringers have large economic goals and consumer infringers have small ones. Neither economic extreme, however, seems to describe the form of infringement now taking place in cyberspace. On the Internet and on the networks that comprise the Internet, users routinely deposit copyrighted materials, not for economic gain, but because they enjoy the process and because they simply do not believe that placing copyrighted music, pictures and computer software on the Internet constitutes piracy" (*Id.*, at 67).

In *MTV v. Curry,* 867 F. Supp. 202 (S.D. N.Y. 1994), MTV sued a former video disc jockey, Adam Curry, alleging trademark violations in connection with his use of "mtv.com" to locate his Internet site. Curry claimed he had the legal right to use MTV's mark to develop an Internet site which dispatched daily music gossip; he also registered "mtv.com" under his own name with his own money and continued issuing his daily Internet reports after MTV terminated him. However, Curry ultimately settled the dispute in March 1995 and relinquished the "mtv.com" domain name to MTV on undisclosed terms.

Domain Names and Cybersquatting[2]

Domain names are made up of a number of characters separated by periods to designate field. Often, domain names consist of a word that will easily identify the holder of that address, such as an individual's or organization's name or brand name or trademark or a nickname.[3] Cybersquatting is the process of individuals attempting to profit from the Internet by reserving and later reselling or licensing domain names to the companies that invested time and money in developing the goodwill of the trademark.

In a WIPO arbitration procedure, *NCAA v. Brown,* Case No. D2009–0491 (Aug. 30, 2004), the contested domain names were <ncaafootball2005.com> and <ncaafootball2006.com>. Plaintiff NCAA owns numerous United States trademark registrations for the mark "NCAA." The NCAA is an association of colleges and universities that supervise intercollegiate athletics in the United States of America. The NCAA has been in use since 1921 in conjunction with the 1921 annual national championships. The NCAA also owns a website regarding intercollegiate football with content mirrored at ncaafootball.com and ncaafootball.net. Several Corporate

Champion and Corporate Partner Programs, including top corporations such as General Motors, Kraft and Coca-Cola, are recognized on the website.

Fantasy Sports Websites[4]

Fantasy sports leagues are an Internet phenomenon with player performance statistics and are an integral part of their popularity. Fantasy baseball is a game that allows ordinary people to act as the owner and general manager of an imaginary baseball team made up of Major League Baseball (MLB) players. "[I]t is a game that owes much of its success to the ease of compiling statistics on the Internet" (Razzano at 1157, footnote omitted).

The Major League Baseball Players Ass'n (MLBPA) struck a five-year, $50 million deal with Major League Baseball Advanced Media, LP (MLBAM) in January 2003 to acquire exclusive rights to players' names, statistics, likenesses, etc., for the development of online content, including fantasy baseball. However, in *C.B.C. Distribution & Marketing, Inc. v. MLBAM*, 505 F.3d 818 (8th Cir. 2007), it soon became very clear that MLBAM intended to enforce these rights in ways that the MLBPA never imagined. On First Amendment grounds, the court found that the video producer's right to use player names and statistics trumped the players' alleged publicity rights (*See* Robert Freeman & Peter Scher, "Fantasy Meets Reality: Examining Ownership Rights in Player Statistics," 23 WTR Ent. & Sports Law 7 [Winter 2006]).

In *Fantasy Sports Properties v. SportsLine.com, Inc.*, 287 F.3d 1108 (Fed. Cir. 2002), the court looked at a controversy between competing computer football games to determine whether they infringed on Fantasy Sports' Properties patent that allowed fantasy football games to award "bonus points." These bonus points were awarded based on the difficulty of the called play. Cable television network ESPN and Internet websites Yahoo and SportsLine.com released similar football games. Fantasy Sports sued for patent infringement, but the court held that the defendants, Yahoo Sports and ESPN, had not infringed the patent because their games did not give bonus points for difficulty of a play. That is, they did not adopt Fantasy Sports' so-called "unique bonus points" system. Although extra points were given in their computer games, the points were based on actual scores and not on the difficulty of a particular football play.

Two of SportsLine's games also fell under the court's interpretation of bonus points; however, a third game did not. That game, found at Commissioner.com, had the ability to be customized to offer bonus points based on the difficulty of a play; therefore, the court held that triable issues of material fact existed and remanded that part only to the lower court for further proceedings (*See also* 19 No. 21 Andrews Computer & Online Indus. Litig. Rep. 8 [May 21, 2002]).

Meta Tags and Trademarks[5]

The web is a graphical interface that is a subset of the Internet; it is an intricate group of links that allows buyers and sellers to engage in commerce. Navigating around the web necessitates the need for a "search engine," which operates like directory assistance. Some search engines search via meta tags, which are descriptive information about a web page inserted in that page's sublevel and are invisible to users. So meta tags are very useful, but, because they are invisible, they may also lure unwilling customers to specific sites (Chinnock at 258–260). Their invisibility can also create unique problems vis-à-vis potential trademark infringement.

In *Playboy Enters. Inc. v. Welles,* 7 F. Supp. 2d 1098, 1104 (S.D. Cal. 19989), defendant uses "Playboy" and "Playmate" as meta tags for her website that features photographs of nude women. The question is whether the web design was operating in good faith.

There are generally two types of metatags: description metatags and keyword metatags. Description metatags describe a website, while keyword metatags contain the keywords related to the content of a website. Search engines use these keyword metatags to pull websites applicable to search terms. On many search engines, the more often a term appears in the metatags of a particular web page, the more likely it is that the web page will be "hit" in a search for the keyword and the higher on the list of "hits" the web page will appear. The problem with metatags is that Internet users entering the trademark owner's mark into the computer may end up at the defendant's website. Although the consumers realize immediately upon accessing the site that they reached a site operated by the defendant and wholly unrelated to the trademark owner, some customers who were originally seeking the trademark owner's website may be perfectly content with the defendant's website. Because those customers would have found defendant's website due to the defendant's misappropriation of the trademark owners goodwill in its mark, a remedy should be available to the trademark owner (Evans at § 10). Evidence of actual confusion between trademarks is the best evidence in deducing infringement. Remember, within a metatag, particularly the description and keyword metatags, the developer of a website can include information describing or identifying the website and its contents.

In *Planned Parenthood Federation of America v. Bucci,* 42 U.S.P.Q. 2d (BNA) 1430, 1441 (S.D. N.Y. 1997), the court granted an injunction against the use of "plannedparenthood" as a domain name. Planned Parenthood operates a website at www.ppfa.org that offers information on family planning, pregnancy, sexually transmitted diseases, and abortion, along with links to similar pages. But because of metatags, some Internet users landed on defendant's page at "www.plannedparenthood .com"; defendant is an antiabortionist and greeted users with "Welcome to the PLANNED PARENTHOOD HOME PAGE!" Of course, this site was designed solely to cause consumer confusion of plaintiff's mark. Defendant intentionally lured an audience intended for Planned Parenthood, which caused a prophylactic effect on those who sought Planned Parenthood's site. Additionally, defendant tried to persuade users not to use Planned Parenthood's services (*See* Chinnock, at 208–209).

In *Playboy Enterprises v. Calvin Designer Label,* 985 F. Supp. 1220, 1221–1222 (N.D. Cal. 1997), the judge granted Playboy a preliminary injunction to prevent Calvin from using Playboy's federally registered trademarks as domain names and meta tags. The Calvin designer ran "www.playboyxxx.com" and "www.playmatelive.com," which visibly displayed the statements "Playmate Live Magazine" and "Get it all here at Playboy." Calvin also repeatedly used the "Playboy" trademark as meta tags. The court blocked Calvin's use of both the computer addresses and the meta tags. The likelihood of confusion argument is heightened by the fact that Playboy runs its own web page at "www .playboy.com," which, like Calvin's web page, offers pictures of nude women on the Internet. Additionally, Playboy's current and potential customers are unknowingly led to Calvin's website through meta tags. Calvin's domain names and meta tags violated Playboy's trademarks, and thus, the judge correctly issued an injunction covering both domain names and meta tags (*See,* Chinnock at 273–275).

Ambush Marketing[6]

Ambush marketing is well-known in the context of bait-and-switch and false and deceptive advertising techniques. It is less known in the altered universe of cyberspace, but one form could certainly be "cybersquatting." In cyberspace, ambush marketing revolves around trademark infringement on the Internet. Now, one uses the Internet to conduct ambush marketing, which can be generally defined as a company's intentional efforts to weaken its competitor's official, trademarked association with another organization, which is usually acquired through the payment of sponsorship fees.

In *NCAA v. Pitkin,* Case No. 2000–0903 (WIPO), one arbitrator ruled that domain name registrations such as "finalfourseats.com" were not transferable to the NCAA. That same arbitrator, however, just a few months earlier, reached the opposite decision in *NCAA v. Freedman,* Case No. 2000–0841 (WIPO), involving the domain name "finalfour -merchandise.com." With "finalfourseats.com" and other domain names held by a ticket broker, the arbitrator found that the use of Final Four was at the outset confusingly similar with an NCAA trademark. But the ticket broker disclaimed any affiliation with the NCAA on the website; therefore, there was a likelihood of confusion that "finalfourseats.com" was an official NCAA ticket site once a consumer accessed the site. The arbitrator's opinion in "finalfourmerchandise.com" found that the registration was in bad faith partly because he knew of the NCAA's interest in the "Final Four" and sought to profit. However, in *NCAA v. Halpern,* Case No. D2000–0700 (WIPO), the NCAA received a favorable outcome against another ticket broker when the arbitrator ruled that initial interest confusion was enough to show bad faith.

In *National Collegiate Athletic Association and March Madness Athletic Association, L.L.C. v. BBF International,* No. Civ. A.01-442-A, 2001 WL8910050 (E.D. Va. May 4, 2001), the court entered an injunction against BBF's use of NCAA trademarks in domain names and on websites related to gambling. The court also prohibited BBFI's depiction of student-athletes on the sites (*See* Bearby & Siegal at 659).

As was said in *Seinfeld,* "It's gold, Jerry, gold," which is the value of the Olympic trademarks and the relationship between corporate sponsors and their attempts to neutralize and punish ambush marketers who would use all available means, including the Internet, to furnish or steal the sponsor's Olympic gold (*See* Batcha at 251).

In *NHL v. Pepsi-Cola,* 92 D.L.R. 4th 349 (B.C. 1992), a Canadian court discussed ambush marketing in the context of sports sponsorships. Here, Pepsi-Cola, although not an official sponsor of the NHL, still purchased the rights to advertise during the hockey broadcasts. Pepsi set up several contests to attract customers. The contests, while not directly using any NHL trademarks or symbols, falsely portrayed an association to the NHL. The court concluded that Pepsi-Cola's contests were legitimate marketing tactics and did not infringe upon any registered trademarks. Luckily for U.S. trademark and domain name holders, this was a Canadian case and has no precedence here, so it could not be used by the pro-ambush marketing lobby (*See* Batcha at 253).

CHAPTER 16

The Branding of Johnny Football

Johnny Manziel, the person, was born on December 6, 1992, and is known by his nickname, Johnny Football. He is a quarterback for Texas A&M. He played in Coach Kevin Sumlin's Air Raid offense during A&M's first season in the SEC. On December 8, 2012, he became the first freshman to win the Heisman Trophy. He was also the first freshman to win the Davey O'Brien National Quarterback Award. On January 4, 2013, Manziel led Texas A&M to victory, 41–13, in the 2013 Cotton Bowl Classic against Oklahoma.[1]

Ryan Tannehill left A&M for the NFL after the 2011 season. Manziel won the starting job over Jameill Showers before the season began. Manziel's football debut was as a redshirt freshman against the University of Florida Gaters at the Aggies' Kyle Field. He broke Archie Manning's 43-year-old total offense record against Arkansas. Two games latter, against Louisiana Tech, Manziel surpassed his own total offense record against #24 Louisiana Tech to become the first player in SEC history to have two 500+ total offense games in one season. After the Auburn blowout, Manziel became a potential Heisman Candidate. Manziel led Texas A&M to a 29–24 upset over #1 Alabama in Tuscaloosa. In that game, he became only the second freshman in NCAA history to pass for 200 yards and rush for 100 yards during a game.

In the November 24, 2012, game against Missouri, he amassed 439 yards of total offense, including 3 passing and 2 rushing touchdowns. He broke the single season record for offensive production in the SEC with 4,600 yards, surpassing Heisman Trophy winners Cam Newton and Tim Tebow. He also became the first freshman and only the fifth player ever to pass for 3,000 yards and rush for 1,000 yards in a season. Manziel won the Davey O'Brien Award on December 6, 2012, and the Heisman Trophy on December 8, 2012. He is the ultimate football icon and brand.

Branding, Generally

A brand is the name, term, design, symbol, or any other feature that identifies one seller's good or service as distinct from those of other sellers. A modern example of a brand is Coca Cola, which belongs to the Coca-Cola Company. A brand is the most valuable fixed asset of a corporation. The Coca-Cola brand, for example, is protected by many intellectual property laws.

So, a brand is a sort of a logo. And now the branding can also apply to a person, such as "Johnny Football." After a while, the brand "Johnny Football" will replace the name Johnny Manziel; this is the stated goal of the Texas A&M athletic department.

Historically, factories introduce mass-produced goods to customers who only were able to obtain local goods. Generic products have difficulty competing with familiar local products, so difficulty arises when manufacturers attempt to convince consumers to try their non-local products. This occurred with slogan and mascots and jingles that began to appear on radio in early television. By the 1940s, manufacturer researchers were able to decipher that managers were developing relationships with products in a social and psychological manner. Marketers began to realize that consumers buy the brand itself rather than the product.

A brand receives brand recognition due to how widely known it is across the populace. Brand franchise is when a brand enjoys a critical mass of positive sentiment in both the general public and the market economy. For example, the Nike swoosh is associated with Nike products such as shoes, bags, and apparel, and their products are identified not by the company's name but through visual signifiers like logos, slogans, and colors, and are eyeballed by the swoosh. For example, Walt Disney's "signature" logo is used in the logo for go.com and is a successful brand because of its particular script font.

Brands typically are made up of various elements, which can include name, the word or words used to identify a company, product, service, or concept; logo, the visual trademark that identifies the brand; tagline or catchphrase; graphics; shapes, colors; sounds; scents; tastes; and/or movements. The brand name and brand to most individuals are somewhat interchangeable to the general public. In this context, a brand name constitutes of trademark if it exclusively identifies the general public. A brand owner may protect proprietary rights known as Registered Trademarks. Advertising spokespersons have also become part of some brands, for example: Mr. Whipple of Charmin toilet tissue and Tony the Tiger of Kellogg's Frosted Flakes; or, in the case of Johnny Football, Johnny Manziel is now associated with Texas A&M's entrance into the SEC. The outward expression of a brand—including its name, trademark, communications, and visual appearance—is brand identity. There is also the question of brand extension and brand dilution.

The "Johnny Football" Brand

Johnny Manziel, his family, and his university are now in the business of protecting his good name and his catchy nickname and are taking steps to trademark "Johnny Football." By seeking a trademark, A&M and the Manziel family can police how the name is used so as to make sure it's not treated in a negative manner, such as the Disney characters associated with a pornographic poster.

No freshman has ever won the Heisman (before), and in this, A&M's first year in the SEC, all "No. 2" jerseys are sold out immediately. A&M's NCAA compliance officer welcomes the opportunity to protect Johnny Football's eligibility. A&M has used more than 400 cease-and-desist letters to manufacturers of everything from knock-off T-shirts to action figures to bobblehead dolls using his trademark Johnny Football. Manziel can't even declare himself eligible for the NFL draft until after the 2013 season. The NCAA, of course, tries to keep as much money as possible, but the athletes now claim, in a class action suit filed by former UCLA basketball star Ed O'Bannon, that they are entitled to a fair share when the NCAA markets their images with exact numbers and jerseys in video games (*See*, e.g., *O'Bannon v. NCAA*, 2009 WL 4899217 [N.D. Cal. 2009]).

A&M has worked diligently to position the A&M brand as the school moves into the SEC, America's most fearsome football conference. No one could have ever foreseen the success of the team, its first-year coach, or its freshman quarterback. The Heisman was a dream that could only be imagined.

Some companies, the "Kenneth R. Reynolds Family Investments" of College Station, Texas, for example, have already filed for the Johnny Football trademark. But it is assumed that the Manziel family will have no problem in eventually securing the Johnny Football trademark.

CHAPTER 17

International Aspects

Intellectual property protection and piracy are now global propositions in a global market. TRIPS, or the Agreement on Trade-related Aspects of Intellectual Property Rights, contains provisions relative to copyrights, patents, trademarks, designs, trade secrets, and semiconductor chips. There are also treaties under U.S. law and global patent, trademark, and copyright registration agreements. There is international domain name protection and litigation. Domain names are unique addresses assigned to particular computers that are connected to the Internet.

It can definitely be said that the entertainment world is international in scope with global implications. Every Monday, Hollywood waits for the foreign weekend movie sales. "In 2003, a broad consortium of film, music, television, and technical services industries formed the Entertainment Industry Coalition for Free Trade (EIC) to reflect the vital interest trade represents for the industry and the importance entertainment represents for the United States" (Garon at 40).

In *Fila U.S.A., Inc. v. Kim,* 884 F. Supp. 491 (S.D. Fla. 1995), plaintiff alleges trademark infringement and unfair competition activities with regard to counterfeit Reebok and Fila footwear. Plaintiffs, Fila and Reebok, sell sportswear, athletic shoes, and related goods using registered, well-known trademarks. Defendant negotiated the sale of 5,000 pairs of Reebok and 3,000 pairs of Fila shoes, all counterfeit.

A trademark is any word, name, symbol device, or any combination thereof used by a manufacturer or retailer of a product, in connection with that product, to help consumers identify that product as different from the product of competitors. A trademark also identifies a particular product as coming from a distinct source, even if the name of the source is unknown to the consumer.

To prevail in an action for trademark infringement under the Lanham Act, the plaintiff must show the following: (1) that its mark is valid (i.e., properly registered, not generic, not abandoned through non-use); and (2) that the defendant's use of the contested mark is likely to cause deception or confusion on part of the consuming public as to the source of goods and services at issue.

With regard to counterfeit goods, the counterfeit merchandise must be a duplicate for the genuine article. Where a counterfeit item is virtually identical to the genuine item, the very purpose of the individuals marking the cheaper counterfeit items is to confuse the buying public into believing that it is buying the "real McCoy."

Defendants do not dispute that plaintiff Reebok has federally registered trademarks and the exclusive right to use those marks. Plaintiff has also established that the shoes sold to Mills and manufactured in Korea were counterfeit. The "smoking gun" here was a document in which defendant Kim writes: "Certificate of origin which states Made in USA will be prepared here. The master box which contains boxes of shoes should not say anything like 'Made in Korea.' The shoe box and shoes must state 'Made in USA.'" Q.E.D.

The modern American "culture," skinny jeans, Quentin Tarantino movies, hip-hop, and NBA basketball, has developed into our best form of "cultural invasion diplomacy." In a bizarre twist, think of Dennis Rodman as our cultural basketball ambassador to North Korea. The U.S. has been very successful in exporting ideas and concepts, which have then been incorporated into the systems of other "parasitic" countries. You see Air Jordans or Reebok Pumps everywhere in the world. In Vietnam, for example, a baseball cap with a Yankees logo is an extremely prized possession. NBA basketball is now the leading American sport and a global brand. These brands, logos, trademarks, and patents must be strenuously protected from counterfeits and knock-offs manufactured, usually, in third-world countries with less than spotless human rights records.

"In the past, less developed countries were skeptical of intellectual property and regarded it as an exploitative device that drains less developed countries of their scarce resources and slows down their economies and catch-up processes. Some of them also considered intellectual property rights to be tools to protect competitive advantage of the developed world by concentrating intellectual property ownership in enterprises based in developed countries, while covertly transferring valuable cultural resources out of less developed countries" (Yu at 245–246; footnotes omitted). Times have changed; many leaders now realize the benefits of promoting foreign intellectual property rights.[1]

So far, the United States has been very successful in exporting its ideas and concepts. From laws to basketball, countries have incorporated American concepts into their systems. By appealing to its ideas and culture, rather than by military means, the U.S. successfully transforms others' preferences by convincing them that the American way is preferable. It is no coincidence that teenagers abroad are wearing Air Jordans or Reebok Pumps or that they are imitating NBA players, longing to be the next Magic, Michael, or Larry (or perhaps even Sir Charles). With aggressive marketing and the ubiquity of the "American [k]ulture," it is no wonder that our system of intellectual property protection is also pervasive, and, in some cases, daunting.

International System for the Enforcement of Intellectual Property Rights

While governments agree to adopt and maintain Intellectual Property Rights (IPRs) at international organizations in Geneva and elsewhere, enforcement usually takes place in national and local courts. Enforcement is initiated by the rights holder in a civil or administrative court in the country where the IPRs are held and where the alleged infringement occurred.

"The Uruguay Round Agreements Act (URAA) which implemented the General Agreement on Tariffs and Trade (GATT) that included the Trade Aspects of Intellectual Property Rights Agreement (TRIPS) and the World Trade Organization Agreement (WTO) was signed into law on December 8, 1994. Under the Act, any work of a foreign author that lost its United States copyright or was denied a United States copyright due to the formalities of United States copyright law may receive United States copyright protection for that work. Under this provision, a work by a foreign author that was published without proper copyright notice, was not properly renewed, or was a pre-1972 sound recording first fixed outside the United States may be given United States copyright protection" (Lind, et al., Entertainment Law 3d: Legal Concepts and Business Practices, § 16:92 [database updated Dec. 2011; footnotes omitted]).

There was no formal international IPR protection until the passage of the 1883 Paris Convention and the 1886 Berne Convention. These conventions were the first attempts to provide right holders with uniform international protection. The problem may be China, which has a history of copying and rote memorization as a part of their educational system. The Confucian system centers on learning that is gained through replication, where public disputes result in loss of face. A criticism is that

China's court system has a lack of independence from other branches of government. China, however, in response to the tremendous pressure from the West to meet the IPR obligations of TRIPS, created an expansive number of administrative agencies that are delegated to enforce IPR violations. TRIPS is the most efficient method to counter China's counterfeits of U.S. intellectual property. China, as a TRIPS signee, is obligated to be involved in their dispute settlement mechanisms. TRIPS also has enforcement procedures, but, again, because of cultural differences, not to mention China's huge economic wallop, it might be wise to tread softly (*See generally* Levine at 223). "International intellectual property protection of technological works is a topic that rests at the forefront of legal scholarship—particularly with the advent of cheap, widely-accessible broadband Internet connections, violations of copyright by overseas actors is a relatively nascent, but nevertheless rampant problem" (Comerford at 633; footnote omitted). E-sports is a favorite target. However, there are IPR protection schemes available. "[T]he United Nations administers most existing international intellectual property treaties through the World Intellectual Property Organization. WIPO is an agency of the United Nations that was created in 1967 in order to advance the global defense of intellectual property. As part of its duties, WIPO administers 24 different treaties related to intellectual property" (*Id.,* at 634–635; footnotes omitted).

Football Ass'n Premier League v. YouTube, LLC, 633 F. Supp. 2d 159 (S.D. N.Y. 2009), discusses the relationship between soccer matches and defendants showing those games on YouTube. Under 17 U.S.C. § 412, there is no exception that excuses foreign works from the requirement of registration to obtain statutory damages for both domestic and foreign works. However, plaintiffs' copyright Act claims for statutory damages are dismissed with respect to all unregistered foreign works, except those claims based on unregistered foreign works which qualify for the "live broadcast exemption" in Section 411(c) of the Copyright Act.

In *Marcinkowska v. IMG Worldwide, Inc.,* 342 Fed. Appx. 632 (Fed. Cir. 2009), the question was asked, what is required for international patent infringement? Here, there is a patent for a dual surface for sports events.

"[T]he exhibition promoted on the Internet and televised throughout the world was held on a tennis court built and housed in the Kingdom of Spain, and it was this Spanish tennis court that provided the playing surface for the Battle of the Surfaces exhibition over which IMG and other entities obtained trademarks, advertised, and licensed broadcast rights throughout the world. In this case, the hybrid tennis court was not 'used' in the United States—it was 'used' in Spain and that use was broadcast in the United States" (*Id.* at 636).

The piracy of motion pictures, both nationally and internationally, is a major problem costing the industry billions of dollars. In *Seinfeld,* Jerry was forced to film counterfeit versions of different movies, and of course, he was worried about his art as a film maker. However, this is no laughing matter for movie studios. It is said that the industry has refocused its promotional efforts overseas, but, unfortunately, actual and potential revenue is eroded by dishonored contracts, foreign trade restrictions, and international piracy. The pirates are lowering the profit margin of the movies' IPRs. The most effective way to stop or slow down foreign piracy is to cooperate more with local government police to bolster enforcements and penalties.[2]

The Olympics

"The Olympic Movement consists of several governing bodies in an elaborate international and domestic organizational structure" (Yasser at 961). At the head is the International Olympic Committee (IOC), a non-profit, non-governmental organization formed and operating from Lausanne, Switzerland, under Swiss Law. Under the Olympic Charter, the IOC is the final authority on all questions concerning the Olympic Games and the Olympic Movement.

By § 380 of the Amateur Sports Act, Congress gave the USOC exclusive trademark rights to the Olympic name, symbol consisting of five interlocking rings, the USOC emblem, and the words "Olympic," "Olympiad," and the motto "Citius Altius Fortius" (faster higher stronger). The United States Olympic Committee (USOC) also has exclusive rights to license commercial and promotional use of Olympic trademarks, as a means to enable the USOC to raise funds to support the United States' Olympic participation (*Id.,* at 991).

The authority for Olympic trademark protection emanates from the International Olympic Committee (IOC), which is the supreme authority for the Olympic Movement. It is a non-governmental, non-profit organization created by Pierre de Coubertin in 1894. It owns all rights concerning the Olympic symbol, the Olympic flag, the Olympic motto, the Olympic anthem, and the Olympic Games. The United States Olympic Committee (USOC) was chartered by Congress in 1950; its purpose is to assist funding of U.S. participation in the Olympic Games. Although chartered by Congress, it is a private non-profit entity and does not receive governmental financial support. USOC raises funds to promote U.S. Olympic efforts by arranging corporate sponsorships, licensing of USOC logos for merchandizing, and revenues from television broadcasting.

Under the Amateur Sports Act of 1978, the U.S. Congress granted the USOC exclusive control over the commercial exploitation of Olympic and Paraolympic related trademarks, symbols, and terminology. The Act grants USOC the remedies afforded to commercial trademarks protection and also imposes civil liability upon any person who uses Olympic name or symbol without USOC consent. The Amateur Sports Act was amended and recodified as the Ted Stevens Olympic and Amateur Sports Act of 1998. Under 36 U.S.C. § 220506(c), USOC was granted exclusive rights to: the United States Olympic committee; the fire ring Olympic symbol; the USOC emblem; the words "Olympic, "Olympiad," "Paralympic," "Paralympiad," and "Pan-American"; the mottos "Citius Altius Fortius" and "America Espirito Sport Fraternite"; and the licenses to exploit the commercial and promotional use of the Olympic trademarks (36 U.S.C. § 380b). However, there are exceptions to USOC's exclusive rights. The word "Olympic" may be used, without sanction, to identify a business or goods or services if (1) such use is not combined with any of the Olympic trademarks; (2) it is evident from the circumstances that such use of the name "Olympic" refers to the naturally occurring mountains or geographical region of the same name and that it does not refer to the corporation or to any Olympic activity where such business, goods, or services are operated, sold, and marketed in the state of Washington, west of the Cascade Mountain range, and marketing in this area is not substantial; and (3) the use commenced before September 21, 1950 (rights are subject to preexisting rights usage prior to September 21, 1950).

In *San Francisco Arts & Athletics, Inc. v. USOC*, 483 U.S. 522 (1987), plaintiff, a gay rights organization in San Francisco, tried to hold the "Gay Olympic Games" in 1982. This nom de guerre was used by plaintiff to sell merchandise to the public under the slogan "Gay Olympic Games." It was proposed as a nine-day event that was specifically designed to mimic the real Olympics, including a "Gay Olympic Flame" that was to be carried from New York City to San Francisco. The Supreme Court held that, because of the statutory grant for use of the word "Olympic," a showing of actual consumer confusion, or even a likelihood of such confusion, is not necessary for USOC to prevail. The word "Olympic" was not classified as generic, thereby entitling it to trademark rights; there was no violation of the First Amendment; and USOC was not a governmental actor. The Olympics are aggressively protected because it is the most effective international corporate marketing platform in the world (reaching billions of people in over 200 countries and territories). Let's use Michael Jordan as an example. When Michael Jordan accepted his Olympic medal on the podium in 1992, he had to drape a towel over the Adidas brand to satisfy his individual contract with Nike. Even though Adidas was the Olympic sponsor, Nike knew those photos of Jordan on the podium would persist for years, and they moved to protect their association with Jordan. Corporations like McDonald's, Coca-Cola, Visa, Kodak, and Xerox pay a multimillion dollar fee for the right to be part of The Olympic Partner (TOP) program which grants sponsors the exclusive worldwide marketing rights in their product categories for both the Winter and Summer Games. The USOC has actively policed its rights to maintain the strength of the Olympic trademarks and thus protect Olympic corporate sponsors against dilution of the value of the Olympic trademarks. Unaided brand awareness for the Olympic Rings was 93 percent according to research conducted in 1998, 1999, and 2000. Of course, the five interlocking rings symbolize the continents of Africa, America, Asia, Australia, and Europe, which are joined together irrespective of race, nationality, religion, or economic differences.

Here is the famous Ravelympics anecdote: In 2012, the knitting social network, Ravelry, hosted a "Ravelympics," a knitting competition for users that includes events like an "afghan marathon," "scarf hockey," and "sweater triathlon." The knitters were supposed to compete in their events while watching the actual Olympic Games on TV. USOC sent Ravelry a cease-and-desist letter, stating that the Ravelympics "denigrated the true nature of the Olympic Games and was disrespectful to our country's finest athletes." This caused uproar among the two million strong knitting communities. The USOC later released an apology on its website but remained firm in its demand that they change the name.

Ambush marketing is defined as a company's intentional efforts to weaken its competitor's official association by capitalizing on the goodwill, reputation, and popularity of a particular event by creating an association without the authorization or consent of the necessary parties. This does cause consumer confusion, which may cause companies that were willing to pay the premium to be an official Olympics sponsor to reconsider because companies conducting ambush marketing campaigns potentially can get as much attention as legitimate advertising campaigns but at a much lower cost. There are four methods of ambush marketing: purchasing advertising time around an event in order to associate a nonsponsoring company as a sponsor of the event; negotiating with individual players or teams who are participating in a larger sponsored event or league to have them endorse a nonsponsoring company; using event tickets in a promotional contest to tie a nonsponsoring company to that event; and aggressively marketing a nonsponsoring company around the location of an event.

During the 1994 Winter Olympic Games, Wendy's aired commercials with its founder, Dave Thomas, participating in traditional Winter Olympic sports. Its competitor, McDonald's, had paid $40 million to be an official Olympic sponsor. The success of Wendy's threatened USOC's ability to charge $40 million for sponsorship fees at future Olympics.[3]

CHAPTER 18

Advocacy and Litigation Strategy

Walter T. Champion, Kirk D. Willis,
Patrick K. Thornton, and Joey Barajas

The key to the growth of intellectual property as an essential element in the sports and entertainment industries is the utilization of advocacy and litigation stratagems to promote your brand. Think "Johnny Football." Sometimes, socially harmful intellectual property litigation occurs because the rights are easy to acquire and could apply broadly.[1] There are many intellectual property lawsuits that are weak and anti-competitive. A lawsuit is weak and anti-competitive if it seeks to impair the defendant's performance in their shared market or even to exclude the defendant from the market completely based on an unlikely or invalid claim.[2]

The scope of intellectual property rights is highly subjective because the vague standards for infringement may cause reasonable judges to often disagree on the interpretation of a patent claim, and the complexity of the evidence can lead to difficulties for a deserving defendant to prevail.[3] A common strategy used by intellectual property plaintiffs with narrow rights is to gamble that a court will grant them broad rights due to the vague standards for infringement.[4] For example, the "Linsanity®" and "Johnny Football" brands must be vigorously enforced to be effective. Texas A&M's athletic department has written about 400 cease-and-desist letters to protect their "Johnny Football" brand. It's like the irritating situation when you order a Coke, but the semi-officious waiter asks with some solemnity whether Pepsi will be all right as a substitute. The drinks are similar in taste and color but the policing of the individual brands is entirely different.

We return to Mickey, in an article entitled "Don't Mess with the Mouse: Disney's Legal Army Protects Revered Image," which highlights Disney lawsuits against art galleries that have paintings in which Mickey

Mouse is handing a Campbell's soup can to a Russian; or a Beloit, Wisconsin, tavern that was called The Mickey Mouse for 50 years. Don't Mess with the Mouse—Disney lawyers will vigorously enforce their trademark and copyrights with the filing of over 2,000 lawsuits (Gail Cox, 11 Nat'l L.J. 2 [Jul. 31, 1989]).

Back to weak lawsuits and their failure to police and protect—a weak lawsuit may present a credible threat to a defendant who has trouble distinguishing weak lawsuits from strong ones because a plaintiff is likely to have better information about the scope and validity of the intellectual property rights in the early stages of litigation.[5]

A weak lawsuit may be credible because of the costs it may impose on the defendant. A defendant may settle an opportunistic lawsuit to avoid the nuisance of mounting a defense.[6] An opportunistic lawsuit is one that is filed by a plaintiff who is merely seeking a settlement.[7] A threat of a weak lawsuit may deter entry into a market if the plaintiff establishes a reputation for prosecuting weak suits through to the end.[8] The problem with opportunistic lawsuits is very serious and getting worse because defendants fear the high cost of intellectual property litigation and settle opportunistic claims to avoid that cost.[9] An example of an opportunistic entertainment lawsuit would be if a writer pitched his story idea to a studio and was turned down, only to find a movie out in theaters years later that embodied a similar idea.[10] Some enterprising plaintiffs strengthen their claims by pitching their ideas to potential defendants; then they can credibly argue that the defendants had access to the works.[11] But here, this litigation is more complex because copyright will not protect a concept for a TV show or a movie because there is no copyright protection for an idea.[12] Copyright protects an "original work of authorship fixed in [a] tangible medium of expression," so if an idea is not written down, it does not fall within the definition.[13] However, under certain circumstances, a writer may be able to claim that a contract had been reached between the writer and the entity that uses his idea based on the theory that there was a bilateral expectation of payment.[14] This means that a writer provides the idea to a producer with the understanding that the writer will be paid if the producer uses that idea.[15] This is considered opportunistic litigation if the writer distributes this idea to many potential defendants then takes a few of them to court merely because a TV show or movie they produced was somewhat similar to the writer's idea in an effort to delay the production and pressure the producer to settle the case.

Aside from patent litigation, trade dress claims related to product design and configuration pose the gravest threat of predatory litigation.[16] Trade dress refers to the total image of a product and may include features such as size, shape, color combinations, texture graphics, or even particular sales techniques.[17] In *Callaway Golf Company v. Golf Clean, Inc.*, golf club manufacturer brought an action against competitor, alleging trade dress of its "Big Bertha" irons was infringed by competitor's "Big Bursar" clubs. The court reasoned that Canterbury's "Big Bursar" club was made "from the same molds sued by Callaway" in an effort to copy Callaway's club and the Canterbury club also includes matching the shape, script, color, and size of Callaway's "Big Bertha."[18] The court stated that the defendants' product is confusingly similar to the Callaway "Big Bertha" and is likely to be confused by the end user as having some connection to Callaway because of the similarity of design, the similarity of the product, the similarity of retail outlets and purchasers, the similarity of advertising media used and the defendant's intent.[19] The court concluded that Big Bertha arbitrarily combines its features in such a manner that the clubs are inherently distinctive; further the clubs have acquired secondary meaning and the features claimed by Callaway as its trade dress are primarily nonfunctional.[20] On Callaway's motion for preliminary injunction, the District Court held that: (1) trade dress of Callaway's clubs was inherently distinctive; (2) trade dress had acquired secondary meaning; (3) trade dress was nonfunctional; (4) Callaway demonstrated likelihood of confusion; and (5) balance of equities favored grant of preliminary injunctive relief.[21]

Predatory litigation is another type of strategy used in intellectual property suits. Predatory litigation can sour a defendant's credit rating and reduces cash flow because of the high cost of intellectual property litigation.[22] A predatory plaintiff can divert customers from a defendant by threatening the defendant's customers with a lawsuit.[23] Furthermore, a plaintiff can use a preliminary injunction to block the defendant's production and sales before trial.[24] The ultimate goal of the predator is to recoup its cost of litigation by reducing the competition and raising prices while litigation is in process.[25]

Broadcasting and Licensing Rights

Sports Broadcasting

Since 1921, Major League Baseball had entered into contracts authorizing the broadcast of World Series games by various radio stations.[26] One of the first licensing disputes in sports broadcasting occurred when Mr. A.E. Newton began to broadcast the 1934 World Series between the Cardinals and the Tigers without negotiating for the right to do so.[27] Mr. Newton provided his audience with "running accounts" of the games based upon information he received while listening to authorized radio broadcasts.[28] This "play-by-play" broadcasting using information provided by other authorized radio broadcasts formed the basis of a challenge to his license renewal before the Federal Communications Commission, who considered Newton's conduct to be "inconsistent with fair dealing" "dishonest in nature," "unfair utilization of the results of another's labor," and "deceptive to the public upon the whole and contrary to the interests thereof" but not in violation of the Communications Act of 1934.[29] Newton's case was the first in a series of decisions involving the right of sports clubs to control the dissemination of the accounts of their games.[30] The forum soon shifted from the FCC to the state and federal courts, where the sports clubs were more effective advocates than they were before the Commission.[31]

The state and federal courts took a different stand on broadcasting and licensing rights in sports. The leading case is *Pittsburgh Athletic Co. v. KQV Broadcasting Co.*[32] The defendant in this case, a Pittsburgh radio station, KQV, had broadcast play-by-play news of the Pittsburgh Pirates games through information obtained from paid observers. While these observers were situated outside Forbes Field, they nevertheless could see over the Field's enclosure, and could observe—and report—the plays as they were made.[33] This practice was done without the consent of the Pittsburgh Pirates, who are owned by the plaintiff, Pittsburgh Athletic Company, and who licensed the exclusive right to broadcast play-by-play descriptions or accounts of their games to General Mills, Inc. The National Broadcasting Company also has a licensing agreement with General Mills, Inc., to broadcast by radio over stations KDKA and WWSW play-by-play descriptions of these games.[34] Pittsburgh Athletics Co. sued to enjoin the unauthorized KQV broadcasts of the Pirates' games.[35] The court enjoined KQV's activities, concluding that the ball club "by reason of its creation of the game, its control of the park, and its restriction of the dissemination of news therefrom, has a property right in such news, and the right to control the use thereof for a reasonable time following the games."[36] The court held that KQV had misappropriated the property rights of the Pirates in the "news, reports, descriptions or accounts" of the Pirates' games; that such misappropriation resulted in KQV's "unjust enrichment" to the detriment of the Pirates; and that KQV's actions constituted "unfair competition," "fraud on the public," and a violation of unspecified provisions of the Communications Act.[37]

The sports property right concept was strengthened by the Supreme Court in *Zacchini v. Scripps-Howard Broadcasting Company*.[38] There, Zacchini's fifteen-second "human cannonball" act, in which he is shot from a cannon into a net some 200 feet away, was, without his consent, videotaped in its entirety, and broadcast at a county fair in Ohio by a reporter for Scripps-Howard Broadcasting Company.[39] Zacchini brought a damages action in state court against the broadcasting company, alleging an "unlawful appropriation" of his "professional property."[40] The broadcasting company responded that it is constitutionally privileged to include in its newscasts matters of public interest that would otherwise be protected by the right of publicity, absent the intent to injure or to appropriate for some nonprivileged purpose.[41] The Court sided with Zacchini.

Congress added a new dimension to the sports property right concept when it enacted the Copyright Act of 1976.[42] At the urging of the professional sports leagues, Congress extended federal copyright protection to live sports broadcasts, thereby vesting the owners of these telecasts with the exclusive right to "perform" them "publicly."[43] To be eligible for copyright protection, the broadcast must be "fixed" simultaneously with its transmission.[44] The remedies afforded by the Copyright Act are particularly valuable because they permit the copyright owner to recover statutory damages of between $250 and $50,000 for each act of infringement without regard to actual damages suffered.[45]

The Sports Broadcast Act of 1961 immunizes from antitrust liability the pooled sale of telecasting rights by certain of the professional sports leagues.[46] It allowed the leagues to negotiate such lucrative network television packages as Sunday afternoon football and the Saturday Baseball Game of the Week without fear of antitrust prosecution.[47] The Act, however, does have at least one significant limiting feature.[48] It restricts the ability of the leagues to define the geographical areas into which the pooled telecasts may be broadcast.[49] Pooling was considered necessary to "assure the weaker clubs of the league continuing television income and television coverage on a basis of substantial equality with the stronger clubs."[50]

It is important to note that the Act sanctions only arrangements of professional football, baseball, basketball, and hockey leagues—not soccer or, more importantly, the colleges.[51] This fact can best be seen in *Board of Regents of the University of Oklahoma v. National Collegiate Athletic Association (NCAA)*,[52] when it states that, while professional basketball, golf, and hockey are consistently held to be within Antitrust coverage,[53] the television plan regarding the regulation of broadcast rights to intercollegiate football is unreasonably restrictive of competitive conditions and therefore unlawful[54] as a violation of the Sherman Act. The district court states that "the controls exercised by NCAA over college football television are not necessary to preserve competitive balance on the playing field[55] and [the NCAA] television controls not only inhibit competition, they destroy it"[56] by not allowing individual institutions to negotiate a television contract outside the NCAA contracts.[57]

Entertainment Broadcasting

Until *FCC v. Pacifica Foundation,*[58] broadcasting principles in media were largely the result of Federal Communication Commission practices and lower federal court decisions.[59] However, in the 1943 decision of *National Broadcasting Corp. v. United States,*[60] the Supreme Court upheld the provisions of the Communications Act of 1934, which allowed the airwaves to be used only in the "public interest" and granted the FCC enforcement powers primarily by means of its control over broadcast licenses.[61] This case gave the FCC enormous discretion in its decisions of what speech was not in the public interest and required only that the FCC could not revoke or deny a license "capriciously."[62] A license is the radio or television station's life force, and the FCC has power to grant, suspend, deny, or grant only a short-term license renewal.[63]

Section 102(a) of the Copyright Act of 1976[64] protects only "original works of authorship fixed in any tangible medium of expression," including "motion pictures and other audiovisual works."[65] Section 102(a) of the Copyright Act lists eight categories of "works of authorship" covered by the Act, including such categories as "literary works," "musical works," and "dramatic works."[66] The list does not include athletic events, and, although the list is concededly non-exclusive, such events are neither similar nor analogous to any of the listed categories.[67] Thus, the underlying games of a sports telecast do not fall within the subject matter of federal copyright protection because they do not constitute "original works of authorship"; otherwise, any team that performs a unique combination or play could claim a copyright in it and enjoin other teams from competing with the same plays or combinations.[68] However, there exists a copyright in a broadcast sporting event because the simultaneous recording of a transmission suffices for the element of fixation in a tangible medium of expression, thereby falling under the protection of the Copyright Act.[69] A broadcast entity that directs, produces, and therefore, creates a protectable work of authorship is often required to transfer some or all of the copyrights in the broadcast to the sports team or club as an initial condition of being authorized to broad-cast the games.[70] Since the broadcast of a sporting event falls under the protection of the Copyright Act, anyone who materially alters this unique selection of images in a sports broadcast transmission without or in excess of a valid license is preparing an unauthorized derivative work and is a copyright infringer.[71]

Jurors' Perceptions in Patent Cases

The truth about patents, especially patents in sports and entertainment, for example, the dimple pattern in golf balls or film quality for 3-D movies, is that the public does not understand the process. However, these regular, untrained people are often called upon to make complicated decisions about patent infringement as jury members. Important in this type of liti-gation is the trial strategies that are developed to win the votes of the jurors.

Many times, it is the belief of corporate greed and malfeasance that color the perceptions of the jurors in intellectual property trials. "Trial attorneys need to know what the public thinks. This is necessary because juries are made up of ordinary people who are pulled out of their normal lives to serve a public duty and a judge in a case in court."[72]

The Schwarzenegger Bobblehead Doll War

The right of publicity is state-law created intellectual property that pro-tects against the unauthorized appropriation of one's likeness, image, or identity. The right of publicity is defined by the struggle between rights of publicity and First Amendment rights of free speech and expression. The issue was raised by defendants' sale of unauthorized bobblehead dolls incorporating the likeness of Arnold Schwarzenegger, who was both a Hollywood movie star and the governor of California (the so-called "Governator"). It was virtually unprecedented, however, for a sitting politician to sue in order to control the use of his commercial image.[73] But then again, everything about Arnold's term as governor was unusual, unprecedented, and strange.

In *Comedy III Productions, Inc. v. Saderup, Inc.*,[74] the court held that an artist's rendering of The Three Stooges on lithographs and silk-screened T-shirts did not warrant First Amendment protection because the depictions used of these three deceased celebrities on these products was not sufficiently "transformative" to meet the requisite threshold for First Amendment protection against a right of publicity claim. However, two years later, in *Winter v. DC Comics*,[75] the court found that a comic book series that depicted the likenesses of two musicians warranted full First Amendment protection. In *Winter,* a comic book series used the likenesses of two musician brothers, Johnny and Edgar Winter, in a fanciful and strange narrative depicting them as "Johnny and Edgar Autumn"— as "villainous half-worm, half-human offspring born from the rape of their mother by a supernatural worm creature." The Autumn brothers were depicted as long-haired albinos (like the Winter brothers) with tentacles coming from their chests, who decapitated livestock and ate the brains of pigs with whom they fornicated. The Winter brothers sued, claiming the comic book portrayal of them as "vile, depraved, stupid, cowardly, subhuman individuals who engage in wanton acts of violence and bestiality for pleasure" wrongfully appropriated their names and likenesses in violation of their right of publicity under California law. The court determined that the comic book depiction of the brothers was not literal and that the brothers' images were distorted "for purposes of lampoon, parody, or caricature;" therefore, it was fully protected speech.

The Application of Trademark Law to Sports Mark Litigation

A trademark is "a word, name, logo, design or symbol used to identify the maker or seller of a product or service."[76] Also, a trademark symbolizes the goodwill built up by a particular business.[77] To create ownership rights in a trademark, one must be the first to use the mark in trade and to make continuous, uninterrupted use in the trade thereafter. To use the mark in trade is to use it in a way that allows consumers to rely on it for its ultimate purpose, to identify and distinguish the user's particular goods or services from those of other producers. Once a trademark is created, it may acquire certain rights. These rights may be secured in two basic manners. Under common law, rights can be acquired by use, whereas under statute, rights can be acquired by registration and use or intent to use. However, pursuant to common law, the right in a trade is not a right in gross. Instead, the trademark owner's property right extends only as far as is necessary to prevent consumer confusion. Pursuant to registration, a trademark right extends across the United States based on the doctrine of constructive notice.

Trademarks also perform a number of significant roles. One role is the so-called "signaling" function, by which the mark identifies a particular good and distinguishes it from those manufactured or sold by others. In the field of sports, this role is crucial as a way to develop and promote team loyalty.

Inherent in the rights of a trademark is the value of the mark. The value is determined from the nexus between the mark and the particular product or service it represents. This value increases as the trademark becomes recognized by the public in association with the goods it accompanies. However, a mark's value is susceptible to damage, even in the absence of confusion, if others use the mark to identify their products.[78]

In an infringement claim, there are two basic inquiries: does the plaintiff have a protectable right in the mark, and, if so, is there a likelihood of confusion due to the defendant's use of the mark? Therefore, the plaintiff's burden of proof has two prongs. First, the plaintiff must establish secondary meaning in their mark. If the mark is registered, the plaintiff will not have to illustrate secondary meaning. The plaintiff must demonstrate that the defendant's activities have created a likelihood of confusion. Both prongs are critical to every trademark infringement case, including sports trademarks.[79]

An example of a descriptive sports mark is the name "Brooklyn Dodgers." Although the term was found not to be fanciful, it obtained secondary meaning due to its strength as the name of a nationally-recognized sports team. Similarly, courts have held that other team names and logos in addition to baseball teams have the ability to attain secondary meaning.

Once a plaintiff establishes that a mark is registered or has attained secondary meaning, the plaintiff must show that the defendant's use created a likelihood of confusion. An inquiry into the likelihood of confusion "focuses on the product bearing the allegedly infringing marks and asks whether the public believes the product bearing the mark originates with or is somehow endorsed or authorized by the mark's owner."[80]

Likelihood of confusion is the key factor in a trademark infringement. Admittedly, there is a connection between secondary meaning and the likelihood of confusion, but the confusion aspect is "the essential finding in any trademark infringement action." One test for confusion rests on whether the defendant's use of plaintiff's mark "would likely create confusion in the minds of potential buyers as to the source, affiliation, or sponsorship of the parties' products." One can infer from this test that the "use of another's trademark is non-infringing so long as the public is not misled as to the affiliation or as to the source or sponsorship of the goods or services in question." This test, however, does not stress which factors are relevant in deciding the likelihood of confusion.[81]

Some courts have found that the use of disclaimers can make a difference. In *NFL Properties, Inc. v. Dallas Cap & Emblem Mfg., Inc.,* the court found that consumer responses to a survey would have been substantially different had there been a legible disclaimer. Furthermore, if a strong public interest is demonstrated, the unauthorized use of an undeniably valid mark will not be an infringement if accompanied by attempts to avoid confusion. Therefore, while the use of a disclaimer is at times not effective, it may be important in a case concerning likelihood of confusion.[82]

Initially, it bears emphasis that team logos and nicknames are protectable as service marks. They serve as service marks because they are used to identify the activities of a specific team or league. These marks may be owned by the individual team, but they are often controlled and licensed by the "properties" arm of each league. As the sale of goods bearing team logos has grown, the licensing of trademarks has developed into a lucrative business. Consequently, the use of infringement actions by the properties arms is a vital way to protect their interests.[83]

One must ask what harm or injury occurs when someone uses a mark without authorization or license. The unauthorized use of a mark is injurious, as the market demand for any product or service is finite and any sales of unlicensed merchandise will reduce licensed sales. Sports merchandising properties also deserve protection from infringement because they invest time and finances into marketing to develop goodwill and reputation and serve to profit from such efforts. Therefore, sports mark owners have a protectable right in their marks. The only question is how far that right extends and how to evaluate such claims.[84]

In *Major League Baseball Properties, Inc. v. Sed Non Olet Denarius, Ltd.*, the United States District Court for the Southern District of New York examined the property rights associated with the mark "Brooklyn Dodgers" in light of the plaintiff's trademark infringement suit. Beginning in 1988, the defendants used the words "Brooklyn Dodger" in the name of their restaurants. At the time the defendants were selecting a name, there was not a registration of "Brooklyn Dodger." In fact, the Los Angeles Dodgers and the MLB Properties made very limited use of the mark following the Brooklyn Dodgers' departure from Brooklyn in 1958. Indeed, the earliest licensing of the name or mark occurred on April 6, 1981. It was not until 1986 that MLB Properties began to actively market the "Brooklyn Dodger" name on a variety of items and merchandise in their "Cooperstown Collection." Based on these facts, the court had to evaluate the plaintiff's assertion that the defendants' use of the name "Brooklyn Dodger" on a restaurant constituted trademark infringement.[85]

To evaluate the likelihood of confusion, the court utilized an eight-factor test. The court easily found that the marks used were strong and obviously similar. However, the court observed that the services were not in close proximity because one party was involved with baseball exhibitions and the other was an eatery. Next the court determined that there was little likelihood that the plaintiffs could bridge the gap because they had shown no intention in the last century of entering the restaurant business.[86]

The court continued its analysis by examining the surveys introduced by the plaintiffs and concluding that they were both unreliable and failed to establish actual confusion. The court also found that defendants acted in good faith, as they attempted to arouse memories of baseball and not to capitalize on the plaintiff's goodwill. Finally, the court determined that sophisticated consumers were not likely to be confused and would not believe that the defendants had authorization by the plaintiffs. Therefore, the district court held that the plaintiffs failed to establish a likelihood of confusion and a claim for trademark infringement.[87]

In addition, the plaintiffs were found to have abandoned the mark by their extensive period of nonuse. The court asserted that "abandonment is an affirmative defense to trademark infringement." In this case, the plaintiffs had made noncommercial use of the "Brooklyn Dodger" mark between 1958 and 1981. Thus, according to the Lanham Act, nonuse for a period of two years with the intent not to resume or more is prima facie evidence of abandonment. Once there is abandonment, resumed use will not alleviate the condition.[88]

The merchandising properties branch of the National Football League is NFL Properties. Consequently, each NFL team has a logo comprised of a name, design, and color. Pursuant to an agreement between the NFL clubs and the NFL Trust, NFL Properties has the power and standing to enforce the league's marks. The teams' symbols are registered by the individual team and NFL Properties with the United States Patent and Trademark Office for entertainment services in the form of professional football games. NFL Properties licenses the NFL marks and logos to be used on a variety of products and services. A licensee must, in turn, pay NFL Properties a royalty of 6.5 percent of the sales of the licensed goods. These royalties supplement the charitable foundation known as NFL Charities.

Through extensive advertising and promotion, NFL Properties has created the perception that merchandise emblazoned with NFL marks is sponsored or authorized by the NFL. By way of this marketing strategy, the NFL marks and logos have attained a "strong secondary meaning of identification of the member clubs." Because the NFL has so much time and money invested in these marks, NFL Properties is incessant with its protection of the club trademarks. NFL Properties has investigators in every NFL city to investigate claims of trademark infringement.

In 1947, a football fan, Charles Evans, originated the name "Baltimore Colts" as part of a contest to name Baltimore's entry in the All-American Football Conference. Seven years later, in 1952, the Dallas Texans, a professional football team located in Dallas, moved to Baltimore and became the Baltimore Colts. The Colts remained in Baltimore until 1984 when, under cover of the night, they covertly fled to Indiana and became the Indianapolis Colts.

The Indianapolis Colts have federal registration for the marks "Colts," "Indianapolis Colts" and the Indianapolis Colts logo. From the time the Colts left Baltimore in April 1984, the Indianapolis Colts made no commercial use of the "Baltimore Colts" mark. NFL Properties began using the mark as part of its "Throwback Collection" in August of 1991, but neither the Indianapolis Colts nor NFL Properties attempted to renew the "Baltimore Colts" trademark, and the registration expired on December 12, 1992. However, on February 17, 1994, the Canadian Football League awarded James Speros and MBFC a new franchise to begin competition in July 1994. Following an inquiry that revealed that the Indianapolis Colts and NFL Properties had allowed the registration to lapse, MBFC and Mr. Speros announced on March 1, 1994, that the team would be called the "Baltimore CFL Colts." Subsequently, MBFC submitted a registration with the United States Patent and Trademark Office for the trademarks "Baltimore Colts" and "Baltimore CFL Colts." NFL Properties, on behalf of the Indianapolis Colts, filed for trademark infringement.

The plaintiffs in the Baltimore CFL Colts litigation sought relief based upon both federal and state trademark infringement and unfair competition. In a preliminary injunction granted June 27, 1994, District Court Judge Larry McKinney stated that the "consumers of Baltimore CFL Colts' merchandise are likely to think, mistakenly, that the new Baltimore team is an NFL team related in some fashion to the Indianapolis Colts, formerly the Baltimore Colts." Judge McKinney utilized a seven-factor test and concluded that there was a likelihood of confusion.

The Seventh Circuit Court of Appeals found that the district court did not commit clear error in holding that the defendant's use of "Baltimore CFL Colts" was likely to confuse a substantial number of consumers. While affirming the lower court's injunction, the court of appeals' decision contains language that suggests that a full exploration of the factors may yield a different result. The Seventh Circuit admitted that confusion is possible but maintained that it is "undesirable to impoverish the lexicon of trade name merely to protect the most gullible fringe of the consuming public."

In this case, the parties' marks are dissimilar. The Indianapolis Colts' and NFL Properties' "Colts" logo is of a horseshoe. In contrast, the Baltimore CFL Colts' logo consists of a silhouette of a horsehead and a maple leaf to denote CFL affiliation. Therefore, examination beyond merely the words used displays a distinct difference between the parties' marks. The second factor employed by the court was the similarity of the products or services. Facially, the NFL and CFL are similar services— professional football. However, there are noticeable differences between the two leagues. For instance, the CFL uses a larger playing field, different rules, more players, and a different season (July through November), than the NFL. While these distinctions may not make the services dissimilar enough, certainly the variances are deserving of consideration in the court's evaluation.

Abandonment often occurs by nonuse of a mark for two consecutive years. Here, the district court found that the Indianapolis Colts abandoned the "Baltimore Colts" trademark when they moved in 1984. Despite this finding, the court of appeals stated that abandonment of the old Baltimore Colts mark did not empower a third party to use it to confuse Colts fans or consumers "with regard to the identity, sponsorship, or league affiliation of the third party, that is, the new Baltimore team." Additionally, the plaintiffs failed to renew their registration that expired on December 12, 1992, indicating that the plaintiffs indeed had abandoned the mark.[89]

CHAPTER 19

Ethical Considerations[1]

Ethical considerations focus on the "what ifs" of life. Here's one "if": was it ethical for a medical doctor to treat a famous celebrity in an unusual, controversial manner, and in the process, allegedly manipulate a famous brand to jump-start his own career? We could call this an abuse of authority and thus a violation of a fiduciary and/or professional duty in an attempt for self-aggrandizement through the manipulation, association, theft, confusion, dilution, pirating, or infringement of a famous person's intellectual property.

Is it ethical to provide steroids to baseball players? Is it ethical for baseball management to instigate a war against steroid use even though steroids fueled a home run mania and saved baseball after the 1994 strike that cancelled the World Series? Of course, the president of the Texas Rangers, George Bush Jr., who later, as President in his January 2004 State of the Union address, said that our country's worst problem is steroid use in professional sports. Is it unethical to gain an unfair advantage? There are many unfair advantages in life; how about money, family, or talent—all can also be "unfair."

To digress, ethics are the universal and unchanging standards of what we should do; that is, what is good. Closely related to ethics is morality; morals are the standards that we adopt from a particular group at a particular time based on what people actually do. Ethics in intellectual property revolve around the theft, usurpation, or confusion (muddying the waters) of a second party's borrowing or tarnishing of the first party's intellectual property for the sole purpose of filthy lucre. Think of the trademarked logo as your team's money, and the unethical mirroring of that logo takes money that should belong to you. Is that an absolute? Probably not.

In *Hawaii-Pacific Apparel Group, Inc. v. Cleveland Browns Football Company LLC and National Football League Properties, Inc.,* 418 F. Supp. 2d 501 (S.D.N.Y. 2006), the question is whether a trademark can be abandoned. In 1984, Browns players and fans started to refer to the team's defense—and, eventually, the team's fans—as the "Dawg Pound," which eventually jump-started the sale of Browns-related merchandise. CLEVELAND BROWNS DAWGS and a design of three dogs in football uniforms was officially registered by the State of Ohio in 1988, as was a similar design for CLEVELAND BROWNS DOGS. Each of these trademark registrations expired ten years after the date of issuance.

In 1995, the Browns franchise moved to Baltimore and became known as the Baltimore Ravens. Thus, the "Dawg Pound" no longer existed. During this period when there was no "Dawg Pound," HP, a private company, sold its DAWG-related apparel in national chains.

In 1999, the Browns and the "Dawg Pound" returned to Cleveland. On March 26, the Browns filed an intent-to-use application with the PTO for the DAWG POUND mark. In August of 1999, the application was rejected on account of its similarity to, and corresponding likelihood of confusion with, HP's LIL DAWG POUND mark, which had been registered successfully in 1996. What are the ethical issues here? Were the HP actions legal? Yes. Were they ethical? Probably yes, as they were just sharp businessmen who could not be accused of diluting the mark, since at the relevant time period, it appeared to be abandoned and thus usable under the "fair use" doctrine.[2]

Fake Movies

In the movie and musical, *The Producers,* Mel Brooks's fabricated play, *Springtime for Hitler,* was a ruse to lure blue-haired old ladies into financing a flop, 10,000 times over. *Argo,* Ben Affleck's Academy Award–winning movie, was about the real-life ruse to produce a fake movie entitled *Argo,* a "science fantasy," that was to be produced in Iran as a means to secretly extract the hostages who were hiding in the Canadian embassy.

In Great Britain, three would-be producers were convicted of tax fraud by creating a "fake" movie:

In some ways 'A Landscape of Lies' was a typical indie film, with a tiny budget, a B-list cast and an award from an American film festival.

What made it special is that it was created solely to cover up a huge tax fraud.

Five people in Britain face jail sentences after being convicted... of attempting to bilk the government of $4.2 million in a moviemaking scam reminiscent of Academy Award-winning hit 'Argo'—without the heroic hostage rescue.

Prosecutors and tax authorities say the fraudsters claimed to be producing a made-in-Britain movie with unnamed A-list actors and an approximately $30 million budget supplied by a Jordanian firm.

In fact, officials say, the project was a sham, set up to claim almost $2.2 million goods and services for work that had not been done, as well as $1.9 million under a government program that allows filmmakers to claim back up to 25 percent of their expenditures as tax relief.

Britain's tax agency... said that the filmmakers had submitted paperwork and already received $2.5 million when checks revealed that the work had not been done and most of the so-called suppliers and film studies had never heard of the gang.

The self-described movie producers were arrested on suspicion of tax fraud in April 2011—and decided their best shot at avoiding criminal charges was to hastily make a film. 'A Landscape of Lies' did garner some fans, winning a commendation called a Silver Ace award at last year's Las Vegas Film Festival. (AP, "5 Convicted of Film-Tax Fraud," Houston Chronicle @A2, March 16, 2013)

Are these ruses unethical? Should Mel Brooks, Ben Affleck, and/or the producers of "A Landscape of Lies" manufacture such fabrications to distort copyright protection? Ethics are our better angels. In *Argo*, the "lie" was for a good cause. In *Springtime for Hitler (and Germany)*, Zero Mostel was not purposefully unethical. And in *A Landscape of Lies*, at the end of the day, an award-winning move was produced (for a pittance!). "Bait-and-switch" maneuvers whose sole goal is to diminish a valued copyright or trademark or patent or trade secret protection for the purpose of pecuniary gain is certainly unethical. We are not sure if the ruses of these three movies are *per se* "unethical"—shady with *The Producers,* not well-intended with *Landscape,* but in *Argo,* since the motivation and process was ethical and patriotic and noble, the result was also ethical (and patriotic and noble). Patriotism trumps copyright, or, in this case, fake copyright.

Ethical Considerations of "Spygate" and the "Bounty" Scandal

The so-called "Spygate" scandal is well-known and involves the theft of trade secrets in the form of plays, formations, and audibles by one Bill Belichick, legendary coach of the New England Patriots, who stole the signals of rival football teams by "spying" on their practices. Coach Belichick instructed an agent to surreptitiously videotape the other teams' coaches and players with the purpose of illegally recording, capturing, and stealing their signals and visual coaching techniques. Coach was fined and punished by the NFL, but he also violated a code of ethics by stealing the trade secrets of the competing teams.[3]

The "Bounty" scandal was NFL Commissioner Goodell's reaction to the New Orleans Saints allegedly specifically paying bounties to injure particular players on the opposing team. Is this unethical or merely unsportsmanlike behavior? Or is it just "gamesmanship?" Is there a difference between "play hard, hurt those guys" and "break number 42's legs?" Probably so; and remember, the soon-to-be-injured football star is not only a person but a conglomerate of intellectual property protections buzzing around his head like so many angry bees. Injuring a player and ruining his career may also tarnish or diminish that player's intellectual property rights.

Cybersquatting

Athletes and entertainers have domain names that protect their valuable trademarks. Other folks who are not associated with the trademark in any way buy the famous domain name and squat on it to gain money and fame. The Anticybersquatting Consumer Protection Act of 1999 is a tool that can be used to fight against cybersquatters. Many times, the usurpers register the famous domain name, or something that sounds similar, so as to use it as a fan website.

In *Eldrick "Tiger" Woods, for Itself, Tiger Woods and His Minor Child, Charlie Axel Woods v. Josh Whitford*, WIPO Claim No. FA0905001263352 (2009), Tiger tried to register his infant son's name as a domain name, but some usurper had gotten there first and tried to sell it on eBay, nine days after the child's birth (<charliesaxelwoods.com>). The panel found that Woods did not have trademark rights in "Charlie Axel Woods."[4] Were the defendant's actions unethical? Yes. Were they illegal? No. The best way to explain it is to say that the legal penalties against cybersquatting have not caught up to the moral imperative of protecting your son's image and intellectual property rights from cross exploitation.

Theft, Piracy, Dilution, Infringement, and Confusion[5]

Athletes and entertainers must take the necessary steps to protect their images and rights of publicity then "police" the authorized or unauthorized use of their image to ensure their rights are not being infringed upon. Universities and amateur athletics associations also must monitor and protect their intellectual property on a global basis to prevent others from diluting or tarnishing their images and logos (think "Johnny Football").

The NFL's Super Bowl is the merchandizing bonanza that enters into contracts with numerous licensees who are contractually authorized to sell NFL-branded goods. But many unlicensed vendors attempt to profit from the goodwill of the NFL's intellectual property. Many individuals sell knock-off goods and illegal merchandise without NFL approval.

The Internet revolutionized the way fans view and participate in sports; for example, the "real-time" gamecasts on the Internet, fantasy websites using player statistics, digital technology, and streaming videos all create ethical and intellectual property issues. What is theft on the Internet? What is copyright piracy?

In *State of Utah v. Ted Frampton*, 737 P.2d 183 (1987), the court discussed the issue of counterfeit merchandise in the form of baseball gloves, in which defendant possessed with the intent to sell counterfeit gloves offered and disguised as genuine Wilson gloves, complete with Wilson's A200 trademark. This is called a "knock-off" and is *de facto* unethical and illegal.

The Internet has magnified the concerns of copyright owners as to how to stop the unauthorized use and infringement of their intellectual property rights. With immediately available information, theft and infringement of copyrighted material is now easier for pirating criminals.

However, parodies are not infringement. For example, the good Dr. Seuss could not successfully sue for infringement when Penguin Books (who should have known better) published a book entitled *The Cat Not in the Hat! A Parody by Dr. Juice*. All you need to know about this book is to compare Dr. Seuss's line "One fish, two fish, red fish, blue fish, black fish, blue fish, old fish, new fish," to Dr. Juice's line, "One knife? Two knife? Red knife? Dead wife" (*Penguin Books, USA, Inc. v. Dr. Seuss Enterprises*, 924 F. Supp. 1559 [S.D. Cal. 1996]).

In *Bouchat v. Baltimore Ravens, Inc.*, 214 F.3d 350 (4th Cir. 2000), Frederick Bouchat, an amateur artist/security guard, created drawings and design for Baltimore's new NFL team, the Ravens, including a Raven holding a shield. Bouchat gave his design as affixed to a mini-helmet to a state official in the building where Bouchat was a guard. The Ravens, of course, initially stiffed him, but Bouchat ultimately obtained a copyright for his shield design. Did the Ravens steal his design? Yes. However, fair use of copyrighted material is not considered to be infringement.

In *Burnett v. Twentieth Century Fox Film Corporation,* 491 F. Supp. 2d 962 (C.D. Cal. 2007), the world famous comedienne and entertainer Carol Burnett sued *Family Guy* for an episode entitled "Peterotica." Near the beginning of the episode, the Griffin family patriarch, Peter Griffin, an "Archie Bunker"-like character, enters a porn shop with his friends. Upon entering, Peter remarks that the porn shop is cleaner than he expected. One of Peter's friends explains that "Carol Burnett works part time as a janitor." The screen then switches for less than five seconds to an animated figure resembling the "Charwoman" from the Carl Burnett Show, mopping the floor next to seven blowup dolls, a rack of XXX movies, and a curtained room with a design above it reading "Video Booths." As the "Charwoman" mops, a "slightly altered version of Carol's Theme from The Carol Burnett Show is playing." The scene switches back to Peter and his friends. One of the friends remarks: "You know, when she tugged her ear at the end of that show, she was really saying goodnight to her mom." Another friend responds, "I wonder what she tugged to say goodnight to her dad," finishing with a comic's explanation, "Oh!" This blaspheme was legal under the doctrines of parody and fair use. Does it make a legal difference that the *Family Guy* producers obviously knew that Carol Burnett did not have an incestuous relationship with her father? No; it was a parody. But the producers were unethical for not doing the right thing. "And for what?" as was asked in *Fargo* by Frances McDormand in the closing shot. "For a little bit of money."

Trademarks are ubiquitous in the business marketplace. Trademarks can define the business and establish goodwill; the trademarks are recognized globally. A trademark can be a word, a name, a symbol, or a device used by a manufacturer or merchant to identify its goods and to help distinguish the goods from other merchants' goods. Knock-offs are the bane of the existence of trademark holders. Sub-par goods may tarnish the actual mark and cause the business to lose customers. It is expensive to create the right snappy jingle that attracts customers. Once established, others might copy or infringe that mark, so the holder must police the mark against infringement.

In *PlayMakers, LLC v. ESPN, Inc.,* 297 F. Supp. 2d 1277 (W.D. Wash. 2003), plaintiff is a small sports agency and ESPN is a multimedia sports entertainment cable network. ESPN promotes a dramatic series called

"Playmakers." Plaintiff could prevail here because it could prove the likelihood of consumer confusion.

In *Dallas Cowboys v. America's Team Properties, Inc.*, C.A. No. 306-CV-1960K (N.D. Tex. 2006), the Cowboys sought to cement their legal claim to the phrase "America's team," which they had been using as a service mark and trademark since 1979. In *Young Jr., v. Vannerson*, 612 F. Supp. 2d 829 (S.D. Tex. 2009), the court discussed a trademark dispute over rights to the marks "VY" and "INVINCEABLE." Vince Young, a professional football player, asserts that he is widely known by his initials—"VY" —and his nickname—"Invincible." Young asserts that he is a senior user of the marks and has a common-law ownership interest in the trademark rights.

Trademark dilution is the "whittling away" of the distinctiveness or goodwill of a mark. Many states have anti-dilution laws to prevent merchants from "free riding" on the goodwill of others. The Federal Trademark Dilution Act of 1995 (FTDA) provides owners of famous trademarks some protection against those parties diluting or tarnishing their trademarks. In *The Heisman Trophy Trust v. Smack Apparel Co.*, 595 F. Supp. 2d 320 (2009), the Heisman Trophy Trust alleged that Smack Apparel Company continues to infringe and dilute The Heisman Trust's trademarks. The Heisman Trust alleges that it has also acquired common law trademark rights through its extensive use of its registered and unregistered trademarks. Smack Apparel is a clothing manufacturer that sells principally to retailers and operates a website through which it also sells its apparel. The Heisman Trust alleges that Smack Apparel first made unlawful use of the Heisman Marks in 1999, when a college football player who was a candidate for the Heisman Trophy that year was arrested for shoplifting. Smack Apparel produced a T-shirt with the word "Heistman" and a depiction of the football player from the Heisman Trophy statuette holding a shopping bag in his hand.

In the years since the settlement agreement, Smack Apparel has occasionally produced T-shirts promoting the candidacies of potential Heisman Trophy winners, including one series of T-shirts in 2002, and another in 2007. In the fall of 2008, Smack Apparel produced thirteen varieties of Heisman Trophy-related T-shirts. The Heisman Trust then filed the underlying suit, alleging breach of contract (referring to the settlement agreement), as well as trademark infringement and dilution. The Smack Apparel T-shirts also use a font that is virtually identical to the font used on the T-shirts licensed by The Heisman Trust and on The Heisman Trust's website.

Sometimes a party will make fun of a copyright or trademark through the use of a parody or spoof. Even though the mark is being used, it may not be an infringement of the mark. The First Amendment to the U.S. Constitution can be a factor in determining whether parody can be a proper defense to the use of a trademark. Trademark infringement is concerned with the consumer being confused by the use of the mark, but that is not the case with a parody. To operate as a parody, the mark must merely "conjure up" or suggest the owner's trademark to the consumer.[6]

Remember Napster? At the time Napster was shut down in 2001, it was estimated that 75 million Napster users were exchanging 10,000 music files every second. During the Napster trial, an expert witness for the music industry observed a disagreeable new attitude in America that downloaded songs should be free. Napster eventually did shut down in a firestorm of copyright infringement claims.

"In a recent *New York Magazine* article, however, Michael Wolff wrote that not everybody—75 million people—could be an outlaw and that it was not so much Napster users who were on the wrong side of the law as the entertainment industry that is on the wrong side of economics laws" (Gardner, 44 IDEA at 239). So, are these 75 million people all criminals? Are they unethical? No.

There is also the intellectual property of the right of publicity, which can be defined as the right to use, without a license, the identity of a real person to attract attention to an advertisement. In the Lew Alcindor case (*Abdul Jabbar v. GMC*, 85 F.3d 407 [9th Cir. 1996]), General Motors ran a television advertisement for Oldsmobile cars. This ad ran during the NCAA men's basketball tournament. The voice-over asked "Who holds the record for being voted the most outstanding player of this tournament?" On screen appeared the answer: "Lew Alcindor, UCLA, '67, '68, '69." Once having attracted the viewers' attention, the advertisement proceeded to laud Oldsmobile, using sports metaphors that echoed Alcindor's accomplishments. This was infringement, since the information was conveyed in an advertisement for a commercial product. This was not only infringement, but it was unethical also, since they knew it was wrong and they borrowed information on him for less than laudable reasons.

The *Cardtoons* case (*Cardtoons v. MLBPA*, 95 F.3d 959 [10th Cir. 1996]) concerns sports trading cards and the question is whether trading cards are communicative—like stories in *Sports Illustrated*—or commercial—like the use of a ball player's name on a model of sports shoe or baseball bat. In the 1996 *Cardtoons* case, the Tenth Circuit applied

Oklahoma law and balanced the right of publicity against a First Amendment defense. In doing this, the court dismissed a right of publicity claim against a company that made baseball cards that parodied prominent professional baseball players. The court found that the parody baseball trading cards were not commercial speech but were to be classified so as to receive "full First Amendment protection." The court said that in order to adequately poke fun at the plaintiffs, defendant had no feasible alternative other than to use plaintiffs' identities and to use the baseball trading card format to do so. The court concluded that parody trading cards are not commercial speech—they do not merely advertise another product.

Is the unauthorized use of a person's identity on a T-shirt protected by the First Amendment? Defendant artist drew a sketch of the Three Stooges and sold prints and T-shirts with the sketch on it. The owner of the post mortem right of publicity of the Three Stooges obtained an injunction, defendant's profits of $75,000.00 and attorney fees. Defendant argued that the First Amendment immunized this use because a T-shirt is a "communicative" medium of expression. The court rejected this, noting that neither defendant's T-shirts nor its prints conveyed any "message" other than a picture of the Three Stooges. Similarly the court rejected the defense that this was "art" and therefore immune (*Comedy III Prods., Inc. v. Gary Saderup, Inc.*, 68 Cal. App. 4th 744 [Cal. Ct. App. 1998]).

In the Tiger Woods painting case, a federal court in Ohio dismissed Woods's claim that his right of publicity under Ohio law had been infringed by defendant's use of Woods's likeness in prints of defendant's painting of Tiger Woods in action on the golf course (*ETW Corp. v. Jireh Publ'g, Inc.*, 99 F. Supp. 2d 829 [N.D. Ohio 2000]). The court found that such an unauthorized use of the image of a famous athlete was protected by principles of free artistic expression because paintings and drawings are protected by the First Amendment. The fact that the painting was reproduced and sold in an edition of 5,000 prints was found not to convert the artistic image into a commercial product. Instead, the court stated that the print at issue is an artistic creation seeking to express a message. The fact that it is sold did not negate its First Amendment protection.[7]

Newcombe contends that his right of privacy was violated, and his likeness was used against his permission for commercial advantage in violation of his statutory and common law rights of privacy. His right to privacy was violated since the likeness in the ad was undeniably a depiction of Newcombe, and it was readily identifiable as him. Defendant had a duty to find out who the player in the picture was. *Sports Illustrated* also had an ethical obligation in the publishing of the ad, especially in light of its content and Newcombe's history.[8]

Ethics in Licensing and Sponsorship Agreements

The licensing of sponsorship agreements is worth billions of dollars. For example, the NCAA protects its intellectual property of logos, etc. The NCAA instituted an "NCAA Trademark Protective Program." They own many marks; here are some of the marks the NCAA constantly monitors:

65 Teams . . . One Dream™
And Then There Were Four™
College World Series™
Final 4™
Frozen Four™
It's More Than A Game™
March Madness™
Middle School Madness™
Midnight Madness™
Men's Elite Eight™
Men's Final Four™
Men's Frozen Four™
The Big Dance™
The Final Four™
The Greatest Show on Dirt™
The Road Ends Here™
The Road to Atlanta™
The Road to Cary™
The Road to Cleveland™
The Road to Detroit™
The Road to Indianapolis™
The Road to Minneapolis™
The Road to New Orleans™
The Road to Omaha™
The Road to San Antonio™
The Road to San Diego™
The Road to St. Louis™
The Road to the Final Four™
We are the Game™
Women's Frozen Four™

Michael Vick's troubles with the NFL are well known. When he first got into trouble for participating in dog fighting, the NFL suspended the sale of "Vick-related merchandise" on NFL.com. The NFL said selling his merchandise was "not appropriate under the circumstances." After Vick returned to the NFL from prison, the NFL began to sell jerseys that could be custom ordered for pets. In September 2009, Vick's jersey was the NFL's top seller.[9]

Because of franchise owners' and leagues' increased emphasis on profits in the modern era of sports, franchises are no longer connected to the city in which they play; instead, franchises have become "free agents." "Franchise free agency" is the tendency of NFL franchises to shop for a new home when their current situation is less than ideal.

In *Indianapolis Colts, Inc. v. Metropolitan Baltimore Football Club Limited Partnership*, 34 F.3d 410 (7th Cir. 1994), the court analyzed the likelihood of confusion between marks. In 1942, a football team began competing in the city of Baltimore under the name "Baltimore Colts." The Colts became one of the most illustrious teams in the history of professional football. In 1984, the Baltimore Colts moved to Indianapolis. The city of Baltimore was awarded a Canadian Football League franchise in 1993, and the citizens of Baltimore succeeded in having the Colts chosen as their mascot. The Indianapolis Colts of the NFL and the NFL itself brought a trademark infringement suit based on likelihood of confusion, seeking to permanently enjoin the Baltimore CFL franchise from calling itself the Colts.

There is also the concept of trademark dilution. The theory behind dilution is that some mark holders should be able to prevent use of their marks on other products, even when use of the mark will not cause confusion. This type of dilution is known as blurring. Blurring occurs when the use of the mark for a different purpose weakens the unique and distinctive significance of the mark in its original use.[10]

Protecting the Celebrity's Image and Right of Publicity

Famous athletes possess a commercial value in their name and likeness. Companies pay large amounts of money to athletes for their endorsement; therefore, athletes must make every effort to protect the use of their image and likeness. In *Ali v. Playgirl, Inc.*, 447 F. Supp. 723 (1978), Muhammad Ali, the former heavyweight boxing champion of the world, brought an action for damages against Playgirl, Inc., for its alleged unauthorized printing, publication, and distribution of an objectionable portrait of Ali in the February 1978 issue of *Playgirl Magazine*.

The portrait depicts a nude black man that resembles Ali seated in the corner of a boxing ring. Ali alleges that the publication of this picture constitutes a violation of his right of publicity. Although the picture is captioned "Mystery Man," the identification of the individual as Ali is further implied by an accompanying verse that refers to "the Greatest," which, undeniably, was his *nom de guerre.*

Should an athlete be able to protect a self-designated nickname such as "The Greatest?" Maybe not; but here the photo infringed on his right of privacy and the commercial exploitation of his name and likeness.

Pitcher Nolan Ryan was sued by a Texas couple who claimed he breached a contract for the exclusive right to sell the likeness of his pitching hand. New England star quarterback Tom Brady sued Yahoo! over the use of his image to promote fantasy football games. Brady said Yahoo! used his photo without his permission in a September 2006 *Sports Illustrated* ad and in its banner ads on Yahoo!

Kareem Abdul-Jabbar was a great NBA player, maybe the greatest (Okay, the greatest center). His "sky hook" dominated the league for many years. Should he capitalize on his "Sky Hook" and be able to use the term in marketing? In fact, that is exactly what he did. Abdul-Jabbar stated he hopes to use proceeds from "Sky Hook" apparel sales to raise money for schools.

The NFLPA dealt with fantasy sports leagues in *CBS Interactive, Inc., v. National Football League Players Association, Inc.* Should football statistics be treated any differently from baseball statistics in dealing with the right of publicity? In January 2010, Shaquille O'Neal sued a Las Vegas company over the word "Shaqtus." When O'Neal played for the Phoenix Suns, he was known as "the Big Cactus" and "the Big Shaqtus." Do you consider this an infringement upon Shaq's right of publicity? Do you consider this stealing?[11]

CHAPTER 20

Hip Hop and Intellectual Property

"I sit alone in my four-cornered room staring at candles" (Ghetto Boyz, "My Mind's Playing Tricks on Me"). Hip-hop is life today. It's music, it's culture, it's a way of life. It also permeates with intellectual property concerns, mostly because of its tendency to "sample" from other songs, motifs, logos, etc. Hip-hop is rife with free speech, First Amendment, and intellectual property concerns. Copyright law affects hip-hop's creativity and accessibility by requiring licenses for even "de minimus" sampling of music.

There is a deep distrust of the law in the urban hip-hop community. Sometimes, such as Ice-T's "Cop Killer" and Dr. Dre and Snoop Dogg's "Deep Cover," the form of expression takes a desire to inflict violence upon police. In *Skyywalker Records, Inc. v. Navarro*, 737 F. Supp. 578 (S.D. Fla. 1990), a complaint was made to the Broward County Sheriff concerning the graphic nature of 2 Live Crew's "As Nasty as They Wanna Be" then being sold in local retail music stores. The deputy assigned to investigate the complaint prepared an affidavit concerning his findings and filed it, along with a tape cassette of the album and a transcript of six of the tape's 18 songs, in the county circuit court. The judge agreed and issued an order finding probable cause to believe that the recording was obscene under Florida law. Local law enforcement "visited" several of the music store managers, provided them with a copy of the order, and warned them "as a matter of courtesy" that any further sale of the album would result in arrest. While the district court agreed that the recording was obscene under Florida law, it also found that the Sheriff's Office violated the First and Fourteenth Amendments by prior restraint of speech. The Eleventh Circuit Court disagreed, however, and found the district court's decision that the album "had no artistic value" was arbitrary.

"Hip-hop" is more than just a style of music. It is the manner of dress, dialect, and language preferred by a large segment of the population born between 1965 and 1984. Three of its four principal elements are grounded in music: emceeing (or "MCing," sometimes "rapping"), disc jockeying ("DJing"), break dancing, and graffiti. Its essence, however, is MCing and DJing. A form of verbal expression deeply rooted in ancient African culture and oral tradition shaped by contributions from the R&B, Caribbean, and other forms in the early 1970s; MCing or rapping is the performance of complex rhyming lyrics that often are spoken against a backdrop of music or a beat rather than sung. Generally, the hip-hop artist composes his or her own lyrics and uses the lyrics of others only to show respect or to call out the author to battle.[1]

"The sampler is a tool and a music instrument. That's how I always thought about it . . . [T]he sampler is an instrument that I play." RZA, from the Wu Tang Clan, continues, "I've always been into using the sampler more like a painter's palette than a Xerox" (The RZA, The Wu-Tang Manual 192 [2005]). The sampler is like a musical instrument or an artistic tool. Sampling is hip-hop; it creates its unique collage-like artistry which is very similar to the oral tradition of adding and supplementing, as witnessed in African-American spirituals and chants.

In *Campbell v. Acuff Rose, Inc.,* 510 U.S. 569 (1994), the Supreme Court ruled in favor of hip-hop artists 2 Live Crew's mocking version of Roy Orbison's "Oh, Pretty Woman." 2 Live Crew parodied (or mocked) Orbison's haunting ballad. Parody is just another version of sampling. This parody was without the consent of the original copyright owner. Here, 2 Live Crew actually offered to pay royalties for the use of the song but was refused. However, 2 Live Crew still included "Pretty Woman" in their 1980 LP release "As Clean As They Wanna Be" with the same opening lyrics, drum beat, and bass riff but transmorphing Roy's icon of feminist beauty into a "big hairy woman."[2]

Sampling and Copyrights

In *Newton v. Diamond,* 349 F.3d 591 (9th Cir. 2003), the famous Beastie Boys sampled a six-second, three-note segment from jazz flautist James Newton. The Beastie Boys, however, obtained a license to sample from Newton's sound recording, but they did not obtain a license to sample from the musical composition. As regards copyright infringement, the standard for hip-hop sampling appears to be measuring the similarity of the two works.

De minimus copying is allowed, and the test is whether the average audience would recognize the appropriation. *Bridgeport Music, Inc. v. Dimension Films,* 401 F.3d 647 (6th Cir. 2003) involved a two-second sample of an arpeggiated guitar chord from a song by George Clinton and the Funkadelics; the sample was lowered, looped, and extended to sixteen beats, extended to seven seconds, and repeated five times in the song "100 Miles and Runnin," which was used in the movie soundtrack for "I Got the Hook Up." This *de minimus* sampling was allowed, at least in the Sixth Circuit.

In *Grand Upright v. Warner Bros. Records,* 780 F. Supp. 182 (S.D.N.Y. 1991), old school hip-hop artist Biz Markie sampled Gilbert O'Sullivan's song "Alone Again Naturally." The court found that Biz Markie requested but was denied permission to sample and had infringed Gilbert O'Sullivan's copyright. The court saw this sampling as "theft."

In *Williams v. Broadus,* 2001 WL 894714 (S.D.N.Y.), rapper Snoop Dogg was sued over his use of an allegedly unauthorized sample. The court utilizes a "substantial similarity" test and finds that a sample that is not qualitatively or quantitatively similar to the sampled sound recording is not a violation of the copyright holder's right to create a derivative work.

In summary of the major digital sampling cases: "In Grand Upright, one person owned both the copyright in the underlying composition and the copyright in the master recording, permission was sought by Biz Markie and not received, and the final court ruling was in favor of the original artist. In Newton, the Beastie Boys paid for the rights to sample the sound recording but did not obtain a license for the underlying musical composition from the original recording artist, but still won the case under the substantial similarity and de minimus tests. In Bridgeport, the defendant-sampler had entered into a license agreement for the musical composition copyright but did not get a copyright to sample the digital sound recording, and eventually lost against the company owning the sound recording copyright under the theory that any sampling of a sound recording is *per se* infringement" (22 St. Johns J. Legal Comment. at 406.)[3]

Hip-Hop and Trademarks

"Hip-hop's view of originality and imitation appears to be tinged with trademark-like ideas as much as explicit ideas about expression and creativity" (20 Tex. Intell. Prop. L.J. at 140). The key is whether the cultural reaction to the copying is based on consent (ghosting) or non-consent (biting), which is more problematic. Another key question is whether the source of the expression is easily identifiable. In some instances of quoting within hip-hop, an explicit shout-out is given to the originator by the imitator; for example, Snoop Dogg shouts out in covering La Di Da Di. Other times, the source material is well known and identified with the originator, so that no shout-out is necessary. For example, Rappers Delight originated with the Sugar Hill Gang, so Def Squad quotes it as accepted homage. If the source material is relatively obscure, however, and if there is no shout-out or other explicit acknowledgment of origin, the copier is biting, and is essentially engaging in the tort of passing off in the hip-hop marketplace. (*Id.*)

> Another question is whether the imitation is used as a springboard for the imitator's own creativity. If that's the case, then it is likely that the copying will be perceived as quoting or sampling, both of which are culturally acceptable.
>
> Is the imitation brand-enhancing for the source? If the imitation calls attention to the source's work and either identifies the source or uses an iconic source that needs no explicit identification, the imitator may reinforce the value of the contribution that the source has made to the music, thereby enhancing the source's brand. Homage quoting and sampling both have this value-reinforcing quality. Even battle quoting may create buzz (and sales) around the source in the course of disparaging it. As such uses enhance the goodwill of the originator and inure to that person's benefit, the hip-hop community is likely to accept them as permissible copying. (*Id.*)
>
> The final question is whether the imitation contributes to an overall conversation in the hip-hop culture. If the imitation is expressive, it will be more acceptable to the community. The bottom line is that the imitation paradigm in hip-hop focuses on marketplace impact. The concern is not with copying *per se,* but copying that constitutes passing off. The verdict on a particular instance of copying is based on at least a tacit examination of the goodwill effects—whether the copying usurps or enhances the goodwill of the originator as a purveyor of creative works in the marketplace. As it mainly condemns passing off and usurpation, the paradigm leaves plenty of room for 'no-trademark' uses of existing works (*Id.*).[4]

Unauthorized Use of Brand Names

The use of product endorsement in entertainment is not new. Product use is generally linked with advertising through paid product placement and integration. With the advent and increased popularity of technologies like TiVo that record shows and bypass traditional commercials, methods of embedding commercial information into the actual media content becomes more important. In hip-hop, it appears that the artists include brand names in their songs without receiving any form of compensation. But see, for example, "Now I got to give a shout-out to Seagram's Gin 'cause I drink it, and they paying me for it" (Petey Pablo in "Freek-a-Leek").

In films, product placement goes as far back as the 1980s. Who can forget the product placement of Reese's Pieces in "E.T.?" "While the movie and television industries have longer and deeper histories of product placement and integration, the music industry appears to be a strong emerging market. Historically, there are some very popular and well-known brand name references in music, such as Janis Joplin's "Mercedes Benz" ("Oh, Lord, won't you buy me a Mercedes Benz"). However, the overwhelming number of brand name mentions in music derives from the rap/hip-hop genre; and while some of those mentions are intentional commercial placements, such as Petey Pablo's shout-out, it is estimated that 90% of the mentions are unpaid (8 Tex. Rev. Ent. & Sports L. at 5).

Hip-hop artists usually refer to well-known and well-protected brand names, so an owner would have no trouble proving validity— "I got Lamborghini doors on my Escalade." After validity, plaintiff must prove actual infringement. The test is to determine the likelihood of confusion among consumers (*Parks v. LaFace Records*, 329 F.3d 439 [6th Cir. 2003]).

The second likelihood of confusion test is the "alternative avenues" test. The Rosa Parks court summarizes the "alternative avenues" test as follows: "A title of an expressive work will not be protected from a false advertising claim if there are sufficient alternative means for an artist to convey his or her idea."

Language from the Rosa Parks case may be misinterpreted, however, to conclude that all song uses are expressive. In criticizing the factors test, the court stated: "This approach ignores the fact that the artistic work is not simply a commercial product but is also a means of communication" (*Id.* at 19).

"In the majority of cases, rap/hip-hop artists are most likely using brand names simply as source-identifiers. If that use is challenged as an infringement, a court should apply the factors test, composed of the traditional eight factors. . . . [H]owever, the first four factors are completely or partially inapplicable to this kind of use, simply because the use is not related to a competing product. The most relevant factors are probably three of the last four: (5) the actual or potential likelihood for confusion; (6) the defendant's intent to confuse the public . . . and (8) the sophistication of consumers" (*Id.*).

In *New Kids on the Block v. News America Pub., Inc.* (971 F.2d 302 [9th Cir. 1992]), the New Kids court ruled that there are three elements to satisfying a nominative fair use defense: "Where the defendant uses a trademark to describe the plaintiff's product rather than its own, we hold that a commercial user is entitled to nominative fair use defense provided he meets the following three requirements: First, the product or service in question must be one not readily identifiable without use of the trademark; second, only so much of the mark or marks may be used as is reasonably necessary to identify the product or service; and third, the user must do nothing that would, in conjunction with the mark, suggest sponsorship or endorsement by the trademark holder."

A standard use of a brand name in a song should easily pass the three requirements: (1) artists are referring to specific items that are only referable by their brand names; (2) artists verbally refer to the name so there is no question of incorporating the brand name's distinctive styling, and (3) there is usually no indication of any kind of sponsorship or endorsement.

Companies may try to bring infringement claims against hip-hop artists for uses they did not authorize; however, it appears that the artists have a good chance to defeat those claims. If a court recognizes the nominative fair use defense, artists may have an even better chance. But even without that, the multi-factor test for source-identifying uses creates a heavy burden of proving a likelihood of confusion.[5]

Notes

Chapter 1

1. See generally W. Champion, Sports Law: Cases, Documents, and Materials, 639, *et seq.* (New York: Aspen, 2005).

2. Andrew Dansby, "Reassessing the Monkees: Songs Ubiquitous for a Reason," *Houston Chronicle* at E1 (Mar. 2, 2012).

3. James Earl Jones as Terence Mann in *Field of Dreams,* a Phil Alden Robinson film (Universal City Studios Inc.; a Gordon Co. Production; written for screen and directed by Phil Alden Robinson; 1989).

4. Eric Berger, "Why Humans Make Cultural Leaps," Houston Chronicle at A4 (Mar. 2, 2012).

5. See generally Paul Goldstein, Intellectual Property. The Tough, New Realities That Could Make or Break Your Business 1, *et seq.* (New York: Portfolio, 2007).

6. See generally Michael Mandelbaum, The Meaning of Sports, Why Americans Watch Baseball, Football, and Basketball and What They See When They Do, 67 *et. seq.* (New York: Public Affairs, 2004).

7. *Id.* at 186 et seq.

8. Don Garber, "Major League Soccer: Establishing the World's Sports in a New America," at 110, *et seq.,* in The Business of Sports. Executives from Major Sports Franchises on How a Team Operates Behind the Scenes (Aspatore, Inc.: 2004).

9. Reprinted from *Open Sources Yoga Unity v. Choudhury,* 74 U.S.P.Q. 2d 1434 (N.D. Cal. 2005).

10. *Reed v. Peterson,* 2005 WL 1522187 (N.D. Cal.).

11. *Sullivan v. Author Solutions, Inc.,* 2008 WL 2937786 (E.D. Wisc.).

12. See generally Bolitho, "When Fantasy Meets the Courtroom: An Examination of the Intellectual Property Issues Surrounding the Burgeoning Fantasy Sports Industry," 67 Ohio St. L.J. 911 (2006); and Massari, "When Fantasy Meets Reality: The Clash Between On-Line Fantasy Sports Providers and Intellectual Property Rights," 19 Harv. J.L. & Tech. 443 (Spr. 2006).

13. See generally Das, "Offensive Protection: The Potential Application of Intellectual Property Law to Scripted Sports Plays," 75 Ind. L.J. 1073 (Summ. 2000); and Mobery, "Football Play Scripts: A Potential Pitfall for Federal Copyright Law?" 14 Marq. Sports L. Rev. 525 (Spr. 2004).

14. See generally Kukkonen, "Be a Good Sport and Refrain from Using My Patented Putt; Intellectual Property Protection for Sports Related Movements," 80 J. Pat. & Trademark Off. Soc. 808 (Nov. 1998); Kieff, Kramen, & Kunstadt, "It's Your Turn, 'But It's My Move: Intellectual Property Protection for Sports 'Moves,' "25 Santa Clara Comp. & High Tech. L. J. 765 (Apr. 2009); and Abromson, "The Copyrightability of Sports Celebration Moves: Dance Fever or Just Plain Sick?" 14 Marq. Sports L. Rev. 571 (Spr. 2004).

15. See *Bouchat v. Baltimore Ravens Football Club, Inc.*, 246 F.3d 514 (4th Cir. 2003); and *Bouchat v. Baltimore Ravens Football Club, Inc.*, 589 F. Supp.2d 686 (D. Md. 2008).

16. See generally McKelvey, "Commercial 'Branding': The Final Frontier or False Start for Athletes' Use of Temporary Tattoos as Body Billboards," 13 J. Legal Aspects of Sports 1 (Wint. 2003).

17. See generally *Id.*, at 7; Bolitho, 67 Ohio St. L.J. 911, 943 *et seq*; Lind, Siememsky, Selz, & Action 2 Entertainment Law 3d, Legal Concepts & Business Practices §§ 11:59, § 13.55, 1213.6213.62, 14.18.50; 20.57 (updated Dec. 2011); Biedermann, *et al.* Law and Business of the Entertainment Industries 260–63, 282–90, 456–459 (Westport, Ct.: Praeger, 5th ed. 2007); Garon, Entertainment Law and Practice 161 *et seq*. (Durham, N.C.: Carolina Academic Press, 2005); and Simensky, Entertainment Law 51–51, 76–94, 221–22 (New York: Matthew Bender, 1997).

Chapter 2

1. This chapter is co-authored by Dr. Lawrence Ruddell, Dean of Faculty at the Houston Campus of Belhaven University. He's a co-author with Prof. Champion and the late Prof. Thornton of Sports Ethics for Sports Management Professionals (Jones-Bartlett, 2012). He is also the author of Business Ethics – Faith That Works – Leading Your Company to Long Term Success (Houston: Halcyon Press, 2004).

2. The following is a general source note for § 2.5: Lori Bean, "Ambush Marketing: Sports sponsorship Confusion and the Lanham Act," 75 B.U.L. Rev. 1009 (Sept. 1995); Scott Bearby, "Marketing, Protection and Enforcement of NCAA Marks," 12 Marq. Sports L. Rev. S43 (Spring 2002); Scott McKelvy and John Grady "Ambush Marketing: The Legal Battleground for Sports Marketers," 21 Ent. & Sports Law 8 (Winter 2004); Anita Moorman and T. Christopher Greenwell, "Consumer Attitudes of Deception and the Legality of Ambush Marketing Practices," 15 J. Legal Aspects Sport 183 (Summer 205); Brian Pelanda, "Ambush Marketing Dissecting the Discourse," 34 Hastings Conn. & Ent. L.J. 341 (Spring 2012); and Patrick Sheridan, "An Olympic Solution to

Ambush Marketing: How the London Olympics Show the Way to More Effective Trademark Law," 17 Sports Law J. 27 (Spring 2010).

Chapter 3

1. See http://uslegal.com/entertainment-law.

2. "Take Me Out to the Ballgame: Patents and Trademarks Related to America's Favorite Pastime." U.S. P.T.O. Press Release, #01–50 (Oct. 26, 2001).

3. See Walter T. Champion, Sports Law Cases, Documents, and Materials, at 641–642 (Aspen 2005).

4. For a general source note for Section 3.3, see: Jeffrey Smith, "It's Your Move—No It's Not: The Application of Patent Law to Sports Moves," 70 U. Colo. L. Rev. 1051 (Summ. 1999); Karl Kukkovien, "Be a Good Sport and Refrain from Using My Patented Putt: Intellectual Property Protection for Sports Related Movements," 80 J. Pat.& Trademark Off. Soc'y 808 (Nov. 1998); Derek Bambauer, "Legal Responses to the Challenges of Sports Patents," 18 Harv. J.L. & Tech. 401 (Spr. 2005); L.J. Weber, "Something in the Way She Moves: The Case for Applying Copyright Protection to Sports Moves," 23 Colum.VLA J. L. & Arts 315 (2000); Robert Kunstadt, "Are Sports Moves Next in IP Law?" Natl. L.J. at C2 (May 20, 1996); and Richard Steuer, "A Patent on Baseball?" 14 SPG Antitrust 4 (Spr. 2000).

5. Ian Rainey, "The War Over Information Technology Patents: How Microsoft Is Reforming the Mobile Entertainment Industry," 2011 U. Den. Sports & Ent. L.J. 137 (Fall 2011).

6. "NASCAR Patent Suit Ends in $4 Million Licensing Deal," *Immersion Entm't v. NASCAR*," 4 No. 9 Andrews Patent Litig. Resp. 13 (Feb. 21, 2008).

Chapter 4

1. *See generally,* Marshall Leaffer, Understanding Copyright Law, 201–236 (3d, 1999, Matthew Bender).

2. Jack Gould, "Radio Music Dispute Raises Complex Issues," New York Times, 9 Feb 1941.

3. Thomas A. DeLong, The Mighty Music Box: The Golden Age of Musical Radio (Los Angeles: Amber Crest Books, 1980), p. 230.

4. Russell Sanjek, American Popular Music and Its Business: The First Four Hundred Years, Volume III: From 1900 to 1984 (New York: Oxford Press USA, 1988), p. 180.

5. Recording Industry Association of America, http://www.riaa.com/aboutus.php

6. Copyright Act of 1976, Pub. L. No. 94–553, 90 Stat. 2541 (for the general revision of copyright law, Title 17 of the United States Code, and for other purposes), October 19, 1976, with effect from January 1, 1978.

7. *See generally,* United States v. American Society of Composers, Authors, and Publishers, 2010 WL 3749292 (2d Cir. 2010).

8. The term "piracy" is generally used to describe the deliberate infringement of a copyright on a commercial scale.

9. A&M Records v. Napster, Inc., 239 F.3d 1004 (9th Cir. Cal. 2001).

10. Jeff Leeds, "Labels Win Suit Against Song Sharer," The New York Times, October 5, 2007. http://query.nytimes.com/gst/fullpage.html?res=9803E 2DD1739F936A35753C1A9619C8B63.

11. Sarah McBride, "Music Industry Wins Digital Piracy Case," The Wall Street Journal, October 5, 2007.

12. Whether making copyrighted works "available" to the public is a right protected by § 106(3) has divided the district courts. *Compare, e.g.,* Atl. Recording Corp. v. Howell, 554 F. Supp. 2d 976, 981–84 (D. Ariz. 2008), and London-Sire Records v. Doe 1, 542 F. Supp. 2d 153, 176 (D. Mass. 2008), with Motown Record Co. v. DePietro, No. 04-CV-2246, 2007 WL 576284, at *3 (E.D. Pa. Feb. 16, 2007), and Warner Bros. Records, Inc., v. Payne, No. W-06-CA-051, 2006 WL 2844415, at *3 (W.D. Tex. July 17, 2006).

13. James Walsh, "Brainerd Music Downloader Ordered to Pay $1.5 Million," Minneapolis StarTribune, November 3, 2010.

14. Capitol Records, Inc. v. Thomas-Rasset, Case 06-cv-01497-MJD/LIB (D. Minn 2011), Document 457: Memorandum of Law&Order," July 22, 2011. http://ia700504.us.archive.org/21/items /gov.uscourts.mnd.82850/gov.uscourts .mnd.82850.457.0.pdf.

15. United States v. ASCAP, 1940–43 Trade Cas. ¶56,104 (S.D.N.Y. 1941); United States v. Broadcast Music, Inc., 1940–43 Trade Cas. ¶56,096 (E.D. Wisc. 1941).

16. United States v. ASCAP, No. 42–245 (S.D.N.Y. 1947).

17. *See* Second Amended Final Judgment, United States v. ASCAP, No. 41–1395 (WCC) (S.D.N.Y. June 21, 2001).

18. United States v. American Society of Composers, Authors and Publishers, 2010 WL 3749292 (C.A. 2).

19. Cartoon Network LP v. CSC Holdings, Inc., 536 F.3d 121, 136 (2d Cir. 2008).

20. *See also,* Columbia Pictures Indus., Inc. v. Prof'l Real Estate Investors, Inc., 866 F.2d 278, 282 (9th Cir. 1989) (holding that renting videodiscs to a hotel guest for playback in the guest's room does not constitute the "transmission" of a public performance).

21. Bright Tunes Music Corp. v. Harrisongs Music, Ltd., 420 F. Supp. 177 (1976).

22. Steele v. Turner Broadcasting System, Inc., 646 F. Supp. 2d 185 (2009).

23. A&M Records, Inc. v. Napster, Inc., 239 F.3d 1004 (9th Cir. 2001), affirming, 114 F. Supp. 2d 896 (N.D. Cal. 2000).

24. 239 F.3d at 1015.

25. *Id.*

26. 239 F.3d at 1019–24.

27. *Id.*

28. Metro-Goldwyn-Mayer Studios, Inc. v. Grokster, Ltd., 518 F. Supp. 2d 1197 (C.D. Cal. 2007).

29. London-Sire Records v. Armstrong, 2006 WL 2349615 (D. Conn.).

Chapter 5

1. See generally, *Walt Disney Productions v. Air Pirates,* 518 F.2d 751 (9th Cir. 1978); Cox, "Don't Mess with the Mouse: Disney's Legal Army Protects a Revered Image, 11 National L.J. 2 (Jul. 31, 1989); and Bob Levin, The Pirates and the Mouse: Disney's War Against the Counterculture (Seattle: Fantagraphic Books, 2003).

2. U.S. Const. art.1, §8, cl. 8.

3. 17 U.S.C. § 102(a) (2012).

4. *Id.*

5. *Id.,* at 102(b).

6. Krasilovsky & Shemel, "This Business of Music" 90 (10th ed., 2007).

7. *Id.*; Copyright Act of 1976, Pub. L. No. 94–533, 90 Stat. 2541 (October 19, 1976).

8. Krasilovsky & Shemel, *supra* note 6.

9. 17 U.S.C. § 106(1) – (6) (2012).

10. Irah Donner, "The Copyright Clause of the U.S. Constitution: Why Did the Framers Include It with Unanimous Approval?" 36 Am. J. Legal Hist. 361 (1992).

11. *Id.* (citing B. Bugbee, Genesis of American Patent and Copyright Law 129 (1967). The patent clause was also included with the copyright clause and it too passed unanimously. *Id.* The actual author of the copyright clause is still unknown. However, most commentators believe that it was either James Madison or Charles C. Pinckney. *See* Fenning, "The Origin of the Patent and Copyright Clause of the Constitution," 17 Geo. L.J. 109 (1929).

12. *See* Krasilovsky & Shemel, *supra* note 60.

13. Krasilovsky & Shemel, *supra* note 1.

14. *Id.,* at 90.

15. *Id.,* at 91.

16. *Id.*

17. *Id.*

18. *Id.*

19. *Id.*

20. *Id.*

21. *See* generally, *Id.,* at 90–91, 110.

22. *Eldred v. Ashcroft,* 537 U.S. 186, 193 (2003).

23. *See Harper & Row, Publishers, Inc. v. National Enterprises,* 471 U.S. 539 (1985).

24. *See Eldred,* 537 U.S. at 197–199, 208, 211.

25. Krasilovsky & Shemel, *supra* note 6, at 112.

26. Biographies of 10 Classic Disney Characters, Walt Disney Archives, http://d23.disney.go.com/archives/biographies-of-10-classic-disney-characters/#MickeyMouse (last visited May 10, 2012).

27. *Walt Disney v. Powell,* 897 F.2d 565, 567–69 (D.C. Cir. 1990).

28. *Walt Disney Productions v. Air Pirates,* 581 F.2d 751–58 (9th Cir. 1978).

29. *Walt Disney Productions v. Mature Pictures Corp.,* 389 F. Supp. 1397, 1397 (S.D.N.Y. 1975).

30. Tom W. Bell, *Copyright Duration and the Mickey Mouse Curve* (Aug. 6, 2009), http://techliberation.com/2009/ 08/06/copyright-duration-and-the-mickey-mouse-curve/.

Chapter 6

1. Walter Champion, Sports Law: Cases, Documents, and Materials, at 669 (New York, 2005).

2. *See* In re NCAA Student Athlete Name & Likeness Litigation, 2011–1 Trade Cas. (CCH) 77448, 2011 WL 1642256 (N.D. Cal. 2011); Keller v. EA, 2010 WL 530108 (N.D. Cal. 2010); Hart v. EA, 740 F. Supp. 2d 658 (D. J.J. 2010), M. S.J. Gr., 808 F. Supp. 2d 757 (D. N.J. 2011); and Andy Latack, "Quarterback Sneak With Its College Football Video Game, EA Sports Is Making an End Run Around the NCAA's Rules," 2006 FEB Legal Aff. 69 (Jan./Feb., 2006).

3. *See* generally, Biederman et al. Law and Business of the Entertainment Industries, at 10.7.1 – 10.7.3, pp. 865–867 (5th, 2007).

4. Dana Howells, "Log Me In to the Old Ballgame: CBC Distribution & Marketing, Inc. v. Major League Baseball Advanced Media, LP," 22 Berkeley Tech. L.J. 471, 488–489 (2007).

5. Parrish v. NFLPA, Inc., 2007 WL 1674601 (N.D. Cal.), 2008 WL 1925208 (W.D. Call.), mot. den. 2009 WL 88484 (N.D. Cal.). See Also, Walter Champion, Fundamentals of Sports Law, at §20.3, p. 425 & §20.2, p. 46, 2012–2013 Ann. Supp. (2d ed., 2004).

6. Robert Trent Jones II, Inc. v. GFSI, Inc., 537 F. Supp. 2d, 1061 (N.D. Cal. 2008).

7. *Id.,* at 1065–1068.

8. 130 S.Ct. 2201 (2010).

9. NFLP, Inc. v. Wichita Falls Sportswear, Inc., 532 F. Supp. 651 (W.D. Wash. 1982).

10. *Id.,* at 654–656.

11. Biederman, Law and Business of the Entertainment Industries, at 865.

12. Fleischer Studios, Inc. v. AVELA, Inc., 636 F.3d 1115 (9th Cir. 2011), opin. w/d w.rev'd opin. 654 F.3d 958 (9th Cir. 2011); *see also* Fleischer Studios, Inc. v. AVELA, Inc., 772 F. Supp. 2d 1155 (C.D. Cal. 2009).

Chapter 7

1. *The Rational Basis of Trademark Protection*, 40 Harv. L. Rev. 813 (1927).

2. Laura Lee Stapleton & Matt McMurphy, "The Professional Athletes Right of Publicity," 10 Marq. Sports L.J. 23 (1999–2000).

3. Sport Supply Group, Inc. v. Columbia Casualty Company, 335 F.3d 453, 461 (5th Cir. 2003).

4. 15 U.S.C. § 1127.

5. Qualitex Co. v. Jacobson Products Co., Inc., 115 S.Ct. 1300, 34 U.S.P.O. 2d 1161 (1995) (finding that a color could constitute a trademark).

6. Half Price Books v. Barnesandnoble.com, 2003 WL 23175436 (N.D. Tex. 2003) at 3.

7. Douglas Laboratories, Inc. v. Copper Tan Inc., 210 F. 2d 453 (2d. Cir. 1954).

8. Kodak Co. v. Weil, 243 N.Y.S. 319 (1930).

9. Abercrombie & Fitch, 537 F.2d at 9, n.6.

10. Half Price Books, 2003 WL 23175436 at 3.

11. Duluth News-Tribune v. Mesabi Pub. Co., 84 F.3d 1093, 1096 (8th Cir. 1996).

12. Big O Tire Dealers, Inc. v. The Goodyear Tire & Rubber Company, 408 F. Supp. 1219 (D. Col. 1976), *aff'd,* 561 F.2d 1365 (10th Cir. 1977).

13. Half Price Books, 2003 WL 23175436 at 4.

14. Fuddruckers, Inc. v. Doc's B.R. Others, Inc., 826 F.2d 837, 841 (9th Cir. 1987).

15. Washington Speakers Bureau, Inc. v. Leading Authorities, Inc., 33 F. Supp. 2d 488, 504 (E.D. Va. 1999).

16. People for the Ethical Treatment of Animals v. Doughney, 2000 WL 943353 (E.D. Va. 2000).

17. Deere & Company v. MTD Products, Inc., 41 F.3d 39 (2nd Cir. 1994).

18. Girl Scouts of USA v. Personality Posters Manufacturing Co., 304 F. Supp. 1228, 1233 (S.D.N.Y. 1969).

19. 2 J. McCarthy, Trademarks and Unfair Competition § 31:38 at 670 (2d ed. 1984).

20. Dr. Seuss Enterprises v. Penguin Books, Inc., 924 F. Supp. 1556, 1569 (D. Neb. 1996).

21. Lyons Partnership, 179 F.3d 384.

22. Dallas Cowboys Cheerleaders, 467 F. Supp. at 376.

23. *See* 15 U.S.C. § 1127, 1995 Federal Trademark Dilution Act (FTDA).

24. Virtual Works v. Volkswagen of America, Inc., 238 F.3d 264, 267 (4th Cir. 2001).

25. Abercrombie & Fitch Stores v. Zuccarini, Case No. D2000-1004 (WIPO Nov. 1, 2001).

26. Major League Baseball Properties, 385 F. Supp. 2d at 253.

27. *See* National Football League v. Jasper Alliance Corporation, 1990 WL 354523 (Trademark Tr. & App. Bd. 1990).

28. Lemon, 437 F. Supp. 2d at 1094.

29. Estate of Tupac Shakur v. Shakur Info Page, AF-0346 (eResolution Sept. 28, 2000).

30. Katie Thomas, "Sports Stars Seek Profit in Catchphrases," The New York Times, at C1, December 9, 2010.

Chapter 8

This chapter is substantially reprinted from Tina Y. Burleson and Walter Champion, "Trade Dress as the Only Club in the Bag to Protect Golf Club Manufacturers from 'Knock-Offs' of Their Prized Boutiques Gulf Clubs," 3 Tex. Rev. Ent. & Sports L. 43 (Spr. 2002). It is reprinted with permission of the authors and the Texas Review of Entertainment and Sports Law. Tina Y. Burleson is a chemist with a J.D. who is finishing her LL.M. in Intellectual Property.

1. Walter T. Champion, Jr., Sports Law in a Nutshell 293 (2000).

2. *Id. See also* Jeff S. Lambert, "Avoiding the Rough: A Two-Case Analysis and Perspective in Defining the Boundaries of Trade Dress Protection for Golf Equipment," 5 Sports Law. J. 61 (1998).

3. *See e.g.,* JOHN JACOBS with KEN BOWDEN, THE GOLF SWING SIMPLIFIED 8 (1993). There are books on swings, on clubs, on balls, and (undoubtedly) on tees, too. In discerning a simplified swing, the authors dissect, in some detail "the 'geometry' of golf." *Id.* at 22.

4. Jeff Jackson, Equipment Fact and Fallacies: Some Questions and Answers That May Surprise You, available at, http://www.golfinsite.net/fact_ and_fallacies .htm (June 24, 20001).

5. William M. Bulkeley, "Callaway's New Computerized Golf Cart Doesn't Carry Clubs, It Designs Them," Wall Street Journal, June 22, 2001 at B-5.

6. Clifton Brown, "Ely Callaway, Golf Club Maker Dies at 82," The New York Times, July 6, 2001, at B-7.

7. W. Champion, *supra* note 1, at 286.

8. Matthew C. McKinnon, Robert A. McCormick, and Darryl C. Wilson, Sports Law 8–1 (1998).

9. *Folsom v. Marsh* (C.C.D. Mass. 1841) (no. 4901) as quoted in Arthur R. Miller and Michael H. Davis, Intellectual Property (2d ed., 1990).

10. Mckinnon, *supra* note 18, at 8–1.

11. 35 U.S.C. § 101 (2000).

12. 17 U.S.C. § 101 (1998).

13. *See generally,* W. Champion, *supra* note 1, at 286.

14. *Id.* at 290.

15. 15 U.S.C. § 1051 (1998).

16. Champion, *supra* note 1, at 291.

17. *Id.* at 286–288.

18. *Id.* at 288–289.

19. National Football League of New Haven v. Rondor, Inc., 840 F. Supp. 1160 (N.D. Ohio 1993).

20. Home Box Office v. Champs of New Haven, Inc., 837 F. Supp. 480 (D. Conn. 1993).

21. See National Football League Properties, Inc. v. Wichita Falls Sportswear, Inc., 532 F. Supp. 651 (W.D. Wash. 1982); and University of Pittsburgh v. Champion Products, Inc., 686 F.2d 1040 (3d Cir. 1982).

22. W. Champion, *supra* note 1, 291–292.

23. Taylor Made Golf Co., Inc. v. Carsten Sports, Ltd., 175 F.R.D. 658, 44 U.S.P.Q.2d 1938 (S.D. Cal. 1997).

24. *See generally,* Taylor Made Golf Co. v. Trend Precision Golf, Inc., 903 F. Supp. 1506 (M.D. Fla. 1995).

25. *See* Callaway Golf Co. v. Golf Clean, Inc., 915 F. Supp. 1206 (M.D. Fla. 1995).

26. *Id.;* Callaway Golf Co. v. Joe Money, No. SACV95-0030 (C.D. Cal. 1995); and Callaway Golf Co. v. Green, No. 4:95-1173-22 (M.D.S.C. 1995).

27. Lambert, *supra* note 2, at 81.

28. Callaway Golf Co. v. Turin Golf Corp., No. SACV95-1086AH5 (C.D. Cal. Jan. 26, 1996) (order granting preliminary injunction) [hereinafter cited as Turin I]; and Callaway Golf Co. v. Turin Golf Co., No. SACV-95-1086AHS (C.D. Cal. May 30, 1996) (Memorandum of Points and Authorities in Support of Ex Parte Application of Callaway Golf for Order to Show Cause Re Contempt) [hereinafter cited as Turin II].

29. Lambert, *supra* note 2, at 81.

30. W. Champion, *supra* note 1, at 286.

31. Duane Grandbois, A Hole New Golf Game, Golf Insite: A Reference Center, available at http://www.golfinsite.net/holenewgame.htm (June 24, 2001).

32. Callaway Golf Co. v. Turin Golf Corp., No. SACV95-1086AH5 (C.D. Cal. Jan. 26, 1996); and Callaway Golf Co. v. Turin Golf Co., No. SACV-95-1086 AHS (C.D. Cal. May 30, 1996).

33. Turin I, *supra* note 28, at 2.

34. Lambert, *supra* note 2, at 64.

35. 15 U.S.C. § 1051.

36. 35 U.S.C. § 1; Turin I, at 2.

37. Turin II, *supra* note 28, at 2.

38. Two Pesos, Inc. v. Taco Cabana, Inc., 505 U.S. 763, 765, n. 1 (1992) (citing John H. Harland Co. v. Clarke Checks, Inc., 711 F.2d 966, 980 [11th Cir. 1983]).

39. Turin I, *supra* note 28, at 13; *See* Lambert, *supra* note 2, at 66; *See also* Gregory T. Talley, Taylor Made Golf Co. v. Trend Precision Golf, Inc.: Golf Club Manufacturer's Ability to Seek Trade Dress Protection for the Color Combinations of Their Products and the 'Inherently Distinctive' Obstacle, 3 Sports Law. J. 63 (1996).

40. W. Champion, *supra* note 1, at 293.

41. Two Pesos, Inc. v. Taco Cabana, Inc., 505 U.S. 763 (1992).

42. *Id.* at 773.

43. Lambert, *supra* note 2, at 76.

44. Two Pesos, 505 U.S. 763, at 773.

45. *Id.* at 764 n. 1 (citing John H. Harland Co. v. Clarke Checks, Inc., 711 F.2d 966, 980 [11th Cir. 1983]).

46. Lambert, *supra* note 2, at 76–77.

47. Pebble Beach Co. v. Tour 18, Ltd., 942 F. Supp. 1513 (S.D. Tex. 1996).

48. W. Champion, *supra* note 1 at 293.

49. Two Pesos, 505 U.S. at 765, n. 1 at 269.

50. Carsten Sports, 17 F.R.D. 658, 662–63. *See* also W. Champion, *supra* note 1, at 294.

51. Trend Precision, 903 F. Supp. at 1507.

52. Taylor Made Loses in Court, Golf World, March 10, 1995, at 9.

53. Lanham Act § 43, 15 U.S.C. § 1125(a) (1998).

54. Talley, *supra* note 59, at 63–64.

55. Callaway Golf Co. v. Golf Clean, Inc., 915 F. Supp. 1206.

56. *Id.*

57. Lanham Act § 43; 15 U.S.C. § 1125 (1998); *See* also Golf Clean, 915 F. Supp. 1206, 1213.

58. Golf Clean, Inc., 915 F. Supp. 1206, 1215.

59. Callaway Golf Co. v. Turin Golf Corp., No. SACV95-1086AH5 (C.D. Cal. Jan. 1996).

60. *Id.; See* also Lambert, 5 Sports Law. J. at 66–67.

61. *Id.*

62. Golf Clean, Inc., 915 F. Supp. at 1211.

63. Carsten Sports, 175 F.R.D. at 663.

64. Golf Clean, Inc., 915 F. Supp. at 1214.

65. *See* contra Trend Precision, 903 F. Supp. at 1507 (finding the Burner Bubble's copper and black trade dress to be inherently non-distinctive and no more than a common design).

66. Golf Clean, Inc., 915 F. Supp. at 1210.

67. Lanham Act § 43, 15 U.S.C. § 1125. *See* John H. Harland, 711 F.2d at 980.

68. Two Pesos, 505 U.S. at 773.

69. *Id.*

70. Golf Clean, Inc., 915 F. Supp. at 1212.

71. *Id.*

72. *Id.*

73. Golf Clean, Inc., 915 F. Supp. at 1214.

74. Exxon, 628 F.2d at 506.

75. Golf Clean, Inc., 915 F. Supp. at 1214.

76. John H. Harland, 711 F.2d at 978 (quoting *Amstar,* 615 F.2d 500, 504 [5th Cir. 1980]).

77. Golf Clean, Inc., 915 F. Supp. at 1214.

78. Carsten Sports, 175 F.R.D. at 664.

79. Lanham Act 35(a), 15 U.S.C. 1117(a) (1998).

80. Carsten Sports, 175 F.R.D. at 662.

81. Nintendo v. Ketchum, 830 F. Supp. 1443, 1445–1446 (M.D. Fla. 1993).

82. 15 U.S.C. 1117(a) (1998).

83. Lindy Pen Co. v. Bic Pen Co., 982 F.2d 1400, 1409 (9th Cir. 1993).

84. Cartsen Sports, 175 F.R.D. at 663, 664.

Chapter 9

SOURCE NOTE: This chapter is co-written by Professor Champion's research assistant, Joey Barajas. For general source notes for Chapter 12, see: Peter J. Wied, *Patently Unfair: State Unfair Competition Laws and Patent Enforcement,* 12 Harv. J. Law & Tech. 469 (1999); George P. Roach, *Counting The Beans: Unjust Enrichment And The Defendant's Overhead,* 16 Tex. Intell. Prop. L.J. 483, 505 (2008); Caprice L. Roberts, *The Case For Restitution And Unjust Enrichment Remedies In Patent Law,* 14 Lewis & Clark L. Rev. 653 (2010); and Stephen A. Smith, *The Structure of Unjust Enrichment Law: Is Restitution A Right Or A Remedy,* 36 Loy. L.A. L. Rev. 1037 (2003).

1. http://www.swlearning.com/blaw/cases/intellectual/0104_intellectual _01.html

2. Jay Shankar, *et al.,* Entertainment Law and Business, § 2.1.2.4 at 121 (3d ed., 2009). See RESTATEMENT OF TORTS § 757 (1937).

3. Victoria Cundiff, "Recent Developments I Trade Secrets Law," 1022 PLI/Pat. 785, 787 (Sept., Oct. 2010).

4. *Id.*

5. *See* Victoria Cundiff, "Trade Secrets Law: The Latest Developments," 1063 PLI/Pat. 691, 693 (Sept.-Oct., 2011).

6. *See* Triple Tee Golf, Inc., 2005 WL 1639317, *1-*3 (N.D. Tex. 2005); Triple Tee Golf, Inc. v. Nike, Inc., 485 F.3d 253 (5th Cir. 2007); and Gillig v. Nike, Inc., 602 F.3d 1354 (Fed. Cir. 2010).

7. Fox Sports Net Worth, LLC v. Minnesota Twins Partnership, 319 F.3d 329 (8th Cir. 2003).

8. Hoffman v. Impact Confections, Inc., 6544 F. Supp. 2d 1121 (S.D. Cal. 2008).

9. Welsh v. Big Ten Conference, Inc., 2008 WL 5070321 (N.D. Ill. 2008).

10. *See* Michael Epstein and Cheryl Davis, "Trade Secrets and Antitrust Protection," 270 PLI/Pat 401, 427–429 (April 1, 1989); and Robert Schwartz and Michael Weil, "United States Law on Restrictive Covenants and Trade Secrets," ST001 ALI-ABA 2291, 2295–2296 (July 28–30, 2011).

11. *See* Schwarts & Weil, "U.S. Law on Restrictive Covenants & Trade Secrets," ST001 ALI-ABA 2291, 2307–2309 (July 28–30, 2011).

12. Cundiff, “Recent Developments in Trade Secret Law," 2011 PLI/Pat 785, 807–809 (Sept.-Oct., 2010).

13. Harry Barnett, Inc. v. Shidler, 338 F.3d 1125 (10th Cir. 2003).

14. Graeme Dinwoodie, *et al.,* International Intellectual Property Law and Policy § 3.0313, C1, at 519–523.

15. Victoria Cundiff, "Avoiding Prosecution under the Economic Espionage Act," in Cundiff, PLI's Fourth Annual Institute for Intellectual Property Law, 533 PLI/Pat 9, 54–59 (October 1998).

16. Rice Ferrelle, "Combating the Lure of Impropriety in Professional Sports Industries: The Desirability of Treating a Playbook as a Legally Enforceable Trade Secret," 11 J. Intell. Prop. L. 149 (Fall 2003) (footnotes omitted).

17. *Id.,* at 150 (footnotes omitted).

18. *Id.,* at 159 (footnotes omitted).

19. *Id.,* at 159–160 (footnotes omitted).

20. *Id.*

21. *Id.,* at 160a (footnotes omitted).

22. *See,* Welsh & Weinbach, "Protection of Trade Secrets and Confidential Business Information in the Internet Age: A Brief Overview," 1166 PLI/Corp. 225, 231–234 (March–April 2000) (footnotes omitted).

23. *Id.*

Chapter 10

1. Elvis Presley Enterprise, Inc. v. Capece, 950 F. Supp 783, 801 (S.D. Tex. 1996).

2. Prosser and Keeton on the law of Torts (5th ed. 1984); Restatement (Second) of Torts 3652A (1971).

3. Sinker v. Goldsmith, 623 F. Supp. 727 (D. Ariz. 1985).

4. *See* Carson v. Here's Johnny Portable Toilets, Inc., 698 F.2d 831 (6th Cir. 1983), *appeal after remand,* 810 F.2d 104 (6th Cir. *1983); also see* White v. Samsung Electronics America, Inc., 971 F.2d 1395 (9th Cir. 1992).

5. Hirsch v. S.C. Johnson & Son, Inc., 280 N.W.2d 129 (Wis. 1979).

6. Invasion of privacy by use of plaintiff's name or likeness in advertising, 23 A.L.R. 3d 865; Restatement (Second) of Torts § 625C, comm. c (1977). Restatement (Second) of Torts § 625C, comment b (1977)

7. *See* Palmer v, Schonhorn Enterprises, Inc., 96 N.J. Super. 72, 232 A.2d 458, 460–461 (Ch. Div. 1967); Uhlaender v. Henricksen, 316 F. Supp. 1277, 1278–1283 (D. Minn. 1970); Rosemont Enterprises, Inc. v. Urban Systems, Inc., 72 Misc. 2d 788, 340 N.Y.S.2d 144, 146–47 (Sup 1973), order modified, 42 A.D.2d 544, 345 N.Y.S.2d 17 (1st Dep't 1973) [Defendant sold "The Howard Hughes Game."] famous golfer sued over his likeness used in a board game). In Whisper Wear, Inc. v. Morgan, 277 Ga. App. 607, 627 S.E.2d 178, 178–191 (2000) *cert. denied,* (May 8, 2000) (A model sued over her photo which was used in advertising by a company who manufactured breast pumps.)

8. Invasion of privacy by use of plaintiff's name or likeness for non-advertising purposes, 30 A.L.R. 3d 203; Restatement (Second) of Torts § 625C (1977).

9. Schlessman v. Schlessman, 50 Ohio App. 2d 179, 4 Ohio Op. 3d 143, 361 N.E.2d 1347, 1349 (6th Dist. Erie County 1975).

10. Gaines, Cork, Chart of the Day: The Top Endorsement Earners in Each *Sport, Business Insider,* January 27, 2011.

11. In *Apple Corps. Ltd. v. Leber,* 12 Media L. Rep. (BNA) 2280, 229 U.S.P.Q. (BNA) 1015, 1986 WL 215081 (An On-Stage Production of "Beatle-Mania," which imitated a Beatles concert, violated N.Y. Civ. Rights law 50, 51.)

12. See a good discussion of a variety of cases dealing with the right of publicity at, Alexander Lindey and Michael Landau, "The Right of Privacy and Publicity, The Right of Publicity," Publicity & The Arts § 3:16 (3d ed.)

13. Hirsch v. S.C. Johnson & Son, Inc., 280 N.W.2d 129 (Wis. 1979).

14. Abdul-Jabbar v. General Motors, 85 F.3d 407 (9th Cir. 1996).

15. *Id.* at 412.

16. Montana, 40 Cal. Rptr. 2d at 640–41.

17. *Pooley,* 89 F. Supp. 2d at 1114.

18. Don Walker, "Does Kareem Own 'Sky Hook?'" *Journal Interactive,* June 1, 2009.

19. Steve Green, "Company Sues in LV over alleged Shaquille O'Neal Trademarks Infringement," *Las Vegas Sun,* January 18, 2010.

20. Dan Siater, "The Verdict: Hits and Whiffs from the Week That Was," *Wall Street Journal,* April 4, 2008; Sara L. Edelman, "Death Pays: The Fight Over Marilyn Monroe's Publicity Rights," *The Metropolitan Corporate Counsel,* July 1, 2007.

21. A federal appellate court noted approximately one-third of American jurisdictions dealing with this issue recognize the right of post-mortem publicity. *See* Merman Miller v. Palazzetti Imports and Exports, 270 F.3d 298, 325–26 and nn. 12–14 (6th cir. 2001).

22. 46 F. Supp. 2d 587 (N.D. Tex. 1999)

23. Restatement (Second) of Torts § 652C, Comm. C (1977).

24. 551 F. Supp. 1060 (N.D. Ill 1982).

25. 203 FED App. 0137 p (6th Cir.)

26. Multiple cases have explored the intersection between the right of publicity and the First Amendment. For a few examples, *see* Barrows v. Rozansky, 111 A.D.2d 105, 489 N.Y.S.2d 481, 485 (1st Dep't 1985); Creel v. Crown Publishers, Inc., 115 A.D.2d 414, 496 N.Y.S.2d 219, 220 (1st Dep't 1985); Geary v. Goldstein, 831 F. Supp. 269, 277, n. 8 (S.D.N.Y. 1993); and Gionfriddo v. Major League Baseball, 114 Cal. Rptr. 2d 307, 314 (Ct. App. 2001).

Chapter 11

This chapter is co-written by Prof. Champion's research assistant, Joey Barajas (B.A., U.T., Hook 'em Horns).

1. Penn Cent. Corp. v. Chicago Union Station Co., 830 F. Supp. 1509, 1522 (Reg'l Rail Reorg. Ct. 1993) (quoting Indyk v. Habib Bank Ltd., 694 F.2d 54, 57 [2d Cir.1982]).

2. Wendy J. Gordon, "On Owning Information: Intellectual Property and the Restitutionary Impulse," 79 Va. L. Rev. 149, 199 (1992).

3. Zacchini v. Scripps-Howard Broadcasting Co., 433 U.S. 562, 582 (1977).

4. Pittsburgh Athletic Co. v. KQV Broadcasting Co., 24 F. Supp. 490 (W.D. Pa. 1938).

5. Oliveira v. Frito-Lay, Inc., 251 F.3d 56 (2d Cir. 2001).

6. Orion Pictures Co. Inc. v. Dell Pub. Co., Inc., 471 F. Supp. 392 (S.D.N.Y. 1979).

7. James W. Hill, "Trade Secrets, Unjust Enrichment, and The Classification Of Obligations," 4 Va. J.L. & Tech. 248 (1999).

8. Kewanee Oil Co. v. Bicron Corp., 416 U.S. 470 (1974).

9. Sun Media Systems, Inc. v. KDSM, LLC, 564 F.Supp.2d 946 (S.D. Iowa 2008).

Chapter 12

1. This chapter is co-written by Professor Champion's research assistant, Joey Barajas. For source notes for Chapter 12 generally, see: Peter J. Wied, "Patently Unfair: State Unfair Competition Laws and Patent Enforcement," 12 Harv. J. Law & Tech. 469 (1999); George P. Roach, "Counting the Beans: Unjust Enrichment and the Defendant's Overhead," 16 Tex. Intell. Prop. L.J. 483, 505 (2008); Caprice L. Roberts, "The Case For Restitution and Unjust Enrichment Remedies In Patent Law," 14 Lewis & Clark L. Rev. 653 (2010); and Stephen A. Smith, "The Structure of Unjust Enrichment Law: Is Restitution A Right Or A Remedy," 36 Loy. L.A. L. Rev. 1037 (2003).

2. Dreamwerks Production Group, Inc. v. SKG Studio, 142 F.3d 1127 (9th Cir. 1998).

3. TGC Corp. v. HTM Sports, B.V., 896 F. Supp. 751 (E.D. Tenn. 1995).

Chapter 13

1. See, I. Nelson Rose, "Internet Gambling: Domestic and International Developments," SC91 ALI-ABA 131, 157 (June 25, 1998).

2. See generally, for § 13.4, Donald Zupanec, "Practices Forbidden by State Deceptive Trade Practice and Consumer Protection Acts," 89 A.L.R. 3d 449 (updated 2013).

Chapter 14

1. Walter Champion, Fundamentals of Sports Law, at § 20.6 (2d ed. 2004; 2012–2013 Ann. Supp.)

2. Patrick Thornton, Walter Champion and Lawrence Ruddell, Sports Ethics for Sports Management Professionals, at 403–404 (2012).

3. Eldrick "Tiger" Woods, for Itself, Tiger Woods and His Minor Child, Charlie Axel Woods v. Josh Whitford, Claim Number FA0905001263352 (2009), as reprinted in Sports Ethics for Sports Management Professionals, at 404–407,

4. Barry Zito v. Stan Andruszkiewicz, Claim Number FA020700011-4773 (2002).

5. Liddell v. Comdot Internet Services Private Ltd., WIPO Case No. D2008-1284 (Nov. 3, 2008).

6. NFL v. Bonner, WIPO Case No. D2008-0605 (May 29, 2008); NFL v. EENation, WIPO Case No. D2011-1228 (Sept. 25, 2011) (<superbowlconcierge.com>).

7. Ain-Jeem, Inc. v. Barto Enterprises, WIPO Case No. D2007-1841 (Jan. 31, 2008).

8. Stanford v. Mohunlal, WIPO Case No. D2008-1188 (Sept. 25, 2008).

9. Ohio State University v. Thomas, 738 F. Supp. 2d 743 (S.D. Ohio, 2010).

10. Cleveland Browns Football Co., LLC v. Dinola, WIPO Case No. D2011-0421 (2011).

11. Russell Brands, LLC v. Cognata, WIPO Case No. D2011-1394 (Oct. 21, 2011).

12. Rugby World Cup Ltd. V. Gyrre, WIPO Case No. D2011-1520 (Nov. 1, 2011).

13. Peter Brown, "Protection of Trademarks and Trade Secrets in E Commerce," GSO PLI/Pat. 127, 133–138, 149–150 (Apr. 23–24, 2001).

14. Roger Cleveland Golf Co., Inc. v. Price, 2010 WL 5019260 (D. S.C.).

15. Bugoni v. Kappas, 2011 WL 5357815 (D. D.C.).

16. Ellen Rony & Peter Rony, The Domain Name Handbook: High Stakes and Strategies in Cyberspace, at 601 (Lawrence, KS, 1999).

17. S. Rep. No. 106–140, at 5 (1999).

18. Matthew Searing, "What's in a Domain Name? A Critical Analysis of the National and International Impact on Domain Cybersquatting," 40 Washburn L.J. 110 (Fall 2000).

19. 202 F.3d 489 (2d Cir. 2000).

20. Searing, "What's in a Domain Name: A Critical Analysis . . . ," 40 Washburn L.J. 110, 126.

21. 202 F.3d 489, 495, 497–498.

22. Id., at 499.

23. 89 F. Supp. 2d 634 (E.D. Pa. 2000).

24. See, Searing, "What's in a Domain Name? A Critical Analysis . . . 40 Washburn L.J. 110, 128–130.

25. Craig Pinters, "Managing the "Team" on the Field, Off the Field, and in Cyberspace: Preventing Cybersquatters from Hijacking Your Franchise's Domain Names," 11 Marq. Sports L. Rev. 299 (Spr. 2001).

26. Con Way, Inc. v. Conwayracing.com, 2009 WL 2252128 (N.D. Cal.).

27. Mine O' Mine, Inc. v. Calmese, 2011 U.S. Dist. LEXIS75236 (D. Nev.).

Chapter 15

1. For a general source note for § 15.1(i), *see* the following: Jean Braucher, "Delayed Disclosure in Consumer E Commerce as an Unfair and Deceptive Practice," 46 Wayne L. Rev. 1805 (Wing. 2000); Audrey Latourette, "Copyright Implications for Online Distance Education," 32 J.C.&U.L. 613 (2006); Yasaman Navai, "*Sporty's Farm L.L.C. v. Sportsman Market, Inc.* —Protecting Against Cybersquatting or Extending the Allowable Reach of Trademark Law on the World Wide Web," 11 DePaul-LCA J. Art. & Ent. L. 191 (Spr. 2001); Don Tomlinson, "Journalism and Entertainment as Intellectual Property on the Information Superhighway: The Challenge of the Digital Doman" 6 Stan. L. & Pol'y Rev. 61 (1994); and Gayle Weiswasser, "Domain Names, The Internet and Trademarks: Infringement in Cyberspace," 20 Santa Clara Computer & High Tech. L.J. 215 (Nov. 2003).

2. For a general source note for § 15.1(ii), *see* the following: Ian Blackshaw, "Settling Sports Domain Name Disputes through WIPO," 10 No. 1 Bus. L. Int'l 61 (Jan. 2009); Thomas McCarthy and Paul Anderson, "Protection of the Athlete's Identity: The Right of Publicity, Endorsements and Domain Names," 11 Marq. Sports L. Rev. 195 (Spr. 2001); § 15.Steve McKelvey, Sheranne Fairley, & Mark Groza," Caught in the Web? The Communication of Trademark Rights and Licensing Policy on University Official Athletic Websites," 20 J.L. Aspects Sport 1 (Winter 2010); Navai, "*Sporty's Farm* . . . Protecting Against Cybersquatting . . . " 11 DePaul-LCA J. Art. & Ent. L. 191 (Spr. 2001); Craig Pintens, "Managing the 'Team' on the Field, Off the Field, and in Cyberspace: Preventing Cybersquatters from Highjacking your Franchise's Doman Names," 11 Marq. Sports L. Rev. 299 (Spr. 2001); Matthew Searling, "What's in a Domain Name? A Critical Analysis of the National and International Impact on Domain Name Cybersquatting," 40 Washburn L.J. 110 (Fall 2000); and Weiswasser, "Domain Names, the Internet and Trademarks . . . " 20 Santa Clara Computer & High Tech. L.J. 215 (Nov. 2013).

3. Weiswasser at 224 (footnotes omitted).

4. For a general source note for § 15.2, see the following: Niki Arbiter, "The Business of Sports: The Evolution of Intellectual Property Law Away from INS v. AP—NBA v. Motorola, . . . ," 17 Temp. Envtl. L. & Tech. J. 43 (Fall 1998); Jan Boswell, "Fantasy Sports: A Game of Skill That Is Implicitly Legal under State Law, and Now Explicitly Legal under Federal Law," 25 Cardozo Arts & Ent. L.J. 1257 (2008); E. Jason Burke, "'Quasi-Property' Rights: Fantasy or Reality? An Examination of *C.B.C. Dist. Marketing, Inc. v. MLB Advanced Media, L.P.* and Fantasy Sports Providers' Use of Professional Athlete Statistics," 27 Wash. U.J.L. & Pol'y 161 (2008); Askan Deutsch, "Sports Broadcasting and Virtual Advertising: Defining the Limits of Copyright Law of Unfair Competition," 11 Marq. Sports L. Rev. 41 (Fall 2000); Andrea Freeman, "*Morris Comm'ns v. PGA Tour* Battle Over the Rights to Real-Time Sports Scores," 20 Berkeley Tech. L.J. 3 (2005); "Intellectual

Property—8th Cir. Holds that the 1st Amendment Protects Online Fantasy Baseball Providers' Use of Baseball Statistics in the Public Domain—C.B.C. Dist. & Marketing, Inc. v. MLB Advanced Media, L.P., . . ." 121 Harv. L. Rev. 1439 (March 2008); Clifford McDonald, "Gamecasts and *NBA v. Motorola*: Do They Still Love the Game," 5 N.C.J.L. & Tech. 329 (Spr. 2004); Michael Mellis, "Internet Piracy of Live Sports Telecasts," 18 Marq. Sports L. Rev. 759 (Spr. 2008); Robert Razzaro, "Intellectual Property and Baseball Statistics: Can Major League Baseball Take its Fantasy Ball and Go Home?" 74 U. Cin. L. Rev. 1157 (Spr. 2006); Gary Roberts, "The Scope of the Exclusive Right to Control Dissemination of Real-Time sports Event Information," 15 Stan. L. & Pol'y 167 (2004); Chia-heng Seetoo, "Can Peer-to-Peer Internet Broadcast Technology Give Fans Another Chance? Peer-to-Peer Streaming Technology and Its Impact," 2007 U. Ill. J.L. Tech. & Pol'y 369 (Fall 2007); Jason Shane, "Who Owns a Home Run? The Battle of the Use of Player Performance Statistics by Fantasy Sports Websites," 29 Hastings Comm. & Ent. L.J. 241 (Winter 2007); and Adam Sheps, "Swinging for the Fences: The Fallacy in Assigning Ownership to Sports Statistics and Its Effect on Fantasy Sports," 38 Conn. L. Rev. 1113 (July 2006).

5. For a general source note for § 15.3, see Adam S. Chinnock, "Meta Tags: Another Whittle from the Stick of Trademark Protection?" 32 U.C. Davis L. Rev. 255 (Fall 1998); and Michelle Evans, "Establishing Liability for Trademark Infringement by the Uses of Website Metatags," 84 Am. Jur. P.O.F. 3d 93 (2005, database updated 2/13).

6. For a general source note for § 15.4, see the following: Erinn Betcha, "Who Are the Real Competitors in the Olympic Games? Dual Olympic Battles: Trademark Infringement and Ambush Marketing Harm Corporate Sponsors—Violations Against the USOC and Its Corporate sponsors," 8 Seton Hall J. Sport L. 129 (1998); Lori Bean, "Ambush Marketing: sports Sponsorship confusion and the Lanham Act," 75 B.U.L. Rev. 1099 (Sept. 1995); Scott Bearby and Bruce Siegal, "From the Stadium Parking Lot to the Information Superhighway: How to Protect Your Trademarks from Infringement," 28 J.C. & U.L. 633 (2002); Daniel Mark, "Marketing Confusion: The Los Angeles Angels of Anaheim and the Lanham Act," 26 SPG Ent. & Sports Law. 25 (Spr. 2008); Steven McKelvey, "Atlanta '96: Olympic Countdown to Ambush Armageddon," 4 Seton Hall J. sport L. 397 (1994); Anita Moorman and T. Christopher Greenwell, "Customer Attitudes of Deception and the Legality of Ambush Marketing Practices," 15 J. Legal Aspects Sport 183 (Summ. 2005); Brian Lee Pelanda, "Ambush Marketing: Dissecting the Discourse," 34 Hastings Comm. & Ent. L.J. 341 (Spr. 2012); Patrick Sheridan, "An Olympic Solution to Ambush Marketing: How the London Olympics Show the Way to More Effective Trademark Law," 17 Sports Law J. 27 (Spr. 2010); and Edward Vassallo, Kristin Blemaster, and Patricia Werner, "An International Look at Ambush Marketing," 95 Trade Rep. 1338 (Nov.-Dec. 2005).

Chapter 16

1. *See also* Brent Zwernemann, "Where A&M Is Concerned, He's the Only 'Johnny Football,'" Houston Chronicle, at A1 (Nov. 13, 2012); and Randy Harvey, "Next Play Should be a Handoff of Cash to Manziel," Houston Chronicle at C1 (Jan. 29, 2013).

Chapter 17

The authors acknowledge the assistance of Kevin Tamer in the outlining of this chapter. Kevin was an ace student in Professor Champion's Sports Law course at the University of Houston School of Law, and President of their Sports and Entertainment Law Society (SELS) Chapter.

1. As a general source note for 17.1, please see the following: Frederick M. Abbott, Thomas Cottier, & Francis Curry, International Property in an Integrated World Economy (NY: Aspen, 2007); Graeme B. Dinwoodie, *et al.,* International Property Law and Policy (Newark: LexisNexis, 2d ed., 2008); and Jon Garon, Entertainment Law and Practice (Durham: Carolina Academic Press, 2005).

See also: Niki Arbiter, "The Business of Sports: The Evolution of Intellectual Property Law Away from *INS v. AP—NBA v. Motorola*," 17 Temp. Envtl. L. & Tech. J. 43 (Fall 1998); Sean Comerford, "International Intellectual Property Rights and the Future of Global E Sports,'" 37 Brook. J. Int'l L. 623 (2012); Brandi Holland, "Moral Rights Protection in the U.S. and the Effect of the Family Entertainment and Copyright Act of 2005 on U.S. International Obligations," 39 Vand. J. Transnat'l L. 217 (Jan. 2006); Bashar Malkawi, "Broadcasting the 2006 World Cup: The Right Fans versus Art Exclusivity," 17 Fordham I.P. Media & Ent. L.J. 591 (Spr. 2007); and Peter Yu, "The Harmonization Game: What Basketball Can Teach about Intellectual Property and International Trade," 26 Fordham Int'l L.J. 218 (Jan. 2003).

2. As a general source for the last paragraph in §17.2, *see* Jan D'Allessandro, "A Trade-Based Response to I.P. Piracy: A Comprehensive Plan to Aid the Motion Pictures Industry," 76 Geo. L.J. 417 (Dec. 1987). *See generally,* Neu, "Bollywood Is Coming! . . . 8 San Diego Int'l L.J. 123; and Anna Tydniouk, "From ITAR-TASS to Films by Jove: The Conflict of Laws Revolution in International Copyright," 29 Brook. J. Int'l L. 897 (2004).

3. As a general source note for §17.3, see the following: Erin Batcha, "Who Are the Real Competitors in the Olympic Games; Dual Olympic Battles: Trademark Infringement and Ambush Marketing Harm Corporate Sponsors—Violations Against the USOC and Its Corporate Sponsors," 8 Seton Hall J. Sport L. 229 (1998); Laura Misener, "Safeguarding the Olympic Insignia: Protecting the Commercial Integrity of the Canadian Olympic Ass'n," 13 J. Leg. Aspects Sport 79 (Wint. 2003); Noelle Nish, "How Far Have We Come? A Look at the Olympic and Amateur Sports Act of 1998, the U.S.O.C., and the Winter Olympic Games of 2002," 13 Seton Hall J. Sport L. 53 (2003); Edward

Vassallo, Kristin Blemester & Patricia Werner, "An International Look at Ambush Marketing," 95 Trademark Rep. 1338 (Nov.-Dec. 2005); Patrick Sheridan, "An Olympic Solution to Ambush Marketing: How the London Olympics Show the Way to More Effective Trademark Law" 17 Sports Law J. 27 (Spr. 2010); and Ray Yasser, *et al.*, Sports Law: Cases & Materials 959–996 (Cincinnati: Anderson, 4th ed. 2000).

Chapter 18

The co-author of this piece is Joey Barajas, a recent graduate of Texas Southern University School of Law.

1. Michael J. Meurer, "Controlling Opportunistic and Anti-Competitive Intellectual Property Litigation," 44 B.C.L. Rev. 509, 510 (2003).

2. *Id.,* at 512.

3. *Id.,* at 513–514.

4. *Id.,* at 514.

5. *Id.*

6. *Id.,* at 515.

7. *Id.,* at 512.

8. *Id.,* at 518.

9. *Id.,* at 516.

10. Shelly Rosenfeld, "Idea Submission Impossible? The Battle between Copyright and Breach of Contract," 20 Eng. & Sports Law. 1, 22 (Nov. 2012).

11. Michael J. Meurer, "Controlling Opportunistic and Anti-Competitive Intellectual Property Litigation," 44 B.C.L. Rev. 509, 518 (2003).

12. Shelly Rosenfeld, "Idea Submission Impossible? The Battle Between Copyright and Breach of Contract," 20 Ent. & Sports Law. 1, 22 (Nov. 2012).

13. *Id.,* at 13.

14. *Id.,* at 22.

15. *Id.*

16. Meurer, at 521.

17. Callaway Golf v. Golf Clean, Inc., 915 F. Supp. 1206, 1212 (M.D. Fla. 1995).

18. *Id.,* at 1211.

19. *Id.,* at 1213.

20. *Id.,* at 1212–1213.

21. *Id.,* at 1206.

22. Meurer, at 524.

23. *Id.*

24. *Id.*

25. *Id.,* at 525.

26. Robert Alan Garrett, Philip R. Rochberg, "Sports Broadcasting and the Law," 59 Indiana L.J. 157 (1984). Available at http://www.repository.law.indiana.edu/ilj/vol59/iss2/1.

27. *Id.*

28. *Id.*

29. *Id.*

30. *Id.,* at 158.

31. *Id.*

32. Pittsburgh Athletic Co. v. KQV Broadcasting Co., 24 F. Supp. 490 (W.D. Pa. 1938).

33. *Id.,* at 491.

34. *Id.,* at 492.

35. *Id.*

36. *Id.*

37. *Id.,* at 493–494.

38. Zacchini v. Scripps-Howard Broadcasting Co., 433 U.S. 562 (1977).

39. *Id.,* at 563.

40. *Id.,* at 564.

41. *Id.*

42. Garrett and Rochberg, "Sports Broadcasting and the Law," 59 Indiana L.J. 161 (1984). Available at http://www.repository.law.indiana.edu/ilj/vol59/iss2/1.

43. *Id.*

44. *Id.*

45. *Id.*

46. *Id.,* at 186.

47. *Id.*

48. *Id.*

49. *Id.*

50. *Id.,* at 187.

51. *Id.,* at 188.

52. Board of Regents of University of Oklahoma v. National Collegiate Athletic Association, 707 F.2d 1147 (10th Cir. 1983).

53. *Id.,* at 1164 (Barrett, J., dissenting).

54. *Id.,* at 1160.

55. Board of Regents of University of Oklahoma v. National Collegiate Athletic Association, 546 F. Supp. 1276, 1310 (W.D. Okla. 1982) aff'd in part, remanded in part, 707 F.2d 1147 (10th Cir. 1983).

56. *Id.,* at 1311.

57. *Id.,* at 1307.

58. Pacifica Foundation v. FCC, 556 F.2d 9 (1977), rev'd FCC v. Pacifica Foundation, 438 U.S. 726 (1978); Andrea L. Bonnicksen, "Obscenity Reconsidered: Bringing Broadcast into the Mainstream Commentary," 14 Val. U.L. Rev. 261, 261 (1980). Available at: http://scolar.valpo.edu/vulr/vol14/iss2/2.

59. Andrea L. Bonnicksen, "Obscenity Reconsidered: Bringing Broadcast into the Mainstream Commentary," 14 Val. U.L. Rev. 261, 263 (1980). Available at: http://scholar.valpo.edu/vulr/vol14/iss2/2/.

60. National Broadcasting Corp. v. United States, 319 U.S. 190 (1943).

61. Andrea L. Bonnicksen, "Obscenity Reconsidered: Bringing Broadcast into the Mainstream Commentary," 14 Val. U.L. Rev. 261, 278 (1980). Available at: http://scholar.valpo.edu/vulr/vol14/iss2/2/.

62. National Broadcasting Corp. v. United States, 319 U.S. 190, 226–227 (1943); Andrea L. Bonnicksen, "Obscenity Reconsidered: Bringing Broadcast into the Mainstream Commentary," 14 Val. U.L. Rev. 261, 264 (1980). Available at: http://scholar.valpo.edu/vulr/vol14/iss2/2/.

63. 47 U.S.C. § 303(m)(1) (2010).

64. Copyright Act § 102(a) (1976).

65. Copyright Act § 102(a)(6) (1976).

66. Copyright Act § 102(a) (1976); Askan Deutsch, "Sports Broadcasting and Virtual Advertising: Defining the Limits of Copyright Law and the Law of Unfair Competition," 11 Marq. Sports. L. Rev. 41, 48 (2000). Available at http://scholarship.law.marquette.edu/sportslaw/vol11/iss1/7.

67. Askan Deutsch, "Sports Broadcasting and Virtual Advertising: Defining the Limits of Copyright Law and the Law of Unfair Competition," 11 Marq. Sports. L. Rev. 41, 48 (2000). Available at http://schoalrship.law.marquette.edu/sportslaw/vol11/iss1/7.

68. *Id.*

69. *Id.,* at 52.

70. *Id.,* at 54–55.

71. *Id.,* at 83.

72. Philip K. Anderson *et al.,* "Intellectual Property Trial Strategies: How Jurors' Perceptions of Corporate America Affect their Judgments in Patent Cases," 875 PLI/Pat 461, 467 (Sept.-Nov. 2006).

73. *See,* William Gallagher, "Strategic Intellectual Property Litigation, the Right of Publicity, and the Attenuation of Free Speech: Lessons from the Schwarzenegger Bobblehead Doll War (and Peace)," 45 Santa Clara L. Rev. 581, 582–583 (2005).

74. 21 P.3d 797 (Cal. 2001).

75. 69 P.3d 473 (Cal. 2003).

76. 15 U.S.C. § 1127 (1988).

77. *See, generally,* Steven Geise, "A Whole New Ballgame: The Application of Trademark Law to Sports Mark Litigation," 5 Seton Hall J. Sport L. 553, 554 (1995).

78. *Id.,* at 554–555.

79. *See,* NFL Properties, Inc. v. Wichita Falls Sportswear, Inc., 532 F. Supp. 651 (W.D. Wash. 1982).

80. Geise, 5 Seton Hall J. Sport L. 553, 559–560.

81. *Id.,* at 560–561.

82. 327 N.E.2d 247 (Ill. 1975).

83. Geise, 5 Seton Hall J. Sport L. 553, 564–565.

84. *Id.,* at 565.

85. 817 F. Supp. 1103 (S.D. N.Y. 1993).
86. *Id.,* at 1118–1121.
87. *Id.,* at 1123–1126.
88. *Id.,* at 1126–1127, 1132.
89. *See,* NFL Properties, Inc. v. Dallas Cap & Emblem Mfg., Inc., 327 N.E.2d 247 (Ill. 1975); *see* generally, Geise, 5 Seton Hall J. Sport L. 553, 567–573.

Chapter 19

1. Author's note on sources: The late co-author of this book, my friend, Pat Thornton, was also the lead co-author of Sports Ethics for the Sports Management Professionals (Jones Bartlett, 2012), along with myself (Champion) and our friend Larry Ruddell. This chapter mirrors much of Sports Ethics' Chapter 11, "Ethical Consideration for Intellectual Property in Sports" (pp. 387–420).
2. Thornton, Champion & Ruddell, Sports Ethics, at 407–409.
3. *See generally,* Carl Kukkonen, "Be a Good Sport and Refrain from Using My Patented Putt: Intellectual Property Protection for Sports Related Movements," 80 J. Pat. & Trademark Off. Soc'y 808 (Nov. 1998); Prolog Das, "Offensive Protection: The Potential Application of Intellectual Property Law to Scripted Sports Plays," 75 Ind. L.J. 1073 (Summ. 2000); and Ferrelle, "Combating the Lure of Impropriety in Professional sports Industries: Desirability of Treating a Playbook as a Legally Enforceable Trade Secret," 11 J. Intell. Prop. L. 149 (Fall 2003).
4. Thornton, Champion & Ruddell, Sports Ethics, at 403–407.
5. The following is a general source note for § 19.2: Phillips Barengolts, "Ethical Issues Arising from the Investigation of Activities of Intellectual Property Infringers Represented by Counsel," 1 NW. J. Tech. & Intell. Prop. 3 (Spring 2003); Jordana Corush, "Cracks in the Great Wall: Why China's Copyright Law Has Failed to Prevent Piracy of American Movies within its Borders," 9 Vand. J. Ent. & Tech. L. 405 (Winter 2006); Aaron Delgado, "Confessions of a Tennis Shop Pirate—Can Proper Pricing of Factors of Production Deter Copyright Infringement?" 8 J. Tech. L. & Pol'y 179 (Dec. 2003); Peter Gardner, "Our Intellectual Property World: Charting a Course from Ancient Native Cultures to the Threshold of the Future on a Roiled Sea of Macroeconomics, Morality, and Ethics," 44 IDEA 247 (2004); James Grimmelmann, "The Ethical Visions of Copyright Law," 77 Fordham L. Rev. 2005 (April 2009); Sunny Handa, "Retransmission of Television Broadcasts on the Internet," 8 SW. J. L. & Trade Am. 39 (2001–2002).; Thomas Inkel, "Internet-Based Fans: Why the Entertainment Industries Cannot Depend on Traditional Copyright Protections," 28 Pepp. L. Rev. 879 (2001); Jeffrey Levine, "Meeting the Challenges of International Brand Expansion in Professional Sports: Intellectual Property Right Enforcement in China through Treaties, Chinese Law, and Cultural Mechanisms," 9 Tex. Rev. Ent. & Sports L. 203 (Fall 2007); J. Thomas McCarthy and Paul

Anderson, "Protection of the Athlete's Identity: The Right of Publicity, Endorsements, and Domain Names," 11 Marq. Sports L. Rev. 195 (Spring 2001); Theresa McElvilly, "Virtual Advertising in Sports Venues and the Federal Lanham Act § 43(A): Revolutionary Technology Creates Controversial Advertising Medium," 8 Seton Hall J. Sport L. 603 (1998); Steve McKelvey, Sheranne Fairley, and Mark Groza, "Caught in the Web? The Communication of Trademark Rights and Licensing Policy on University Official Athletic Websites," 20 J. Legal Aspects Sport 1 (Winter 2010); John Mills, "Entertainment on the Internet: First Amendment and Copyright Issues," 79 J. Pat. & Trademark Off. Soc'y 461 (July 1997); "Nothing But Internet," 110 Harv. L. Rev. 1143 (March 1997); Craig Pintens, "Managing the 'Team' on the Field, and in Cyberspace: Preventing Cybersquatters from Hijacking Your Franchise's Domain Name," 11 Marq. Sports L. Rev. 299 (Spring 2001); Jeffrey Samuels, "Ethical Considerations for Attorneys Practicing Before the PTO in Trademark Cases," 848 ALI-ABA 177 (April 15, 1993); John Steele, "Ethics Issue in Trademark, Copyright and Unfair Competition Practice," SF87 ALI-ABA 461 (March 22, 2001); Joseph Storch and Heidi Wachs, "A Legal Matter: Peer-to-Peer File Sharing, the Digital Millennium Copyright Act, and the Higher Education Opportunity Act: How Congress and the Entertainment Industry Missed an Opportunity to Stem Copyright Infringement," 74 Alb. L. Rev. 313 (2010–2011); Don Wiesner and Anita Cava, "Stealing Trade Secrets Ethically," 47 Md. L. Rev. 1076 (Summer 1988); and Marc Williams, "Copyright Preemption: Real-Time Dissemination of sports Scores and Information," 71 S. Cal. L. Rev. 445 (Jan. 1998).

6. Thornton, Champion, & Ruddell, Sports Ethics, at 388–403.

7. McCarthy and Anderson, Protection of the Athlete's Identity, 11 Marq. Sports L. Rev. 195, 196–209.

8. Thornton, Champion & Ruddell, Sports Ethics, at 412, 418.

9. Thornton, Champion, & Ruddell, Sports Ethics, at 409–411.

10. Nottingham, "Keeping the Home Team at Home . . .," 75 U. Colo. L. Rev. 1065, 1067–1097.

11. Thornton, Champion, & Ruddell, Sports Ethics, at 411–416, 419–420.

Chapter 20

Professor Champion appreciates and acknowledges the vibes of his colleague, Dock Sanders, in the "metaphysicalization" (with apologies to Bush, Jr.) of this chapter.

1. Tonya M. Evans, "Sampling, Looping and Mashing . . . Oh My!: How Hip-Hop Music is Scratching More than the Surface of Copyright Law," 21 Fordham Intellectual Property, Media & Ent. L.J. 843, 852–854 (Summ. 2011).

2. As a general source note for the section entitled "Sampling and Copyrights," please see the following: Harold A. Anderson, Jr., "No Bitin' Allowed: A Hip-Hop Copying Paradigm for All of Us," 20 Tex. Intell. Prop. L.J. 115 (fall 2011);

Olufunmilayo Arewa, "From J.C. Bach to Hip-Hop: Musical Borrowing, Copyright and Cultural Context," 84 N.C.L. Rev. 457 (Jan. 2006); Tonya M. Evans, "Sampling, Looping and Mashing . . . Oh My!: How Hip-Hop Music Is Scratching More than the Surface of Copyright Law," 21 Fordham Intellectual Property, Media & Ent. L.J. 843 (Summ. 2011); John W. Gregory, "A Necessary Global Discussion for Improvements to U.S. Copyright Law on Music Sampling," 15 Gonz. J. Int'l L. 4 (2011–2012); Candace G. Hines, "Black Musical Traditions and Copyright Law: Historical Traditions," 10 Mich. J. Race and L. 463 (Spr. 2005); L.J. Jackson, "Hip-Hop at Law," 98 SEP A.B.A. J. 11 (Sept. 2012); David M. Morrison, "Bridgeport Redux: Digital Sampling and Audience Recoding," 19 Fordham Intell. Prop. Media & Ent. L.J. 75 (Autumn 2008); Jason E. Powell, "R.A.P. Rule Against Perps (Who Write Rhymes),: 41 Rutgers L.J. 479 (Fall & Winter 2009); Andre L. Smith, "Other People's Property: Hip Hop's Inherent Clashes with Property Laws and Its Ascendance as Global Counter Culture," 7 Va. Sports & Ent. L.J. 59 (Fall 2007); and Amanda Webber, "Digital Sampling and the Legal Implications of Its Use After *Bridgeport*," 22 St. John's J. Legal Comment. 373 (Summ. 2007).

3. As a general source note for the section entitled "Hip-Hop and Trademarks," please see the following: Anderson, "No Bitin' Allowed: A Hip-Hop Copyright Paradigm for All of Us"; Arewa, "From J.C. Bach to Hip-Hop: Musical Borrowing Copyright, and Cultural Context"; Evans, "Sampling, Looping, and Mashing . . . Oh My!: How Hip-hop Music Is Scratching More than the Surface of Copyright Law"; Gregory, "A Necessary Global Discussion for Improvements to U.S. Copyright Law on Music Sampling,"; Hines, "Black Musical Traditions and Copyright Historical Tensions" 10 Mich. J. Race & L. 463 (Spr. 2005); Brett Kaplicer, "Rap Music and De Minimus Copying: Applying the Ringold and Sandoval Approach to Digital Samples," 18 Cardozo Arts & Ent. L.J. 227 (2000); Morrison, "Bridgeport Redux: Digital Sampling and Audience Recoding"; "Rap Artist Wins Sanctions Against Record Company Over Copyright Claims: *Fharmacy Records v. Simmons*," 18 No. 1 Andrews Ent. Indus. Litig. Rep. 4 (Feb. 8, 2006); Ronda Robinson, "Rap Parody Gets Supreme Nod as Fair Use," 8 AUG NBA Nat'l B.A. Mag. 11 (July/August 1994); Smith, "Other People's Property: Hip-Hop's Inherent Clashes with Property Laws and Its Ascendance as Global Counter Culture"; and Webber, "Digital Sampling and the Legal Implications of Its Use after *Bridgeport*," 22 St. John's J. Legal Comment 373 (Summer 2007).

4. As a general source note for the section entitled "Unauthorized Use of Brand Names," please see the following: Anderson, "No Bitin' Allowed: A Hip-Hop Copying Paradigm for All of Us"; Brian Goldman, "Putting Lamborghini Doors on the Escalade: A Legal Analysis of the Unauthorized Use of Brand Names in Rap/Hip-Hop," 8 Tex. Rev. Ent. & Sports L. 1 (Spr. 2007); and Smith, "Other People's Property: Hip-Hop's Inherent Clashes with Property Laws and Its Ascendance as Global Counter Culture."

5. As a general source note, please see the following: Goldman, "Putting Lamborghini Doors on the Escalade: A Legal Analysis of the Unauthorized Use of Brand Names in Rap/Hip-Hop."

Selected Bibliography

Abbott, Frederick M., Thomas Cottier, and Francis Curry. *International Property in an Integrated World Economy*. New York: Aspen, 2007.

Biederman, Donald E., Martin E. Silfen, Robert C. Berry, Edward P. Pierson, and Jeanne A. Glasser. *Law and Business of the Entertainment Industries*. 5th ed. Westport, CT: Praeger, 2007.

Champion, Walter T. *Sports Law: Cases, Documents, and Materials*. New York: Aspen, 2005.

Dinwoodie, Graeme B., William O. Hennessey, Shira Perlmutter, and Graeme W. Austin. *International Intellectual Property Law and Policy*. 2nd ed. Newark, NJ: LexisNexis, 2008.

Garon, Jon. *Entertainment Law and Practice*. Durham, NC: Carolina Academic Press, 2005.

Goldstein, Paul. *Intellectual Property: The Tough, New Realities That Could Make or Break Your Business*. New York: Portfolio, 2007.

Leaffer, Marshall. *Understanding Copyright Law*. 3rd ed. New York: Matthew Bender, 1999.

Mandelbaum, Michael. *The Meaning of Sports: Why Americans Watch Baseball, Football, and Basketball and What They See When They Do*. New York: Public Affairs, 2004.

Sanjek, Russell. *American Popular Music and Its Business: The First Four Hundred Years, Volume III: From 1900 to 1984*. New York: Oxford Press USA, 1988.

Simensky, Melvin, Thomas D. Selz, Barbara A. Burnett, Robert C. Lind, and Charles A. Palmer. *Entertainment Law*. 2nd ed. New York: Matthew Bender, 1997.

Thornton, Patrick, Walter Champion, and Lawrence Ruddell. *Sports Ethics for Sports Management Professionals*. Burlington, MA: Jones Bartlett, 2012.

Yasser, Ray, James R. McCurdy, C. Peter Goplerud, and Maureen A. Weston. *Sports Law: Cases and Materials*. 4th ed. Cincinnati: Anderson, 2000.

Index

About the Authors

Walter T. Champion is the George Foreman Professor of Sports and Entertainment Law at Texas Southern University School of Law and adjunct professor in sports law at the University of Houston School of Law, at ISDE (Instituto Superior de Derecho y Economía) in Madrid, Spain, and at St. John's University. He is also an Institutional Relations Officer with ISDE Worldwide. He is the author of *Fundamentals of Sports Law*; *Sports Law in a Nutshell*; *Sports Law: Cases, Documents and Materials*; and coauthor of *Sports Ethics for Sports Management Professionals* and *Gaming Law in a Nutshell*.

Kirk D. Willis is managing partner of The Willis Law Group in Dallas, TX.

The late **Patrick K. Thornton** was associate professor in sports management at Rice University and coauthor of *Sports Ethics for Sports Management Professionals*.